African American Biographies

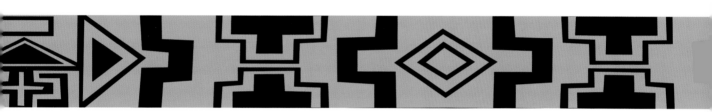

Volume 6

Jakes, T. D.—Loury, Glenn C.

GROLIER

an imprint of

■SCHOLASTIC

www.scholastic.com/librarypublishing

First published 2006 by Grolier,
an imprint of Scholastic Library Publishing,
Old Sherman Turnpike
Danbury, Connecticut 06816

Set ISBN 978-0-7172-6090-4
Volume ISBN 978-0-7172-6096-6

Library of Congress Cataloging-in-Publication Data
African American biographies.
    p. cm.
    Includes index.
    Contents: v.1. Aaliyah–Blyden, Edward W.—v.2. Bond, Horace
Mann–Clarke, John Henrik—v.3. Cleaver, Eldridge–Edmonds, Kenneth
"Babyface"—v.4. Edwards, Herman–Greener, Richard —v.5. Greenfield,
Elizabeth–Jacobs, Harriet—v.6. Jakes, T. D.–Loury, Glenn C.—v.7. Love,
Nat–Oliver, Joe "King"—v.8. O'Neal, Shaquille–Satcher, David—v.9.
Savage, Augusta–Tyson, Cicely—v.10. Tyson, Mike–Zollar, Doris
    ISBN 978-0-7172-6090-4
    I. African Americans—Biography—Juvenile literature. I.
        Scholastic Library Publishing

E185.96.A439 2006
920'.009296073–dc22
[B]

                                2005050391

For information address the publisher:
Grolier, Scholastic Library Publishing,
Old Sherman Turnpike
Danbury, Connecticut 06816

FOR THE BROWN REFERENCE GROUP PLC

Project Editors: Sally MacEachern, Aruna Vasudevan
Design: Q2A Solutions
Picture Researcher: Laila Torsun
Index: Kay Ollerenshaw
Design Manager: Lynne Ross
Production Director: Alastair Gourlay
Senior Managing Editor: Tim Cooke
Editorial Director: Lindsey Lowe

Academic consultants:

        Molefi Kete Asante, Professor,
            Department of African American
            Studies, Temple University
        Mario J. Azevedo, Chair and Frank Porter
            Graham Professor, Department of Africana
            Studies, University of North Carolina at
            Charlotte
        Scott M. Lacy, University of California Faculty
            Fellow, Department of Black Studies,
            University of California
        Mawusi Renee Simmons, Development
            Consultant and Museum Docent, University
            of Pennsylvania Museum Philadelphia,
            Pennsylvania

Printed and bound in Singapore

ABOUT THIS SET

This is one of a set of 10 books about the African Americans who have helped shape the past of the United States and who play a vital part in the nation's life today. Some were leaders of the abolitionist movement against slavery in the latter half of the 19th century; others excelled in their fields despite being born into slavery themselves. The abolition of slavery after the Civil War (1861–1865) did not mark the end of the prejudice that prevented most black Americans from fulfilling their potential, however. During the first half of the 20th century the African Americans who made their names in the arts, entertainment, sports, academia, or business remained exceptions who reached prominence as the result of a determined struggle to overcome discrimination and disadvantage.

The civil rights advances of the 1950s and 1960s removed legal and institutional barriers to African American achievement, but pioneers in many fields still faced greater difficulties than their white peers. By the start of the 21st century, however, black Americans had become prominent in all fields of endeavor, from space exploration to government.

This set contains biographies of more than a thousand of the many African Americans who have made a mark. Some are household names; others are largely—and unjustly—overlooked or forgotten. Their entries explain not only what they achieved, but also why it was important. Every entry has a box of key dates for quick reference. Longer entries also include boxes on the people who inspired great African Americans or people they themselves have influenced in turn. Most entries have a "See also" feature that refers you to related articles elsewhere in the set. If you want to find out more about an individual there are suggested books and Web sites. Addresses may change, however, and the accuracy of information on sites may vary.

Throughout the set are a number of guidepost articles. They provide an overview of particular aspects of African American experience, such as the civil rights movement or the Harlem Renaissance of the 1920s, and help place the individuals featured in the biographies in a wider context.

The biographies are arranged alphabetically, mostly by last name but also by stage name. Each volume contains an index that covers the whole set and will help you locate entries easily.

CONTENTS

JAKES, T. D.
Religious Leader

Thomas Dexter Jakes, one of the most popular African American evangelists of the late 20th century, began his independent ministry in 1982, but did not gain national prominence until the early 1990s. By 2000 he was one of the most recognizable religious figures in the United States. Some commentators have compared Jakes to Martin Luther King, Jr., and Billy Graham (1918–), arguably two of the most visible and influential American ministers in modern history. Although Jakes's audiences were primarily black and his message of economic empowerment was directed mainly toward African Americans, his ability to transcend racial, ethnic, sexual, and socioeconomic differences contributed to his wide appeal. Jakes's emphasis on emotional healing, racial equality, economic empowerment, and spiritual renewal was popular with American evangelicals, especially pentecostals and charismatics.

Making a difference
A native of South Charleston, West Virginia, Jakes was born on June 9, 1957, to Odith and Ernest Jakes. When the boy was 10, his father was diagnosed as having a kidney disease; Jakes spent much of his teenage years caring for his sick father. He dropped out of high school to care for his mother when she also became ill. Both of these experiences, he later claimed, contributed to his commitment to emotional healing in his ministry: "I think it's because I was in such pain myself that I can relate to people who have been through trauma."

Jakes began to preach part time while attending West Virginia State University. He dropped out of college after a

▲ *T. D. Jakes has worked hard to eradicate racism. He said, "It's the contents of your heart" that matters.*

year to work in a chemical plant, although he later earned a BA, MA, and PhD through correspondence courses.

In 1980 Jakes helped found the Greater Emanuel Temple of Faith, still working as a part-time preacher to the 10 members. Two years later he began to devote himself to preaching full time after his father died. By 1996 the congregation had grown to around a thousand members. He established social programs for convicts, the homeless, AIDS victims, drug addicts, and alcoholics.

In 1993 Jakes published *Woman, Thou Art Loosed!*, based on a 1992 sermon. It sold more than a million copies and in 2004 was made into a movie. His subsequent books were also bestsellers, and his evangelistic meetings drew tens of thousands of people. In 1996 Jakes moved his ministry to Dallas, Texas, and with his wife, Serita, founded Potter's House, a multiracial, nondenominational church, which ran programs to help the needy, as well as literacy and prostitute's outreach programs.

See also: King, Martin Luther, Jr.; Religion and African Americans

Further reading: Jakes, T. D. *Woman, Thou Art Loosed!* Shippensburg, PA: Treasure House, 1994.
http://www.tdjakes.org/ (T. D. Jakes's Ministries site).

KEY DATES

1957   Born in South Charleston, West Virginia, on June 9.

1980   Helps establish the Greater Emanuel Temple of Faith in Montgomery, West Virginia.

1982   Begins his first radio ministry, known as "The Master's Plan."

1990   Moves his church to Charleston, West Virginia.

1993   Publishes *Woman, Thou Art Loosed!*; starts a national television broadcast called *Get Ready with T. D. Jakes.*

1996   Establishes Potter's House Church in Dallas, Texas.

JAMES, Daniel, Jr.
Military Officer

In 1975 Daniel "Chappie" James, Jr., was the first black American to become a 4-star general. James was a popular public speaker, who frequently lectured to minority groups, particularly youth groups.

Born in Pensacola, Florida, on February 11, 1920, James was the son of a farm laborer and a local schoolteacher. His mother was a particularly strong influence on the young boy, encouraging him to strive for achievement and never quit in the face of trouble. James subsequently did well academically, graduating from Washington High School in 1937. From there he went to study at Tuskegee Institute, taking a BS in physical education. He also learned to fly under the Civilian Pilot Training Program. On graduation in 1942 James stayed on at Tuskegee as a flying instructor on the Army Air Corps Aviation Cadet Program.

A military career

The United States entered World War II (1939–1945) in 1941. Early in 1943 James entered the Army Air Corps training program. He took a commission as a second lieutenant in July of that year, undergoing training in flying fighter aircraft. He spent the rest of the war instructing the African American pilots of the 99th Pursuit Squadron.

James's combat career began in 1950 with the onset of the Korean War (1950–1953), during which he flew 101 fighter missions. He returned to the United States in July 1951, where he worked his way up through a series of command positions. Between 1953 and 1956 he was based at Otis, Massachusetts, during which time he was appointed a major. James was also given the Young Man of the Year award by the Massachusetts Junior Chamber of Commerce in 1954.

In 1957 James was assigned to staff duty in Washington, D.C. Over the next years he was based in England (1960–1964), Arizona (1964–1966), and Vietnam (1966–1967). As the deputy operations commander for the 8th Tactical Fighter Wing (TFW) based in Thailand, James flew 78 combat missions over North Vietnam.

After returning to the United States in late 1967, James became vice commander of the 33rd TFW. In August 1969 he was appointed commander of Wheelus Air Force Base in Libya, having risen to the rank of brigadier general. Subsequent positions included deputy assistant secretary of defense (1970) and vice commander Military Airlift

▲ *Daniel James, Jr., spoke out about U.S. racial policies as well as its military policies.*

Command (1974). From 1975, when James became a full general, he was also commander-in-chief of the North American Air Defense Command (NORAD). James's final position was as special assistant to the chief of staff, U.S. Air Force, a role he took up in 1977 and held until his death from a heart attack on February 25, 1978.

KEY DATES	
1920	Born in Pensacola, Florida, on February 11.
1942	Begins working as a flying instructor.
1950	Serves in the Korean War.
1966	Serves in the Vietnam War (1964–1973).
1975	Becomes a general and commander-in-chief of NORAD.
1978	Dies in Colorado Springs, Colorado, on February 25.

Further reading: McGovern, James R. *Black Eagle: General Daniel "Chappie" James, Jr.* Tuscaloosa, AL: University of Alabama Press, 1985.
http://www.africanamericans.com/ChappieJames.htm
(Biography featuring photographs).

5

JAMES, LeBron
Basketball Player

Basketball player LeBron James was named 53rd in *Forbes* magazine's 2005 Top 100 list of celebrities. An outstanding athlete, James has inspired many young African Americans.

Early life

Born in Akron, Ohio, on December 30, 1984, James was brought up by Gloria, his young but devoted single mother, in a tough area of the city. James's childhood was hard and this affected his academic performance in elementary school. He did, however, show great promise in both basketball and football. In the fourth grade James began to skip school and a sports coach named Frankie Walker took James to live with his family: his mother agreed that he needed a more stable home life. Although he moved back in with his mother 18 months later, the Walkers remained an important and stabilizing influence.

Exceptional talent

By the eighth grade James had already shown himself to be a talented basketball player. He was a star player in St. Vincent–St. Mary High School, where he was named High School Basketball Player of the Year by *USA Today* in 2002 and 2003; he was also featured in *Sports Illustrated* magazine. James's awesome talents—he averaged 31.6 points per game—drew huge crowds, and many of his high school games were televised nationally. James was also titled "Mr. Basketball" for Ohio by the Associated Press. The only blip in his high school career came in January 2003 after he accepted a contribution of free clothes worth $845 even though taking gifts was prohibited. He was banned from playing for the rest of the season. An Ohio judge overruled the ban a week later, however.

▲ **LeBron James during a game against Lithuania at the 2004 Olympic Games in Athens, Greece.**

Pro game

As James's high school years came to an end, a career as a National Basketball Association (NBA) professional beckoned. In the 2003 NBA draft he was picked to play for the Cleveland Cavaliers: the first pick of the 2003 draft. Far from being overwhelmed, James continued to excel. He was named NBA Rookie of the Month six times consecutively from November 2003, and in 2004 was the Rookie of the Year—the youngest person in NBA history to receive the award—and named to the NBA All-Rookie First Team. In his first pro season he averaged 20 points per game, and in March 2004 he scored 41 points against the New Jersey Nets. In 2004 James played on the U.S. Olympic basketball team in the Olympic Games held in Athens, Greece. He made headlines in 2005 when he fired his agent, Aaron Goodwin, who had negotiated millions of dollars worth of endorsement deals for the player, in favor of a new agency run by friends.

Further reading: Morgan, David Lee, Jr. *LeBron James: The Rise of a Star.* New York, NY: Gray & Company Publishers, 2003. http://www.lebronjames.com (Official site).

KEY DATES	
1984	Born in Akron, Ohio, on December 30.
1994	Begins playing basketball.
2002	Named High School Basketball Player of the Year by *USA Today*.
2003	Drafted to the Cleveland Cavaliers.
2004	Named NBA Rookie of the Year; plays on U.S. Olympic basketball team in Athens.

JAMISON, Judith
Dancer, Choreographer

One of the United States's leading choreographers (creator and arranger of dances), Judith Jamison is the artistic director of the Alvin Ailey American Dance Theater (AAADT), the world-renowned, multiracial modern-dance troupe founded by dancer Alvin Ailey in 1958. During the 1970s Jamison's impassioned, graceful dancing inspired Ailey to create some of the finest female roles in the modern repertoire for her.

KEY DATES

1944 Born in Philadelphia, Pennsylvania, on May 10.

1966 Joins the AAADT.

1989 Becomes artistic director of the AAADT.

1999 Receives the Kennedy Center honor for lifetime contribution to the arts and culture.

The dancer

Jamison was born in Philadelphia, Pennsylvania, on May 10, 1944. Her father was a steelworker and her mother a part-time teacher and former athlete. At age six Jamison

▼ *Judith Jamison (center) joins Maria Llorente (left) and Lazaro Carreno (right), two stars of the National Ballet of Cuba, at City Center.*

began taking ballet classes at Philadelphia's Judimar School of Dance, where she quickly showed her extraordinary talent.

After graduating from high school in 1961, Jamison went to study psychology at Fisk University, Tennessee, but she quickly returned to dance, enrolling at the Philadelphia Dance Academy instead. In 1964, while at the academy, she made her debut at the American Ballet Theater, New York City, dancing in choreographer Agnes de Mille's (1905–1993) *The Four Marys*. A year later Jamison moved to New York City, where she joined AAADT and soon established herself as its principal dancer. Among her many outstanding performances for AAADT were a 15-minute solo in *Ailey's Cry* (1971) and a duet with Russian dancer Mikhail Baryshnikov (1948–) in *Pas de Duke* (1976), set to music by Duke Ellington. Jamison's immaculate technique and emotive presence, together with her striking good looks, also won her guest appearances with dance companies all over the world, including the Swedish and Vienna royal ballets.

After leaving AAADT in 1980, Jamison, then in her late thirties, continued to dance freelance. She also began to choreograph her own works: The first, *Divining,* was premiered by AAADT in 1984. Four years later Jamison took the plunge and set up her own dance troupe, the Jamison Project, but the following year she was invited by the dying Ailey to return to AAADT as its director. She subsequently choreographed some of the troupe's most popular and significant works, including *Hymn* (1993) and *Double Exposure* (2000).

See also: Ailey, Alvin; Ellington, Duke

Further reading: Jamison, Judith. *Dancing Spirit*. New York, NY: Doubleday, 1993.
http://www.alvinailey.org/pf/jamisonbio_pf.asp (Biography).

JAY-Z
Musician, Record Label Executive

Grammy-winning rapper Jay-Z is also a successful music executive. In 2005 he was appointed president and chief executive officer (CEO) of Def Jam Recordings.

Shawn Carey Carter was born in Brooklyn, New York, in 1969. He grew up in the tough Marcy Projects of the city, where he attended George Westinghouse Technical High School. Called "Jazzy" by friends, he shortened the nickname to "Jay-Z."

Roc-a-Fella Records

After showing early musical promise, Jay-Z tried several times to launch a career as a rapper before making the decision to start his own record label. Together with friends Damon Dash and Kareem "Biggs" Burke, Jay-Z launched Roc-a-Fella Records in 1994. Jay-Z's debut album, *Reasonable Doubt*, was released in 1996; it mixed hard-hitting street lyrics and rhymes. The album became a classic among hip-hop devotees and went on to achieve gold record sales.

In 1997 Jay-Z released *In My Lifetime, Vol. 1*, which reached No. 3 on the *Billboard* album charts. The album saw Jay-Z trade his gangsta-rap style for a more mainstream pop-rap, which doubled his audience. His decision to move in a more accessible direction alienated many of his core fans.

The following year saw Jay-Z release *Vol. 2: Hard Knock Life*. The album included several huge hit singles, including "Hard Knock Life (Ghetto Anthem)," which featured a chorus sampled from the Broadway show *Annie*. The album stayed at the top of the *Billboard* chart for five weeks and won the 1999 Grammy for Best Rap Album.

Jay-Z also wrote, produced, and directed the semi-autobiographical short film *Streets Is Watching* in 1998.

▲ *Jay-Z is considered by many to be one of the best hip-hop artists in the music industry.*

The gold-selling soundtrack introduced several of Roc-A-Fella's up and coming stars, including Memphis Bleek, Rell, and Diamonds In The Rough. In December 1999 the release of *Vol. 3: Life And Times of S. Carter* confirmed Jay-Z's status as one of hip-hop's most popular artists when it topped the album charts in January 2000. *The Blueprint* (2001) sealed his position at the top of the New York rap scene. It is considered by many to be one of the best hip-hop albums ever produced. He released *The Blueprint 2: The Gift & the Curse* in 2002. In September 2003, after nine platinum albums, Jay-Z announced his retirement from recording, releasing *The Black Album* in November.

See also: Dash, Damon

Further reading: Bankston, John. *Jay-Z* (Blue Banner Biographies). Hockessin, DE: Mitchell Lane Publishers, 2004.
http://www.jayzonline.com/ (Jay-Z site with links).

KEY DATES	
1969	Born in Brooklyn, New York, on December 4.
1994	Together with Damon Dash and Kareem "Biggs" Burke launches Roc-a-Fella Records.
1996	Releases his debut album *Reasonable Doubt.*
1999	Wins Grammy for Best Rap Album with *Vol. 2: Hard Knock Life.*
2005	Appointed CEO of Def Jam Recordings.

JEAN, WYCLEF
Musician

Wyclef Jean first became famous as part of the acclaimed group the Fugees, in which he performed with Lauryn Hill and his cousin Prakazrel "Pras" Michel. He later established a successful solo career as a rap artist.

Early life
Born Nelust Wyclef Jean in Croix-des-Bouquets, Haiti, on October 17, 1970, Jean and his family moved to Brooklyn, New York, when he was 10; they settled in northern New Jersey. He began playing the guitar and studying jazz in high school. Musically inclined, Wyclef learned to play several instruments including the piano. He performed throughout his neighborhood and formed a group called the Transformaz with his cousin Pras and friend Lauryn Hill. They later renamed the group the Fugees, short for refugees. Jean drove taxis until the group was signed to Ruffhouse Records.

▼ **As well as being a musician and songwriter Wyclef Jean has turned to acting; he has appeared in the drama Third Watch and several independent films.**

Musical success
In 1993 the Fugees released their debut album, *Blunted on Reality*, which did not do well commercially. The band followed it with the 1996 classic hip-hop offering *The Score*. Featuring the hit songs "Fugee-la" and "Killing Me Softly," *The Score* sold more than 17 million copies and earned two Grammys for Best R&B Performance by a Duo or a Group with Vocal ("Killing Me Softly") and Best Rap Album. Creative differences later led to the band's break up.

In 1997 Jean released his debut solo album, *Wyclef Jean Presents the Carnival Featuring the Refugee All-Stars*, known more simply as *The Carnival.* Featuring Pras, Hill, and Jean's brother and sister as guest musicians, the album went platinum. Jean's later albums *The Ecleftic: 2 Sides II a Book* (2000), *Masquerade* (2002), *The Preacher's Son* (2003), and *Sak Pase Presents: Welcome to Haiti* (2004) were commercial successes, although some music critics claimed that they lacked the musical cohesion of *The Carnival.*

Jean has written and produced songs for many other musicians, including the Black-Eyed Peas, Destiny's Child, and Whitney Houston. He has contributed to several film soundtracks, including *The Manchurian Candidate* (2004) and *Hotel Rwanda* (2005), for which he received a Golden Globe nomination for the song "A Million Voices." Jean has branched out into acting, appearing on TV and in film. He established the Wyclef Jean Foundation, which promotes musical education among children, and he is a well-known campaigner for HIV/AIDS awareness in Haiti.

See also: Hill, Lauryn; Houston, Whitney

Further reading: Roberts, Chris. *Fugees.* New York, NY: Virgin Books, 1998.
http://www.mtv.com/bands/az/jean_wyclef (Biography).

JEFFRIES, Leonard
Educator

Leonard Jeffries is a leading voice and theoretician in African-centered education. He was a founding member of the Association for the Study of Classical African Civilizations and professor of Africana studies at the City College of New York.

A whole village

Born in Newark, New Jersey, on January 19, 1937, Jeffries was raised in an environment in which neighbors took care of each other; Newark summed up the African adage that it "takes a whole village to raise a child." Both Jeffries's grandparents lived in the same neighborhood and provided him with love and support. His neighbors also included several leading members of the African American community—the Reverend Harry Spelman and his family lived across the street.

Like other members of the community, Jeffries's family attended the Mount Sinai Baptist Church and this and the close-knit community helped shape Jeffries and give him a pride in himself and his race. Studying in local public schools, Jeffries graduated from Sussex Avenue School in 1951, where he was president of his graduating class.

Jeffries went on to study at Lafayette College in Easton, Pennsylvania. During his time there he encountered the Crossroads program, which emphasized the importance of working in Africa. Jeffries took his first trip to the continent with Crossroads; it was so successful that he joined the Crossroads staff, leading several trips to Africa. Jeffries's experiences there inspired him to change his major from law to political science. He received an MA in international affairs and eventually wrote his doctorate on the politics and economics of Ivory Coast in West Africa.

Jeffries's studies and experience of teaching at the City College of New York (CUNY) brought the realization that African studies was mostly taught from a colonial point of view and therefore did not represent the true history of black people. In 1969 he set up the African Heritage Studies Association with the historian John Henrik Clarke. In the same year Jeffries was asked to set up one of the first black studies programs, at San Jose State University in California. Jeffries aimed to link black history to the period prior to slavery, as well as linking academic study back to the African American community.

Jeffries became the focus of media attention following a speech he made in 1991 at the Empire State Black Arts and

▲ *Leonard Jeffries took part in the Million Youth March in Harlem, New York, in 1998.*

Cultural Festival in Albany, New York, in which he asserted that rich Jews controlled the slave trade and that Hollywood was the center of a Jewish-dominated conspiracy to systematically denigrate blacks. Under great pressure, Jeffries was removed as chair of the black studies department at CUNY. His dismissal was overturned in 1993 on the grounds that the university had violated his First Amendment Rights to free speech. Jeffries continues to speak and write about African studies.

KEY DATES	
1937	Born in Newark, New Jersey, on January 19.
1969	Sets up the African Heritage Studies Association; sets up one of the first black studies programs at San Jose State University.
1993	Wins court case against CUNY for unfair dismissal.

See also: Clarke, John Henrik

Further reading: http://www.nbufront.org/html /MastersMuseums/LenJeffries/LenJeffriesVMuseum.html (Leonard Jeffries Virtual Museum site).

JEMISON, Mae C.
Astronaut, Physician, Educator

Scientist and astronaut Mae Carol Jemison made history in 1992 when she became the first African American woman in space. Her desire to soar above the heavens was strengthened by her ability to fly on Earth, to break through barriers in education and science, and excel in fields often out of reach for women of color. Museum president Christy Coleman of the Charles H. Wright Museum of African American History in Detroit said, "Dr. Jemison embodies self-determination, creativity.... She's about living a legacy, but also about creating a legacy through her foundations and other efforts."

Early life
Jemison was born in Decatur, Alabama, on October 17, 1956, the daughter of Charlie and Dorothy Jemison. Her father worked as a carpenter and roofer, and her mother was a teacher. Jemison's parents taught her and her

▼ *Mae C. Jemison was already a qualified physician when she was accepted onto the NASA program.*

siblings not to be restricted in their thinking about race, gender, or education. They moved the family to Chicago, Illinois, where there were better opportunities for black people. They also wanted to ensure that Mae, brother Charlie, and sister Ada, would receive a fair and equal education. Although the Supreme Court's ruling in *Brown v. Board of Education* (1954) had effectively made segregation in public schools illegal, some areas in the United States remained resistant to integrated education.

Jemison was interested in science from an early age. Graduating from high school at age 16, she entered Stanford University, California, where she earned undergraduate degrees in chemical engineering and African American studies. She went on to study medicine at Cornell University, New York, receiving her MD in 1981. After graduation Jemison did further training at the University of Southern California Medical Center before going to work as a Peace Corps medical officer. She traveled the world trying to improve health care in developing countries, and was assigned to manage pharmacy and laboratory research to combat tuberculosis, asthma, and dysentery. Jemison also went to such countries as Kenya, Sierra Leone, Cuba, and Thailand, serving as a medical supervisor and researching vaccines for hepatitis B and rabies.

Making it to NASA
Jemison went into general medical practice in 1985, working for the CIGNA Health Plans of California. She also enrolled in night classes at UCLA to study engineering because she had been fascinated by the night sky and the mysteries of space since childhood.

In October 1985 Jemison decided to apply to NASA to enter the space program. The disaster on the space shuttle *Challenger*, which exploded shortly after takeoff in 1986, interrupted NASA's recruitment program, however. Two years later it resumed its shuttle program and renewed its efforts to recruit women, minorities, and people of color.

In 1987 Jemison was one of 15 people chosen out of more than 2,000 applicants to train to be an astronaut. She was the first African American woman admitted into the training program at the Johnson Space Center in Houston, Texas. During the one-year program Jemison learned about space shuttle techniques and hardware procedures.

INFLUENCES AND INSPIRATION

Mae C. Jemison is often held up as a role model for young African Americans, particularly women. Jemison herself was inspired by both real and fictional figures in her reach for the stars. Like many young Americans, Jemison watched the cult TV series *Star Trek*, and was inspired by the black engineer, Lieutenant Uhuru, played by Nichelle Nichols (1933–).

Noble Prize-winning biochemist Linus Pauling (1901–1994) made the idea of experiment and discovery attractive to Jemison. Her parents also instilled in her the belief that she could achieve anything she wanted to if she worked hard enough.

When asked what she thought about her achievements, in an interview given to *Ebony* magazine, Jemison replied "The only thing that I have done throughout my life is to do the best job that I can and to be me. In terms of being a role model … what I'd like to be is someone who says, 'No, don't try to necessarily be like me, or live your life or grow up to be an astronaut or physician unless that's what you want to do.'"

Jemison works hard to inspire a love of science in children. She cosponsored an annual international science camp for 12- to 16-year olds, and also was the National School Literacy Advocate for the Bayer Corporation's "Making science makes sense."

First space flight

Between September 12 and September 20, 1992, Jemison was the science mission specialist on STS-47 Spacelab-J, *Endeavour*. The craft orbited the Earth 127 times, while 44 Japanese and American scientists carried out experiments. The mission was notable because Jemison was the first African American female in space, and N. Jan Davis and Mark Lee were the first married astronauts on a space mission. Jemison spent 190 hours performing experiments on weightlessness, tissue growth, and semiconductor metals. She also tested procedures on frogs, embryologic development, and the loss of calcium in women.

After completing her mission Jemison served as an administrator with NASA until 1993, when she left to found the Jemison Group Inc. in Houston, Texas.

KEY DATES

1956	Born in Decatur, Alabama, on October 17.
1977	Graduates with BA from Stanford University.
1981	Receives degree in medicine from Cornell University.
1983	Becomes a medical specialist in the Area Peace Corp in Africa until 1985.
1987	Becomes the first African American woman admitted to the NASA space program.
1992	Makes first space flight in *Endeavour*.
1993	Leaves NASA; founds the Jemison Group Inc.
1994	Founds founds the Dorothy Jemison Foundation for Excellence.

Life beyond space

At the Jemison Group, Jemison directed a series of programs to promote technologies for developing countries. She also established science camps for youth (*see box*), and founded the BioSentient Corporation in 1999, which teaches people how to use technology to control stressful situations.

In 1995 Jemison became a professor of environmental studies at Darmouth College, New Hampshire, and joined the faculty of Cornell University as the A. D. White Professor-at-Large. She also made a guest appearance on *Star Trek: The Next Generation* and hosted a television series on the Discovery Channel from 1994 to 1995 called the *World of Wonders.* Her autobiography, *Find Where the Wind Goes: Moments from my Life,* was published in 2001 and is an inspirational exploration of her life and achievements written for teenagers.

Chosen as one of *People* magazine's "50 Most Beautiful People in the World" in 1993, Jemison has received many honors and awards. She was inducted into the National Medical Association Hall of Fame and elected into the National Academy of Sciences' Institute of Medicine. In 2001 she received the Outstanding Achievement Award from the Congress on Racial Equality. Educational academies in Chicago, Illinois, and Detroit, Michigan, are named in her honor, and she has received many honorary doctorate degrees.

Further reading: Jemison, Mae. *Find Where the Wind Goes: Moments from My Life.* New York, NY: Scholastic, 2001.
www.africanamericans.com/MaeJemison (Biography).
www.jsc.nasa.gov/Bios/htmlbios/jemison-mc.html (NASA page).

JENNINGS, Thomas
Inventor

Although he is less well known than other African American inventors such as George Washington Carver, Garrett Morgan, and Elijah McCoy, Thomas Jennings is widely acknowledged as being the first African American to hold a patent. Like Sarah E. Goode, the first African American woman to receive a patent, Jennings was probably born into slavery. In later life his energies were directed toward the abolition of slavery.

Few details
Very little is known about Jennings's early life. The only fact of any certainty is that he was born in 1791. The details of his upbringing are unknown. However, much, if not all, of his family was enslaved. It is therefore very likely that Jennings too was born a slave, and was later freed or else escaped through the Underground Railroad, the secret network that helped slaves escape from the South.

Only a little more is known about Jennings's later life. By the time he reached adulthood he had succeeded in becoming a free tradesman, with his own tailoring and dry-cleaning business in New York City.

Slavery was ended in New York in 1827, but Jennings was already established as a freedman by that time. Most of his family remained slaves beyond this time, however, so it is probable that Jennings had grown up in another state, or at least escaped before being moved elsewhere. As a businessman, Jennings began saving money to pay for his family's freedom and he also became involved in more general abolitionist activities.

Invention
When he was 30 years old Jennings invented a new process for cleaning clothing. He named it "dry scouring." As a free African American he was allowed under the U.S. patent law of 1793 to patent his invention, which he did on March 3, 1821 (U.S. patent No. 3306X). In doing so he became the first African American to hold a patent, more than 30 years after the United States first began issuing patents. No copy of Jennings's patent is known to exist today, and so the precise details of his invention are unknown.

Although the 1793 patent law appeared to allow slaves (as well as free blacks) to patent their inventions, the legislation was challenged in the *Oscar Stuart v. Ned* case of 1858, in which it was ruled that slaves were not citizens and so could not be granted patents. The 1858 decision was overturned a few years later in 1861, when the Confederate States passed legislation granting slaves patent rights. In the wake of the Civil War (1861–1865), patent laws were changed to allow anyone to hold a patent, and the number of patents issued to African Americans rose significantly.

Buying freedom
Jennings must have used his invention to improve the service provided by his cleaning operation. It is not known if he licensed the process at all. Nevertheless, the invention proved to be a success and Jennings's profits rose.

Records indicate that Jennings was able to use the profits from his invention to purchase his family's freedom. He also used the increased funds available to continue his work as an abolitionist.

Jennings began paying for the publication of petitions that advocated rights for African Americans and an end to slavery across the United States. In 1831 he began serving as assistant secretary for the First Annual Convention of the People of Color, which took place in Philadelphia, Pennsylvania. The meeting agreed to build a college for blacks in New Haven, Connecticut, although the project ended in failure. Jennings died in 1859.

KEY DATES	
1791	Born in this year.
1821	Receives patent for dry-cleaning process known as "dry scouring" on March 3.
1831	Becomes assistant secretary for the First Annual Convention of the People of Color in Philadelphia.
1859	Dies.

See also: Carver, George Washington; Goode, Sarah E.; McCoy, Elijah; Morgan, Garrett

Further reading: Stewart, Jeffrey C. *1001 Things Everyone Should Know About African American History.* New York, NY: Main Street Books, 1997.
http://inventors.about.com/library/inventors/bljennings.htm (Biography)
http://inventors.about.com/library/blblackinventors.htm (Information on other African American inventors).

JETER, Derek
Baseball Player

Derek Jeter is seen by many as one of the best baseball players of his generation. In 2005 he ranked No. 38 in *Forbes*'s Top 100 celebrities.

Jeter was born in Pequannock, New Jersey, on June 26, 1974. His father Charles was black, his mother Dorothy white. Growing up in Kalamazoo, Michigan, Jeter's childhood dreams were to play baseball for the New York Yankees and wear a single-digit number jersey, both of which he eventually achieved.

As a junior high school student, Jeter was voted the "most likely to play shortstop for the New York Yankees" and was named 1992 High School Player of the Year by the American Baseball Coaches Association. On graduating Jeter won a baseball scholarship to Michigan State University, but the New York Yankees drafted him in the first round. Jeter left the Wolverines to follow his dream.

▼ **Derek Jeter at the Skippy Peanut Butter Day at Yankee Stadium in New York City in 2001.**

KEY DATES	
1974	Born in Pequannock, New Jersey, on June 26.
1992	Named High School Player of the Year by the American Baseball Coaches Association.
1995	Replaces Tony Fernandez in major league game on May 29.
1996	Wins Rookie of the Year honors; sets up the Turn 2 Foundation to provide young people with motivation.
2000	Wins All Stars MVP and World Series MVP honors.
2002	Awarded Best Play Award by ESPY.

Jeter's big break in the major leagues came on May 29, 1995, when he was 30 days short of his 21st birthday. He had to replace an injured Tony Fernandez and earned a starting spot with the team in 1996. That same year Jeter earned Rookie of the Year honors. Four years later he won the All Stars Most Valuable Player (MVP) and World Series MVP honors.

In 2004 Jeter won an American League Gold Glove. In 2005 he had a .306 postseason batting average and ranked among the leaders in many postseason categories: He was second in runs, first in hits, second in total bases, second in doubles, seventh in home runs, sixth in RBIs, fifth in walks, first in singles, and sixth in stolen bases.

Other ventures

In 1996 Jeter established the Turn 2 Foundation to support youth-orientated programs and motivate young people to achieve academic success and a healthy lifestyle and to turn away from drugs and alcohol.

Jeter also became the face of baseball's attempt to move into the multibillion-dollar video game industry. In 2005 Take-Two, a video game development company, contracted Jeter as the spokesperson and cover athlete for the licensed 2K5 Sports baseball simulation series. He has received a number of awards, including the *Sporting News* Good Guy in Sports Award and Best Play Award from ESPY.

Further reading: Rizzuto, Phil, et al. *Derek Jeter: A Yankee For the New Millennium*. Dallas, TX: Beckett Pub., 2000. http://www2.turn2foundation.org/events/upcoming.asp (Turn 2 Foundation site).

JOHNS, Vernon
Preacher, Religious Leader

Vernon Johns was one of the leading orators and preachers of his time. In 1949 he became the focus of attention when he announced that he planned to give a sermon entitled "It's Safe to Murder Negroes in Montgomery" from the pulpit of the Dexter Avenue Baptist Church in Montgomery, Alabama. Although he was arrested and questioned by a judge, Johns gave the sermon and continued to speak out against racism and segregation.

Early life
Born near Farmville, Virginia, on April 22, 1892, into a poor farming family, Johns had little formal education. He had an inquiring mind, however, and is believed to have had a photographic memory, which made it easier for him to teach himself Greek, Hebrew, Latin, and German.

In 1918 Johns managed to get a place to study theology at Oberlin College in Ohio; he persuaded the dean, Edward Increase Bosworth, to let him attend the college on a trial basis. So impressed was Bosworth with the young man that he accepted Johns as a full-time student and also found him part-time work as a preacher to enable him to finance his studies. Johns later went on to study at the University of Chicago Graduate School of Theology.

An original man
Brilliant, outspoken, and viewed as eccentric by several of his contemporaries, Johns moved between the pulpit, academic positions, and his Virginia farm throughout his career. His brilliance as an orator led to many job offers to preach, but he was also very quick tempered.

In 1926 he became the first black American minister to have a sermon published in the series *Best Sermons*. He served as president of the Virginia Theological Seminary from 1929 to 1934, and later preceded Martin Luther King, Jr., as the pastor of the Dexter Avenue Baptist Church in Montgomery, Alabama, between 1948 and 1952.

At Dexter Avenue Baptist Church Johns clashed both with whites in Montgomery and with his own middle-class congregation, whom he felt were more concerned with improving their own personal positions than with the position of black people in general. He was an outspoken critic of segregation and discrimination against blacks, and he personally challenged the racist practices of Montgomery by refusing to get on the back of the bus as African Americans were forced to do at the time and by demanding service in white-only restaurants. He also encouraged black women raped by white men to bring charges against their attackers.

Johns urged the African American community to fight white oppression. He preached that blacks should defend themselves against white racism. A believer in the importance of practical labor, Johns also encouraged his congregation to build their own businesses. His views were often outspoken, however, and drew criticism from members of his parish. Johns offered his resignation; it was accepted in 1952.

Johns was a strong influence on important activists, including Martin Luther King, Jr., Ralph Abernathy, and Wyatt Tee Walker. Abernathy said that Johns prepared the way for the black civil rights activism in Montgomery in the mid-1950s. Johns was also a role model for his niece Barbara Johns, who challenged the inadequate facilities of the black high school in Farmville in what became one of the five cases in the landmark 1954 case against segregation in schools *Brown v. Board of Education*.

KEY DATES

1892	Born near Farmville, Virginia, on April 22.
1918	Attends Oberlin College.
1926	Publishes the sermon "Transfigured Moments" in the series *Best Sermons*; he is the first African American to be published in the series.
1948	Assumes pastorship at Dexter Avenue Baptist Church in Montgomery, Alabama.
1952	Resigns from position at Dexter Avenue Baptist Church; his successor is Martin Luther King, Jr.
1965	Dies in Washington, D.C., on June 11.

See also: Abernathy, Ralph; King, Martin Luther, Jr.; Walker, Wyatt Tee

Further reading: Branch, Taylor. *Parting the Waters: America in the King Years 1954–63.* New York, NY: Simon & Schuster, 1989.
http://www.ralphluker.com/vjohns (Outline of Johns's life).

JOHNSON, Charles
Writer

Charles R. Johnson is a prominent writer known for his philosophical novels and complex views on race relations. He believes that black writing should enable African Americans "as a people—as a culture—to move from narrow complaint to broad celebration." Johnson has written novels, essays, screen plays, and literary criticism, as well as achieving success as a cartoonist.

Born in Evanston, Illinois, in 1948, Johnson was a skilled artist. He first published political cartoons in local magazines at age 17 and created, coproduced, and hosted a PBS program called *Charlie's Pad* in 1971. Johnson studied at Southern Illinois University (SIU), where he was influenced by novelist and literary theorist John Gardner, who became his mentor and had a great influence on his early writing. Johnson earned a BA in philosophy and went on to receive an MA in 1973.

Influenced by the work of African American writers Richard Wright, Ralph Ellison, and Jean Toomer, Johnson published his first novel *Faith and the Good Thing* (1974) while he was studying for a PhD in phenomenology (the study of the development of human consciousness) and literary aesthetics at the State University of New York (SUNY). He went on to acquire his doctorate in 1988.

▲ *Charles Johnson was a talented cartoonist before he achieved success as a novelist.*

Two years later Johnson published *Oxherding Tale* to critical acclaim: The book won the Washington State Governor's Award for Literature. Johnson is probably best known for his 1990 novel *Middle Passage*, which won several awards and established his reputation nationally. His 1998 novel *Dreamer* explored Martin Luther King, Jr's life and career.

Achievements
Much honored for his work, Johnson has been awarded honorary degrees from Northwestern University, SIU, and SUNY. In 2005 he was the S. Wilson and Grace M. Pollock Endowed Professor of English at the University of Washington, Seattle, where he worked for almost 30 years. His other accomplishments include 20 screenplays, for which he received several awards, and more than 50 reviews and articles. Johnson was one of the 12 most influential 20th-century black authors featured in a 1977 series of stamps.

See also: Ellison, Ralph; Toomer, Jean; Wright, Richard

Further reading: Storhoff, Gary. *Understanding Charles Johnson*. Columbia, SC: University of South Carolina Press, 2004.
http://charlesjohnson.wlu.edu/ (Charles Johnson Society site).

KEY DATES

1948   Born in Evanston, Illinois.

1965   Publishes first cartoons.

1971   Creates, coproduces, directs, and hosts *Charlie's Pad*, a television production.

1974   Publishes first philosophical novel, *Faith and the Good Thing*.

1983   *Oxherding Tale* wins the Washington State Governor's Award for Literature.

1989   *Being and Race* wins the Governor's Award for Literature.

1990   *Middle Passage* wins the National Book Award.

1998   Appointed a MacArthur fellow.

2000   Receives the Lifetime Achievement in the Arts Award.

2005   Elected to membership in the American Academy of Arts and Sciences.

JOHNSON, Charles S.
Educator

A sociologist and educator, Charles Spurgeon Johnson played a key role in promoting the Harlem Renaissance, the black arts movement that flourished in Harlem, New York City, in the 1920s. His magazine *Opportunity* championed many African American causes and launched the careers of many eminent writers.

Early life
Johnson was born in Bristol, Virginia, on July 24, 1893. His father, the Reverend Charles Henry Johnson, gave his son a grounding in a classical education. Johnson graduated in 1916 with a BA from Virginia Union University in Richmond. He then moved to Chicago to pursue graduate studies at the University of Chicago, where he was mentored by sociologist Robert E. Park (1864–1944).

An illustrious career
After serving in France during World War I (1914–1918), Johnson returned to Chicago in 1919 to a city paralyzed by race riots. Appointed to the interracial Chicago Commission on Race Relations, Johnson cowrote *The Negro in Chicago: A Study in Race Relations and a Race Riot,* published in 1922. In 1921 he moved to New York City, where he worked for the National Urban League. Two years later he started the league's magazine *Opportunity: A Journal of Negro Life,* which he edited until 1928. The magazine was pivotal in promoting Harlem Renaissance poets, writers, and intellectuals, including Alain Locke and Zora Neale Hurston.

In 1928 Johnson moved to Nashville, Tennessee, to become chair of the social sciences department at the historically black Fisk University. He held the position until 1946, when he became the university's president, the first

▲ *Charles S. Johnson published some of the leading African American intellectuals of the 1920s.*

African American to hold the position. Johnson hired many leading African American intellectuals to work there, including Aaron Douglas.

While at Fisk Johnson also produced several reports about the position of African Americans in U.S. society. He established his reputation in the area of race relations not just through his research but also his commitment to training a new generation of social scientists. Presidents Hoover, Roosevelt, Truman, and Eisenhower all asked Johnson to serve on race commissions. Johnson died of a heart attack on October 27, 1956, in Louisville, Kentucky. His invaluable contribution to the study of race relations has been recognized by many commentators.

See also: Douglas, Aaron; Harlem Renaissance; Hurston, Zora Neale; Locke, Alain

Further reading: www.aaregistry.com/africanamericanhistory/1019/CharlesSJohnson (Biography).

KEY DATES	
1893	Born in Bristol, Virginia, on July 24.
1922	Publishes *The Negro in Chicago.*
1923	Founds *Opportunity* magazine.
1928	Becomes chair of the social sciences department at Fisk University.
1946	Becomes president of Fisk University.
1956	Dies in Louisville, Kentucky, on October 27.

JOHNSON, Earvin "Magic"
Basketball Player, Businessman

Basketball player, businessman, and humanitarian, Earvin Johnson, Jr., is better known as Magic Johnson. Some accounts claim that he earned his nickname as a teenager, when he would use his famous smile to lull opponents on the basketball court into a false sense of security before making a move; others cite sportswriter Fred Stabley, Jr., as the source. Stabley called him "Magic" after the 15-year-old scored 36 points and had 16 rebounds and 16 assists during a high school game.

Johnson's impressive height—6 feet 9 inches (2.05m)—meant that he was the tallest point guard in basketball. He also made it acceptable for basketball players to have fun while playing the game. Johnson shocked the sporting world when he announced that he was HIV positive. He is an active campaigner for HIV/AIDS, and has also set up a nonprofit foundation to help inner-city young people. Johnson is also a successful businessman.

The rise to stardom

Born in Lansing, Michigan, on August 14, 1959, Johnson was called "Junior," or "June Bug" by his nine brothers and sisters. His father, Earvin, was a General Motors plant worker and his mother, Christine, was a devout Seventh-Day Adventist and a school custodian. Johnson attended Everett High School in Lansing, where his talent at basketball became obvious. Johnson said, "I practiced all day. I dribbled to the store with my right hand and back with my left. Then I slept with my basketball."

In 1977 Johnson went to Michigan State University, where he led the basketball team to victory in the National Collegiate Athletic Association (NCAA) Championship in 1979 against arch rival Larry Bird (1953–) and the Indiana State University team. Johnson was also named Most Valuable Player (MVP) in the NCAA Final Four.

When Johnson turned professional in 1979, he was selected first overall in the National Basketball Association's (NBA) draft and signed to the Los Angeles Lakers, for whom he played until 1991. Johnson led them to five NBA championships in 1980, 1982, 1985, 1987, and 1988. He led the NBA with 3.43 steals per game in 1981 and 2.67 steals per game in 1982, and was named NBA All-Star 12 times in 1980 and between 1982 and 1992. He was NBA All-Star MVP in 1990 and 1992 and held the NBA All-Star career record for most assists with 127, and the career record for highest assists per game average with 11.2.

Shock announcement

On November 7, 1991, two months after getting married to Earletha "Cookie" Kelly, Johnson made the shocking announcement that he was retiring from the sport on the advice of his physician: He had tested HIV positive during a routine physical exam. Despite this news Johnson continued to play the game over the next few years. He was elected to the 1992–1993 All-Star team and was a member of the Olympic Basketball gold-medal winning Dream Team in Barcelona, Spain (1992).

Johnson also became a part-owner of the Los Angeles Lakers and was head coach for the last 16 games of the 1993–1994 season.

In 1995–1996 Johnson returned to play for the Lakers, but the experience was not a happy one: Several players refused to play with him because of his illness. Johnson decided to leave the game, saying that if he stayed the game would have to change.

▼ *In addition to his sports achievements Earvin "Magic" Johnson has helped many young Americans achieve their dreams through the programs run by his nonprofit foundation, including promoting new technology training in poor neighborhoods.*

INFLUENCES AND INSPIRATION

While "Magic" Johnson earned millions of dollars as a professional basketball player, he claimed that he wanted to play basketball as much as he wanted to be a successful and respected businessman. He was talented enough to achieve both ambitions. His interest in business stemmed from visiting the General Motors plant where his father worked when he was a child. Johnson helped his father clean the executive offices there. Johnson said, "I would sit in the chair behind the desk and dream I was the CEO."

Earvin Johnson, Sr., provided his children with a good example. He taught them to work hard, take pride in any task, and to be committed to doing an exemplary job. Johnson said of his father, "He didn't care if I scored 40 points for my high-school team Friday night. I had to be up at 6 o'clock Saturday to help him work." Johnson said he emulated his father. "[He] is my idol, so I always did everything like him. He used to work two jobs and still come home happy every night. He didn't do drugs or drink, and he wouldn't let anyone smoke in his house. Those are rules I adopted, too."

A man with big heart

After his retirement, Johnson committed himself to promoting awareness about HIV/AIDS. In 1991 he created the Magic Johnson Foundation, a nonprofit organization that focused on improving and addressing the health, educational, and social needs of inner-city youth and communities. Among other things the foundation helped set up university scholarships, mentoring programs, and internships across America.

In 1993 Johnson set up the Johnson Development Corporation (JDC), which established high-quality entertainment and restaurant venues in underserved communities. Johnson explained, "Those kids who come to my [movie] theaters have to know they have someone they can look up to in the business community, so that's why I want to be the best and the biggest. I also have to show athletes they can be more than just a basketball player, football player, and so on."

The company also provided much-needed jobs in high-crime areas in which major companies usually refused to do business. JDC formed a business partnership with several companies, including the transnational corporation Starbucks, with which it created Urban Coffee Opportunities (UCO) in 2005. In that year UCO set up 70 Starbucks in 38 cities in 13 different states, all located in ethnically diverse neighborhoods. Johnson said that African Americans would "drive anywhere to get a cup of Starbucks, but now we have it in our own communities, and that's why our [company's] numbers have been so high."

The bigger picture

Johnson has been heavily involved in charitable work for a number of organizations, including the United States National AIDS Committee, the United Negro College Fund, the Muscular Dystrophy Association, the American Heart Association, the Urban League, the Make-A-Wish Foundation, and the Starlight Foundation.

Johnson was a member of former Vice President Al Gore's White House Community Empowerment Board; he participated in business community efforts designed to encourage leaders and businesses to invest in neglected neighborhoods. Johnson is also Ambassador of Peace for the United Nations.

Among the many awards Johnson has received is the Summit 2000 Ronald H. Brown Award for Leadership. In 2002 he was inducted into the Basketball Hall of Fame.

KEY DATES

1959	Born in Lansing, Michigan, on August 14.
1979	Drafted by the LA Lakers.
1991	Announces that he has HIV/AIDs; establishes the Magic Johnson Foundation.
1992	Wins Olympic gold medal with Dream Team.
1995	Plays for the Los Angeles Lakers until 1996.
2002	Inducted into the Naismith Memorial Basketball Hall of Fame.

Further reading: Johnson, Earvin "Magic", with William Novack. *My Life.* New York, NY: Fawcett, 1993.
www.magicjohnson.org (Magic Johnson Foundation official site).
http://www.nba.com/history/players/johnsonm_summary.html (NBA page).

JOHNSON, George E.
Entrepreneur

One of the most successful African American businesspeople of the 20th century, George E. Johnson is the founder of Johnson Products Co., the maker of a leading brand of "ethnic" hair-care products and the first African American–owned company to trade on the American stock exchange. Johnson's entrepreneurial skill, together with his dedication and loyalty to the African American community, has made him an influential and inspirational figure for generations of young black businesspeople. He once said that the thing that he was most proud of "is the impact that my success has had upon the black youth in our community."

Early life
George Ellis Johnson was born in a three-room shack in Richton, Mississippi, on June 16, 1927. His parents separated when he was two years old. Like many young African Americans from the South at this time, Johnson and his mother migrated north in search of new opportunities and a new way of life. His mother worked in the cafeteria of a hospital and Johnson shined shoes from an early age to help out. He left school while still a teenager to work as a busboy and to wait tables in a bowling alley. At age 18 his luck changed when he obtained a job as a salesman with Fuller Products, a highly successful black hair-care company owned by S. B. Fuller (*see box*).

The hair-care entrepreneur
At that time hair products were one of the few areas of business in which African Americans could succeed, in part because hairdressing and barbering had themselves long been an economic mainstay of black Americans. Some of the first black millionaires, including Madam C. J. Walker, had made their fortunes in the hair-care sector by running their own companies.

By the 1950s Johnson had risen to be a manager at Fuller and was eager to set up his own business. Working with a black Chicagoan barber named Orville Nelson and the head of Fuller's research laboratory, German-born chemist Herbert A. Martini, Johnson developed an effective hair-straightening product, which was then successfully tried out in Nelson's shop. In 1955, with just $250 each to invest, Johnson and Nelson set up their own hair-care business, launching the product Ultra Wave Hair Culture.

Nelson left the business after just three months, but Johnson persisted with the enterprise and in 1957 incorporated it as the Johnson Products Company.

Adapting to changing fashions
Johnson's company particularly began to flourish after 1958, when an even more efficient hair-straightening product, Ultra Sheen, was introduced to the market. In the late 1950s African American women usually straightened their hair by using a hot pressing comb, a time-consuming and cumbersome process that often ended up damaging the hair. Johnson's products revolutionized black hair-care, enabling women to straighten their hair cheaply, simply, and safely at home.

Johnson also proved himself adaptable to changing fashions. During the 1960s he launched the Afro-Sheen line, as a response to the popularity of the "Afro" look, a fashion in tune with the political and cultural assertions of black ethnicity at this time.

In 1971 Johnson Products was listed on the stock exchange, and by 1975 the company's sales were $37.6 million. However, the profitability of the black hair-care sector attracted mainstream beauty-product manufacturers, such as Revlon, into the market who began to aim both competitively priced products and sleek advertising at African American women.

Black pride
In 1981 the black-owned industry fought back to regain black customers: 10 leading companies, including Johnson Products, founded the American Health and Beauty Aids Institute (AHBAI) and launched the "Proud Lady" product symbol as a way of appealing to consumers' ethnic pride. Despite such efforts, Johnson Products' profits fell dramatically, and in 1988, in an attempt to revive the company's fortunes, Johnson appointed his son Eric as the company president. The following year Johnson's former wife, Joan B. Johnson, became the controlling shareholder, and in 1993 she and her son sold the company for $67 million to the IVAX Corporation.

The sale of a black-owned and black-controlled business to a white corporation provoked an outcry in the African American community. Johnson himself had always vowed to keep his company "black," and his wife's and son's decision to sell was widely viewed as a betrayal

INFLUENCES AND INSPIRATION

Johnson has often cited as his inspiration the wealthy black Chicago businessman S. B. Fuller (1905–1988), the man to whom he owed his training in the black hair-care industry. African American success in the sector had always depended in part on the mentorship of talented young employees by successful entrepreneurs. Fuller was himself a protégé of the Illinois cosmetics manufacturer Anthony Overton (1865–1946) who went on to mentor not only Fuller but

also Joe Dudley (1937–), founder of Dudley Products Inc.

During his career Fuller developed an extraordinary entrepreneurial empire that encompassed not only the beauty- and cleaning-product company Fuller Products Inc., but also businesses such as a black newspaper chain, a black Chicago theater (the Regal), and a department store. Fuller Products reached the height of its success during the 1960s, when the company ran 85 stores across

the United States and had a multiracial staff of some 5,600 people.

Fuller also owned a white cosmetics company, Boyer International Laboratories, a fact that he was able to keep secret from its many white southern customers until the early 1960s. At that point white supremacist groups, such as the Ku Klux Klan, organized an effective boycott of Boyer's products, causing Fuller's empire to collapse.

not only of their husband and father's values but also of the whole black community. In 1998, IVAX sold Johnson Products to another black company, Carson Products, then the leading manufacturer of ethnic products. In 2000 Carson was bought by L'Oréal USA, who were forced by the Department of Justice to divest the Johnson Products brand, which was bought by the Wella Group.

A model businessman

Meanwhile, Johnson, who had openly condemned the selling of his former company in the black press, continued to be viewed as a model black businessman. He was perceived as an acute, tough-minded entrepreneur who had also served the community that had helped bring him his success and fortune. Throughout his career, Johnson has supported numerous civic organizations, notably Operation PUSH, the African American campaign group set up by Jesse Jackson in 1971. Johnson also set up charitable groups such as the George E. Johnson Foundation and the George E. Johnson Educational Fund. He is on the board of Chicago's Lyric Opera and is a trustee of Northwestern University.

Johnson is also a leading shareholder of Indecorp, one of the largest black-owned financial institutions in the United States, which also owns Chicago's Independence Bank and Drexel National Bank. Johnson's achievements and charitable work have won him wide recognition. In 1978 he was honored with an American Black Achievement Award by *Ebony* magazine. He has also been awarded honorary doctorates by nine universities, including Fisk University and Tuskegee Institute.

Johnson believes that his success is inspiring for other African Americans. "Today you can count black cosmetic and hair-care companies in the dozens. When I started the company in 1954, you could count black hair-care companies on one hand. So our success has really been a beacon for a lot of blacks who had ambition to try to do something and were encouraged by the fact that we were successful."

KEY DATES

1927 Born in Richton, Mississippi, on June 16.

1945 Begins work for the Chicago-based Fuller Products.

1955 Launches the black hair-care product Ultra Wave.

1971 Johnson Products becomes the first African American company to trade on Wall Street.

1988 Appoints his son, Eric Johnson, as president of Johnson Products.

1993 Johnson Products is sold to IMAX and later becomes part of the Wella Group.

See also: Black Identity and Popular Culture; Jackson, Jesse; Walker, Madame C. J.

Further reading: Walker, Juliet E. K. *(ed.) Encyclopedia of African American Business History.* Westport, CT: Greenwood Press, 1999.
www.businessandindustryhalloffame.com/
Johnson_George.html (Biography).

JOHNSON, Georgia Douglas
Poet

Georgia Douglas Johnson was a talented poet and playwright whose Washington, D.C., home was a literary salon for many of the artists from the early days of the Harlem Renaissance, the literary movement that was centered in Harlem, New York City, during the 1920s. Douglas's literary reputation has grown in recent years and her contribution to African American literature has been recognized.

Early life
Georgia Blanche Douglas Camp was born in Atlanta, Georgia, on September 10, probably in about 1877. She was educated in Rome and then Atlanta, Georgia, before graduating from Atlanta University's Normal School in 1893. Douglas started to teach at Marietta, Georgia, immediately afterward. In 1902 she quit teaching to study music, first at the Oberlin Conservatory of Music and then at the Cleveland College of Music. She left Ohio the following year to return to teaching.

Johnson's husband, lawyer Henry Lincoln Johnson, discouraged his wife's literary aspirations, but she

▼ *Georgia Douglas Johnson held literary gatherings at her home in Washington, D.C.*

KEY DATES	
1877	Born in Atlanta, Georgia, on September 10 at about this time.
1903	Marries Henry Lincoln Johnson.
1918	Publishes first book of poetry.
1926	Publishes first play.
1962	Publishes last book of poetry.
1966	Dies in Washington, D.C., on May 14.

published a poem, "Omnipresence," in the June 1905 issue of the *Voice of the Negro*. When she moved to Washington, D.C., with her husband and two sons, Johnson continued to write poetry. In 1918 her first book of poetry, *The Heart of a Woman and Other Poems*, was published, followed by *Bronze: A Book of Verse* four years later.

A literary salon
When Johnson's husband died in 1925 she had to take on several jobs to pay for her sons' college tuition, leaving her little time to write. However, she did find time to host literary evenings. W. E. B. DuBois, Langston Hughes, Alain Locke, and Jean Toomer were just some of her guests. Douglas's literary salon was instrumental in creating a feeling of community for many of the artists who went on to later success in New York.

During the 1920s Johnson wrote plays. Of the almost 30 she is known to have written, few survive. Her short stories have also been lost. From the mid-1940s until her death from a stroke in 1966, Johnson published the 200 or so poems that she wrote in publications such as the *Journal of Negro History*. She applied for fellowships to allow her more time to write, but with little success.

See also: DuBois, W. E. B.; Hughes, Langston, Locke, Alain; Toomer, Jean

Further reading: Johnson, Georgia Douglas. *The Selected Works of Georgia Douglas Johnson*. New York, NY: G.K. Hall, 1997.
http://www.english.uiuc.edu/maps/poets/g_l/ douglas-johnson/johnson.htm (Comprehensive biography).

JOHNSON, Jack
Boxer

Decades before Jackie Robinson broke the color bar in baseball, Jack Johnson became boxing's first African American world heavyweight champion. After winning the world title in 1908, Johnson faced enormous antagonism from white mainstream America, demonstrating the huge racial chasm that existed in the nation in the early 20th century. Apart from Jackson's domination in the ring, his flamboyant personality and refusal to appear humble and cower before white America only fueled hostility and resentment toward him. To the chagrin of many white people, Johnson's victories in the ring also challenged notions of white superiority and served to instil pride and hope in many black Americans.

Born in Galveston, Texas, in 1878, Johnson developed his boxing skills by participating in battle royals. In these degrading events, organized by whites for entertainment value, a large group of young blacks entered the ring and fought until the last man was standing. By 1903

▼ *Jack Johnson was the first black American world heavyweight champion boxer. He took the title from Tommy Burns on December 26, 1908.*

KEY DATES	
1878	Born in Galveston, Texas, on March 31.
1908	Beats Tommy Burns on December 26.
1910	Beats Jim Jeffries on July 4.
1915	Defeated by Jess Willard on April 5.
1946	Dies in Raleigh, North Carolina, on June 10.

Johnson had emerged as the premier African American boxer in the nation and he traveled across the country looking for challengers.

Making a mark
Johnson's break came in 1908, when the world champion, Canadian Tommy Burns, agreed to fight him in Sydney, Australia. Johnson won the match in 13 rounds and took the title. Bowing to pressure from white Americans who were appalled by the idea of a black champion, former champion Jim Jeffries, deemed "The Great White Hope," agreed to come out of retirement. On July 4, 1910, in Reno, Nevada, Johnson convincingly defeated Jeffries in 15 rounds. His victory resulted in race riots across the nation.

Owing largely to his fast lifestyle and relationships with white women, in 1912 the fighter was convicted of violating the Mann Act, which forbade the transportation of women across state lines for immoral purposes. Although the law was created to restrict trafficking in prostitution, Johnson was prosecuted for traveling with his white girlfriend, later his wife, who had formerly been a prostitute. To avoid imprisonment Johnson moved to France. After losing his title to Jess Willard in 1915 in Havana, Cuba, Johnson returned to the United States in 1920 and served a year in prison. In the 1920s Johnson fought in a few bouts but his career was essentially over. He died in a car crash in Raleigh, North Carolina, in 1946.

See also: Color Bar and Professional Sports

Further reading: Ward, Geoffrey C. *Unforgivable Blackness: The Rise and Fall of Jack Johnson.* New York, NY: A. A. Knopf, 2004.
http://www.cyberboxingzone.com/boxing/jjohn.htm (Johnson's fight record).

JOHNSON, James Weldon
Writer, Activist

James Weldon Johnson was a man of many talents. The author of the National Association for the Advancement of Colored People's (NAACP) official song, he was a poet, novelist, songwriter, and editor, as well as an academic and diplomat who worked to promote African American culture.

A man of great intellect
Johnson was born in Jacksonville, Florida, in 1871, into a middle-class, church-going family. He attended Stanton School, one of the only schools in Florida at the time to accept African Americans, before going to Atlanta University. While there Johnson began to write poetry.

After graduation Jackson returned to Jacksonville, where he was employed as principal at Stanton School. At the same time he founded the *Daily America,* a newspaper for African Americans, which was published for eight months between 1895 and 1896. He also studied law and became the first African American to pass the bar exams in Florida.

▼ *James Weldon Johnson's most famous book of poems was* **God's Trombones: Seven Negro Sermons in Verse** *published in 1927.*

Johnson collaborated with his brother John Rosamond Johnson (1873–1954) on many songs. John wrote the music and James the lyrics. Their most famous song "Lift Ev'ry Voice and Sing" became popular throughout the black American community. In 1920 the NAACP adopted it as their anthem and the song became a favorite choice for the civil rights movement. The brothers moved to New York to write songs, with some success.

Johnson embarked on a successful career as a diplomat between 1906 and 1913 in Latin America. While in Venezuela he wrote his only novel, *The Autobiography of an Ex-Colored Man*, published anonymously in 1912. He did not claim authorship until 1927. The book explored white society from an African American perspective.

On his return to the United States Johnson worked for the NAACP, first as field secretary and then as executive secretary, a position he held until 1930. Based in New York, he also promoted young black writers involved in the Harlem Renaissance and became friends with Charles Spurgeon Johnson, editor of *Opportunity*. He later joined Johnson at Fisk University, Nashville, Tennessee, and also taught at New York University before his death in a car crash in Great Barrington, Massachusetts, on June 26, 1938. More than 2,000 people attended Johnson's funeral.

KEY DATES	
1871	Born in Jacksonville, Florida, on June 17.
1900	Writes lyric for "Lift Ev'ry Voice and Sing."
1912	Publishes anonymously *The Autobiography of an Ex-Colored Man*.
1920	Appointed executive secretary of the NAACP.
1929	Becomes professor of creative writing at Fisk University under Charles Spurgeon Johnson.
1934	Joins New York University.
1938	Dies in Great Barrington, Massachusetts, on June 26.

See also: Harlem Renaissance; Johnson, Charles S.

Further reading: Witalec, Janet (ed.). *Harlem Renaissance. A Gale Critical Companion*. Vol 3. Detroit, MI: Gale, 2003. www.poets.org/poet/jwjohfst.htm (Biography).

JOHNSON, John H.
Publisher, Entrepreneur

John Harold Johnson was the publisher of the very successful magazines *Ebony* and *Jet*. At a young age Johnson noticed that rich people were well dressed and wore suits and that not many black people dressed that way. He became determined to wear a suit when he grew up. He said that he hoped that his example would show young black people that the American Dream is still alive, well, and working.

Early life
Born in Arkansas City, Arkansas, on July 19, 1918, Johnson was the only son of Leroy Johnson and Gertrude Jenkins. His father was killed in a sawmill accident when Johnson was eight years old, and his mother raised him alone, working as a cook and washerwoman to support them both. After the eighth grade Johnson moved with his mother to Chicago, where he discovered that middle-class black people existed. This inspired him and he became an honor student at DuSable High School and managing editor of the school paper. Singer Nat King Cole and comic Redd Foxx were among his classmates.

Harry Pace
Johnson's speech to the Chicago Urban League after his graduation so impressed Harry Pace, president of the Supreme Liberty Life Company, one of most prominent black companies in Chicago, that he offered Johnson a job. As part of his duties Johnson collected articles from national publications and this gave him the idea of publishing the material and marketing it to the black community. In 1939, aged 21, Johnson became editor of Pace's in-house magazine. He also attended the University of Chicago part time while he was working, funded by a scholarship, which Pace made available.

Following dreams
In 1941 Johnson married Eunice Walker, and they had a daughter, Linda. Shortly afterward Johnson decided to put into practice an idea that he had nurtured for a long time: He wanted to publish a magazine similar to the *Reader's Digest* for black Americans. However, Johnson was refused a loan by the First National Bank and when he went to prominent members of Chicago's black community, including Roy Wilkins, head of the NAACP, for help, they tried to talk him out of the venture. In November

▲ *John H. Johnson in 1974. His mother Gertrude helped procure the loan that originally financed his business empire.*

1942 Johnson borrowed $500 from the Citizens Loan Corporation using his mother's furniture as collateral (*see box on p. 26*). He used the money to start Johnson Publishing, naming his first publication the *Negro Digest*.

Johnson located his business in the office of attorney Earl B. Dickerson, on the second floor of Pace's insurance building. He initially used the policyholder's list of Supreme Life to get subscriptions. Although successful, Johnson knew that he needed to do something to make people buy his publication on a wider level. He made friends and family ask for the digest at newsstands and he was soon getting mass orders. The *Negro Digest* became

JOHNSON, John H.

John H. Johnson often claimed that his mother Gertrude Johnson was the greatest influence in his life. In a 1987 interview with *Crisis* he said that his mother "was strong; she had great faith in the ultimate triumph of justice and hard work. She believed passionately in education."

At the time Johnson grew up, Arkansas City, Arkansas, did not offer many educational opportunities to black people beyond the eighth grade. In fact, rather than be out of school for a year Johnson ended up repeating eighth grade. When Mrs. Johnson heard that there were better opportunities for African Americans in Chicago, Illinois, she decided to move there with her son. She worked hard and saved for two years to finance the relocation.

Johnson was a naturally ambitious young man, but living in Chicago showed him that black Americans could be successful if they were determined, even if many other people believed otherwise. In 1942 Mrs. Johnson showed how much she believed in her son when she allowed him to borrow $500 against her furniture in order to start his first business. It paid off: In 1990 Johnson had an estimated personal fortune of $150 million.

extremely popular. It featured work by some of the leading African American and white writers: Johnson, who was very persuasive, even managed to get First Lady Eleanor Roosevelt to contribute an article in 1943.

Building an empire

Not content with running one successful journal, Johnson wanted to build a publishing empire. He decided to launch a publication based on *Life* magazine. The first issues of *Ebony* were published in November 1945, and it proved a successful venture from the start, soon overtaking the *Negro Digest*. The *Negro Digest* was discontinued in 1951, although there were attempts to revive it in later years, the last in 1976. *Ebony* became the Johnson Publishing Company's main magazine, and Johnson began looking for other publishing ventures. Although some were shortlived, *Jet*, a tabloid version of *Ebony* that concentrated on celebrities and gossip, became a huge success.

A man of influence

Johnson was soon recognized as one of the most influential black people in the United States. In addition to publishing he became actively involved in politics. In 1961 President John F. Kennedy appointed him Special U.S. Ambassador to the Independence Ceremonies of the Ivory Coast. Similarly, in 1963 President Lyndon B. Johnson appointed him Special U.S. Ambassador to the Independence Ceremonies of Kenya. In 1966 Johnson also made him a member of the National Selective Service Commission. In 1970 President Richard M. Nixon appointed him to the presidential Commission for the Observance of the 25th Anniversary of the United Nations.

In 1982 Johnson was the first African American to be listed in *Forbes* magazine's annual list of the 400 richest Americans. A well-known philanthropist he donated $4 million to Howard University, Washington, D.C., which renamed its School of Communications in his honor. Johnson received numerous awards, including the NAACP's Spingarn Medal, the *Wall Street Journal*/Dow Jones Entrepreneurial Excellence Award, the Black Journalists' Lifetime Achievement Award, and the Presidential Medal of Freedom.

In 2002 Johnson retired, handing over his company to his daughter Linda Johnson Rice, who became CEO and president. Johnson died of heart failure in 2005.

KEY DATES	
1918	Born in Arkansas City, Arkansas, on January 19.
1942	Establishes Johnson Publishing Company.
1943	Eleanor Roosevelt's article helps increase readership from 50,000 to 100,000.
1965	Awarded the NAACP's Spingarn Medal.
1996	Receives the Presidential Medal of Freedom.
2005	Dies in Chicago, Illinois, on August 8.

See also: Black Identity and Popular Culture; Cole, Nat King; Dickerson, Earl P.; Foxx, Redd; Pace, Harry Herbert; Wilkins, Roy

Further reading: Johnson, John H. *Succeeding Against the Odds.* New York, NY: Penguin 1993.
www.johnsonpublishing.com (Official site).

JOHNSON, Judy
Baseball Player, Coach, Scout

Judy Johnson played for some of the most important teams in the Negro League, including the Darby Daisies, Hilldale, and the Homestead Grays. He was considered the greatest third baseman in the Negro Leagues in the 1920s and 1930s and was team captain of the Pittsburgh Crawfords. Johnson was the first African American to be elected to Baseball's Hall of Fame.

Early life

William Julius Johnson was born in the town of Snow Hill in Worcester County on the Lower Eastern Shore of Maryland on October 26, 1899. He was the youngest of three children born to William Henry Johnson and Annie Lane. Johnson's father, who was a boxing trainer and athletic director of the Negro Settlement House, taught his children, including his daughter, Mary Emma, the rudiments of boxing; Johnson, however, preferred other sports. When his family moved to Wallington, Delaware, Johnson served as a batboy for his father's local team. He quit school after 10th grade, when he realized, as he said later, that his "greatest ambition was to play baseball."

In pursuit of a dream

In 1918 Johnson began playing for the Chester Giants on weekends. He moved on to sign a professional contract with the Atlantic City Bacharach Giants for a fee of $5 per game. The following year he played for the semi-professional Madison Stars of Philadelphia. Hilldale purchased Johnson for $100 in 1920, and the next year gave him $150 a month to be their starting third baseman. Hilldale won a championship in 1921 and played in the

▲ *Judy Johnson's father originally wanted him to become a boxer, but Johnson wanted to play baseball.*

Negro League World Series in 1924 and 1925, winning the latter. Johnson's teammates called him "Judy," owing to his striking resemblance to a Chicago American Giants player, Judy Gans.

Johnson was the Negro Leagues' top third baseman in the 1920s and 1930s. He served as team captain of the Pittsburgh Crawfords until 1936. The Crawfords had a talented line-up, including catcher Josh Gibson and fellow Hall of Famer James "Cool Papa" Bell. Johnson's career was greatly influenced by Hall of Famer John Henry Lloyd: "He's the man I give the credit for polishing me; he taught me how to play third base," Johnson said.

In 1954 Johnson became the first African American coach in the majors when he accompanied Philadelphia Athletics to spring training in Florida. He worked for the Phillies from 1959 to 1973. In 1975 Johnson was elected to the Baseball Hall of Fame. He died on June 15, 1989, in Wilmington, Delaware. Johnson Field at Wilmington's Frawley Stadium is named for him.

See also: Bell, James "Cool Papa"; Gibson, Josh

Further reading: Rendle, Ellen. *Judy Johnson: Delaware's Invisible Hero.* Wallington, DE: The Cedar Tree Press, 1994.
http://www.hsd.org/DHE/DHE_who_johnson.htm (Biography).

KEY DATES	
1899	Born in Snow Hill, Maryland, on October 26.
1918	Begins playing for the Chester Giants; signs with Atlantic City Bacharach Giants.
1920	Purchased by Hilldale.
1933	Joins Pittsburgh Crawfords; remains there until 1936.
1954	Becomes first African American coach in the majors.
1975	Inducted into the Baseball Hall of Fame.
1989	Dies in Wilmington, Delaware, on June 15.

JOHNSON, Katherine G.
Mathematician, Astrophysicist

A gifted mathematician and scientist, Katherine G. Johnson played a significant role in the development of the U.S. space program during the 1950s, 1960s, and 1970s, while working for the National Aeronautics and Space Administration (NASA). As an African American woman working in an overwhelmingly white, male domain, Johnson has been an important role model for younger generations of astrophysicists and space technicians.

Early life
Katherine G. Johnson was born in Sulphur Springs, West Virginia, on August 26, 1918. Her parents were eager that Johnson should receive the best education possible and sent her across the state to study. From an early age Johnson showed a special talent for mathematics. She went on to study French and mathematics at West Virginia State College, graduating summa cum laude ("with highest praise"), after which she taught in various high schools across the state.

Making a difference
Johnson's mathematical gifts eventually brought her to the attention of NASA, where she was employed at the newly established (1917) Langley Research Center in Hampton, Virginia, which focuses primarily on aeronautical research. Johnson became part of a team working on the complex mathematical problems associated with space navigation and the orbits and trajectories of spacecraft and satellites.

NASA
It was an exciting time in the development of the United States's space industry. NASA was first set up in 1958 in response to the launch of Sputnik, the first artificial Earth satellite, by the Soviet Union in 1957. The following years saw a frantic "space race" as the two superpowers each struggled to become the first nation to put a human into space.

NASA mathematicians like Johnson worked under huge pressure, using pencil-and-paper methods to fine-tune the trajectories of spacecraft. The accuracy of these calculations was essential as it could mean the difference between life and death for the astronauts involved. Johnson said of the 1950s, "It was a time when computers wore skirts," referring to the fact that the women in the math pool were the computers of the time.

KEY DATES	
1918	Born in Sulphur Springs, West Virginia, on August 26.
1961	Is a member of the team that puts Alan Shepherd into space on a 15-minute suborbital flight.
1962	Charts course for John Glenn to make the first orbital flight.
1969	As part of NASA's Lunar Spacecraft and Operations team helps achieve the first moon landing.
1986	Retires from NASA.
1999	Is honored as the "Outstanding Alumnus of the Year" by her alma mater, West Virginia State College.

Johnson played a significant research role in key NASA programs. She was part of the 1961 team that placed the United States's first astronaut, Alan Shepherd, (1923–1998) into space during a 15-minute suborbital flight. Johnson helped chart the course for John Glenn (1921–) nine months later, when he made the first orbital flight. She also worked on the 1969 program that put the first man on the moon when Neil Armstrong (1930–) took his first step on its surface on July 20. In addition Johnson made major contributions to the development of the space program, working on the first emergency navigation systems and on satellites such as the Earth Resources Satellite, which was used to help locate underground minerals and other earth resources.

Honors
Johnson retired from NASA in 1986 after a long and illustrious career. She has been widely honored for her pioneering work in the field of navigation. As a member of NASA's Lunar Spacecraft and Operations team, she was a joint recipient of a Group Achievement Award. Johnson received an honorary doctor of law degree from SUNY Farmingdale in 1998. A year later West Virginia State College honored her as the "Outstanding Alumnus of the Year."

Further reading: U.S. Department of Energy. *Black Contributors to Science and Energy Technology.* Washington, D.C.: Office of Public Affairs, 1979.
www.scienceyear.com/outthere/black_history/johnson.html (Biography).

JOHNSON, Michael
Athlete

Michael Johnson was one of the world's most outstanding athletes during the 1990s, when he dominated the 200-meter and 400-meter sprint events, and the 4 x 400-meter relay. Johnson ran with a straight back and short stride, a style unlike that of other runners. He was also known for his trademark scowl, which showed that he was getting into the "danger zone" necessary to win his races.

Early life

Michael Duane Johnson was born the youngest of five children in Dallas, Texas, on September 13, 1967. While a pupil at the Skyline High School, Dallas, he became one of the top 200-meter runners in Texas. In 1986 he won a sports scholarship to Baylor University in Waco, Texas. Under the guidance of coach Clyde Hart, who remained his trainer throughout his career, Johnson continued to excel over 200 meters and also began to compete at the 400-meter sprint and the 4 x 400-meter relay. In 1990 he won gold for the 200 meters at the Good Will Games in Seattle; he also graduated with a BA in marketing.

Achieving dreams

In 1991 Johnson won the World Championship 200-meter title in Tokyo, Japan. Favored to win a gold in the 200 meters at the 1992 Summer Olympics, he failed to make the final owing to a bout of food poisoning. He was still part of the gold-medal-winning Olympic 4 x 400-meter relay team at Barcelona, Spain, however.

In the 1994 Good Will Games, Johnson won golds in the 400 meters and 4 x 400-meter relay. The following year he took gold in the 200 meters, 400 meters, and

▲ *Michael Johnson at the World Championships in Seville, Spain, in 1999, where he set a world record.*

4 x 400-meter relay at the World Championships in Gothenburg, Sweden. By the time of the 1996 Olympics in Atlanta, Georgia, Johnson had won 54 consecutive finals at 400 meters and had not been beaten at the distance in seven years. In a pair of specially made gold shoes, Johnson ran to another 400-meter victory at the Olympics. He also won a gold in the 200 meters, setting a new world record of 19.32 seconds and becoming the first man to win Olympic golds at both distances. This achievement led some sports commentators to compare him to long-jumper Bob Beamon. At the World Championships in 1999 Johnson smashed the world record for the 400 meters with a time of 43.18 seconds. At the 2000 Olympics in Sydney, Australia, he again won gold in the 400 meters, and in the 4 x 400-meter relay after which he announced his retirement. Johnson now works as a sports commentator for television and radio.

See also: Beamon, Bob

Further reading: Rosenthal, Bert. *Michael Johnson: Sprinter Deluxe.* St. Charles, MI: GHB Publishers, 2000. http://www.abc.net.au/news/olympics/athletes/johnson.htm (Biography).

KEY DATES	
1967	Born in Dallas, Texas, on September 13.
1992	Wins first Olympic medal at the Barcelona Games in 4 x 400-meter relay.
1995	Wins gold medals in 200 meters, 400 meters, and 4 x 400-meter relay at World Championships.
1996	Wins gold medals in 200 meters and 400 meters at the Atlanta Olympics.
2000	Wins gold in 400 meters and in 4 x 400-meter relay at Sydney Olympics; announces retirement.

JOHNSON, Rafer
Athlete

Rafer Johnson was a decathlete who won silver and gold medals at consecutive Olympic Games in Helsinki, Finland, and Rome, Italy.

Early life

Johnson was born in Hillsboro, Texas, on August 18, 1935, but spent the early part of his childhood in Dallas, Texas, where his family lived in the segregated black part of town. During World War II (1939–1945) he moved with his family to a small town near Fresno, California. Johnson later said that he had no time for the discrimination and prejudice in Texas and that if he had stayed there he would never as a black man have achieved a successful sports career.

At Kingsburg High School in California, Johnson emerged as the leading sportsman of his year, playing football, basketball, and baseball and starring on the track team. He won a football scholarship to UCLA, but soon decided to concentrate exclusively on track and field. In 1955, while still a freshman, he won the decathlon at the Pan-American Games in Mexico City. This was only the fourth time he had competed in the event at any level. Shortly afterward he set a new world record points total—7,985—in a welcome-home decathlon back at Kingsburg.

A great career

At the start of 1956 Johnson won the national decathlon championship. He was the favorite to win the same event at that year's Olympics in Helsinki, but his performance was restricted by a swollen knee and a torn stomach muscle and he had to settle for the silver medal, finishing second to U.S. teammate Milt Campbell.

Johnson never lost another decathlon. Although the world record was taken from him by Vassily Kuznetsov of the Soviet Union early in 1958, Johnson regained it within

▲ *Rafer Johnson cools down after the 1,500 meter run at the 1960 Olympics in Rome.*

the year in Moscow. Johnson then missed most of the 1959–1960 season while recovering from back injuries sustained in an automobile accident. The Russian set another world record, but in July 1960 Johnson regained his title at a meeting in Eugene, Oregon. Later in the year Johnson crowned his career by taking the gold medal in the decathlon at the Olympics in Rome. He then retired from sports, and worked mainly as a sportscaster. He also appeared in several movies, including *None But the Brave* (1965).

Johnson supported Robert F. Kennedy's campaign for the 1968 presidential election. He was with Kennedy when he was shot dead, and was one of the people who wrestled the assassin, Sirhan Sirhan, to the ground.

In 1984 Johnson lit the flame that signaled the opening of the Olympic Games in Los Angeles, California.

See also: Campbell, Milt

Further reading: Johnson, Rafer, with Philip Goldberg. *The Best That I Can Be: An Autobiography.* New York, NY: Doubleday, 1998.
http://espn.go.com/sportscentury/features/00016405.html (ESPN article).

KEY DATES	
1935	Born in Hillsboro, Texas, on August 18.
1955	Wins decathlon at Pan-American Games.
1956	Wins silver medal in decathlon at Helsinki Olympics.
1960	Wins gold medal in decathlon at Rome Olympics.
1968	With Robert F. Kennedy when he is assassinated.

JOHNSON, Robert
Musician

Robert Johnson was one of the greatest blues musicians of all time. He was also among the first African American blues guitarists to have his works recorded. His musical legacy is incalculable, with many of the most successful rock musicians of the 1960s being heavily influenced by his music and guitar skills. When people first heard his distinct guitar, they wondered who the second guitarist was. Others who were similarly impressed with Johnson's blues concluded that a talent so great could only be achieved by supernatural means. This led to the legend that Johnson purchased his unearthly talents by selling his soul to the devil, and then related the event in his most famous and enduring song "Crossroads."

Life on the move
Julia Dodds gave birth to Robert Johnson in 1911 in Hazlehurst, Mississippi. Noah Johnson, his father, was Dodds's companion while her husband Charles Dodds, Jr., was away or otherwise preoccupied with his mistress Selena. Shortly after Robert was born, Julia took her young son and his baby sister and became a migrant laborer. After enduring great hardship, Julia returned to Memphis and briefly took up residence with her husband, along with his mistress and all their children—a total of five, including Robert. For four years Johnson lived in the household of Charles Dodds (known then as Charles Spencer), even after his mother left Memphis to live in northern Mississippi.

Musical beginnings
At about age seven Johnson moved to Robinsonville, Mississippi, to join his mother and her new husband, Willie "Dusty" Willis. At that time Johnson was using Spencer as his family name, but he finally found a home with his mother and stepfather. As a teenager he learned the true identity of his biological father, and he started introducing himself as Robert Johnson. Johnson attended the Indian Creek School in Commerce, Mississippi, but it was music that captured his attention. Starting with a mouth harp and then the harmonica, Robert passed many of his teenage years playing and singing songs with friends.

In the late 1920s Johnson picked up the guitar, the instrument that would make him a legend. Johnson learned from the musicians playing at venues in Robinsonville, including Charlie Patton (1881–1934) and local star Willie Brown.

▲ *Robert Johnson only recorded 29 songs but his influence on later music is still heard today.*

KEY DATES	
1911	Born in Hazlehurst, Mississippi, on May 8.
1929	Marries Virginia Travis in Penton in February.
1930	Son House moves to Robinsonville; inspires and teaches Johnson the blues.
1936	Records first of two sessions for Vocalion.
1938	Dies in Greenwood, Mississippi, on August 16.

INFLUENCES AND INSPIRATION

In his short life Robert Johnson changed American popular music, laying the foundations of what became rock 'n' roll. Some of the countless superstars directly influenced by Johnson's recordings include Muddy Waters, Cassandra Wilson, Led Zeppelin, the Rolling Stones, and the Grateful Dead. The significance and importance of Johnson's music is clearly reflected in the following tributes from two music icons who were deeply inspired by his music.

Guitar legend Eric Clapton said "Robert Johnson to me is the most important blues musician who ever lived. He was true, absolutely, to his own vision, and as deep as I have gotten into the music over the last 30 years, I have never found anything more deeply soulful than Robert Johnson. His music remains the most powerful cry that I think you can find in the human voice. I knew it when I first heard it... it seemed to echo something I had always felt."

According to Rolling Stones' guitarist Keith Richard, "To me Robert Johnson's influence—he was like a comet or a meteor that came along and, boom, suddenly he raised the ante, suddenly you just had to aim that much higher. You can put the record on now, and it's as fresh and interesting as the first day you heard it. Everybody should know about these 29 titles. Everybody should know Robert Johnson....You want to know how good the blues can get? Well, this is it."

Johnson spent most of his free time playing music, but he worked as a farmer. He met and married Virginia Travis in 1929, but the very next year Virginia and her baby died in childbirth.

Learning the guitar

Two months after he lost his wife and first child, Johnson found a new teacher. Blues legend Son House (1902–1988) moved to Robinsonville in 1930. The intense, raw music House played at local juke joints spoke to Johnson's grieving heart. Eventually Johnson left Robinsonville for Hazelhurst, Mississippi, in search of his birth father.

In Hazlehurst Johnson met and secretly married Calletta "Callie" Craft in 1931. Craft lovingly supported Johnson, tolerating his late nights learning from and playing with bluesman Ike Zinnerman (whose work was never recorded). Johnson played guitar almost constantly, practicing all hours and playing at local juke joints for bustling Saturday night crowds. He quickly became popular in the area, and he moved with Callie and her children to Clarksdale, Mississippi, which had a larger music scene. The move eventually ended his marriage, but Johnson was clearly becoming a master bluesman.

One of a kind

Johnson would eventually make a home in Helena, Arkansas, but after leaving Clarksdale at the end of his marriage, he returned to Robinsonville to visit his mother and his former teachers. Johnson amazed Son House and Willie Brown with his playing. Both older men saw that Johnson had become a one-of-a-kind bluesman.

Johnson traveled throughout the South, and as far north as Canada, playing in juke joints, clubs, and all kinds of gatherings. Although he was known as an intrepid road musician, ready to travel for any gig, it was in Helena, Arkansas, that Johnson met and played with legendary performers like Howlin' Wolf (1910–1976) and Sonny Boy Williamson, among others.

In 1936 and 1937 Johnson recorded 29 songs in two sessions for Vocalion in San Antonio and Dallas, Texas. One of the tracks, *Terraplane Blues*, became a considerable hit, bringing him new fame and bigger audiences.

While on the road with Johnny Shines (1915–1992), Johnson stopped to play at a country roadhouse near Greenwood, Mississippi, called Three Forks. He shared the stage with Honeyboy Edwards (1915–) on August 13, 1938. During the set Johnson first lost his voice and then went outside to be sick. Edwards thought that Johnson's whiskey had been poisoned by a jealous customer because Johnson had been eying his girl. Three days later Johnson died at the early age of 27. Some say he was shot, others that he died of syphilis. His death certificate simply says "no doctor" under cause of death. The first Johnson album *King of the Delta Blues Singers* was compiled in 1961.

See also: Waters, Muddy; Williamson, John Lee; Wilson, Cassandra

Further reading: Wald, Elijah. *Escaping the Delta: Robert Johnson and the Invention of the Blues.* New York, NY: Armistad Press, 2004.
http://www.deltahaze.com/johnson/bio.html (Biography).

JOHNSON, Robert L.
Entrepreneur

Robert L. Johnson is an entrepreneur and founder of Black Entertainment Television (BET), the first network to specifically target African Americans. The first African American billionaire, Johnson was also the first black person to own a high-profile professional sports franchise.

Robert Louis Johnson was born in poverty in Hickory, Mississippi, on April 8, 1946. His mother taught in a segregated, one-room elementary school and his father cut and sold lumber. In 1963 his parents moved Johnson and his nine siblings to Freeport, Illinois, where his parents worked in the local factories. As a teenager Johnson had a number of part-time jobs, ranging from delivering newspapers to a summer job cleaning the animal pens and the public restrooms at the local fairground. At school Johnson was athletic, playing for the football and basketball teams and running track.

▼ **Robert L. Johnson and Sheila Crump Johnson built up a billion-dollar broadcast company, training and employing many African Americans in the media.**

Although Johnson originally planned to follow his brother into the Air Force, he changed his mind when his advanced English teacher asked which students intended to apply for college. The only African American in the class, Johnson discovered that he was also the only student without his hand up and raised it only to avoid humiliation. Johnson was swept along by his teacher's determination to make sure that all her students saw guidance counselors and completed their applications on time, but he gradually came to realize the importance of taking advantage of every opportunity that presented itself.

Entering the University of Illinois in 1964, Johnson became the only one of his brothers and sisters to go to college. Majoring in history, Johnson met his future wife Sheila Crump in his junior year. Upon his graduation in 1968, Johnson won a place at the Woodrow Wilson School at Princeton University, New Jersey. However, Johnson found he was not fully concentrating on his studies because he missed Crump, and he dropped out of Princeton to return to Illinois. The couple were married in 1969 and Johnson became a high school teacher while his wife completed her music degree. He later returned to Princeton, earning an MA in public administration in 1972, supported financially by his wife, who gave music lessons.

Moving in the right direction

Moving to Washington, D.C., Johnson was first employed by the Corporation for Public Broadcasting before being appointed press secretary to Congressman Walter E. Fauntroy. In 1976 Johnson became vice president of

KEY DATES	
1946	Born in Hickory, Mississippi, on April 8.
1976	Becomes a lobbyist for cable television.
1978	Begins developing plans to produce television to target African Americans.
1980	Cofounds Black Entertainment Television (BET).
1991	BET is the first African American company to be listed on the New York Stock exchange.
2000	Sells BET to Viacom for $3 billion.
2003	Buys the NBA team the Charlotte Bobcats.

government relations for the National Cable & Telecommunications Association (NCTA). While lobbying the government on behalf of cable television, Johnson became aware of a niche market that had yet to be exploited: television aimed at middle-class African American viewers.

Johnson began to formulate his plans for a black-owned cable television network; he set about approaching potential investors. The president of the NCTA, Tom Wheeler, invested $15,000 and John Malone, president of TeleCommunications, provided Johnson with $500,000. A chance meeting at the NCTA annual convention with the president of UA-Columbia Cablevision, Bob Rosencrans, supplied Johnson with the cable TV satellite slots he needed to launch his channel. On January 8, 1980, at 11:00 P.M., Black Entertainment Television (BET) aired its first program. The channel initially broadcast only two hours of television a week.

Eventually broadcasting 24 hours a day, the station gradually broadened its range of programs to include music videos, talk shows, Christian programs, news, sports, and comedy, cultivating viewers throughout the United States and the Caribbean. In 2005 it boasted a viewership of more than 70 million households. In 1991 BET also became the first African American owned company to become a public corporation, when it was listed on the New York Stock Exchange. The network continued to prosper, developing music channels, a Web site, publishing and film divisions; Johnson and his partners gained private control of BET once more in 1998.

In 2000 Johnson became the first African American billionaire when he sold the network for approximately $3 billion to the media group Viacom, agreeing to continue as chief executive officer of the company. After dividing the proceeds of the company's sale with his wife when they divorced in 2002, Johnson's assets were believed to be worth around $1.3 billion.

Life after BET

Johnson established the RLJ Companies, which owns shares in businesses operating in the fields of hospitality, real estate, gaming, recording, and professional sports. The company also owns the Barnett–Arden Collection, the United States's oldest and biggest collections of African American art. In 2003 Johnson also realized his ambition of purchasing a National Basketball Association franchise when he bought North Carolina's Charlotte Bobcats, for an estimated $300 million. The deal also gave him ownership of the Women's National Basketball Association team the Sting. In 2004 Johnson founded a sports and entertainment channel for Carolina, the Sports Entertainment Network, known as C-SET.

Johnson has been awarded a NAACP Image Award, the *Broadcasting & Cable Magazine*'s Hall of Fame Award, and Cablevision Magazine's 20/20 Vision Award.

In June 2005 Johnson appointed Debra L. Lee (*see box*) as BET's CEO and president. In October, at a star-studded Silver Anniversary party for BET, he retired.

See also: Johnson, Sheila Crump

Further reading: Pulley, Brett. *The Billion Dollar BET: Robert Johnson and the Inside Story of Black Entertainment Television.* Hoboken, NJ: Wiley, 2004.
http://www.who2.com/robertljohnson.html (Biography and interview).

JOHNSON, Sheila Crump
Entrepreneur, Philanthropist

Business woman, philanthropist, musician, and cofounder of the powerful Black Entertainment Television (BET), Sheila Crump Johnson is the first female African American billionaire.

Early life

Born in McKeesport, Pennsylvania, in 1949, Sheila Crump moved frequently during her childhood with her government accountant mother and her neurosurgeon father. At age five Crump developed a passion for the violin, often waking in the middle of the night to practice.

After winning a scholarship to the University of Illinois, Chicago, to study music, Crump became the university's first African American cheerleader. She met Robert L. Johnson while studying. They married in 1969 and moved to Princeton, New Jersey, where Johnson gave violin lessons to fund her husband's graduate studies. When he was appointed as a congressional aide, the couple moved to Washington, D.C. Johnson continued to teach violin, later working in private schools.

Between 1973 and 1989 Johnson coordinated the Young Strings in Action orchestra and became a U.S. Information Agency cultural liaison to the Middle East, holding the post for five years and helping found a National Music Conservatory in Jordan.

BET

During this time Johnson also supported her husband's television venture. Robert L. Johnson wanted to start a cable network aimed at African American viewers, and he did so with his wife's help: She signed the loan agreements that helped fund BET. The network aired at 11.00 P.M. on

▲ *Sheila Crump Johnson, pictured here with her then-husband Robert at a charity gala in 2000.*

January 8, 1980. Sheila Johnson continued to be involved in the network, developing the acclaimed Teen Summit discussion program for black teenagers. BET was hugely successful and created hundreds of jobs for black Americans in the media. The Johnsons sold BET in 2000 for around $3 billion in stock.

The couple divorced in 2002 and Johnson was awarded a fortune of $1.5 billion. Putting the money to use, she hosted charity events and supported the United Negro College Fund, the Parsons School of Design, the State University of New York at Morrisville, and the Hill School in Middleburg. Johnson was awarded an honorary doctorate from Morrisville and created the Crump-Johnson Institute at the university to encourage diversity and provide scholarships.

KEY DATES	
1949	Born in McKeesport, Pennsylvania.
1969	Marries Robert L. Johnson.
1980	Cofounds Black Entertainment Television (BET).
1986	Helps establish the National Conservatory of Music in Jordan.
2000	Sells BET for about $3 billion in stock.
2002	Divorces Robert L. Johnson; awarded $1.5 billion.

See also: Johnson, Robert L.

Further reading: Pulley, Brett. *The Billion Dollar BET: Robert Johnson and the Inside Story of Black Entertainment Television.* Hoboken, NJ: Wiley, 2004.
http://www.morrisville.edu/campus/inst_diversity/Johnson Inst/index.htm (Crump–Johnson Institute site).

JOHNSON, William H.
Painter

William Henry Johnson was a versatile artist who is best known today for his "primitive" style paintings in which he dealt with themes of African American life and ancestry using simplified shapes and bold colors.

Early life
Born in Florence, South Carolina, on March 18, 1901, Johnson was the eldest of the five children of Henry Johnson and Alice Smoot. Johnson was very light-skinned and this promoted rumors that he was not the son of dark-skinned Henry, especially since Alice worked in the household of a rich white landowner.

While attending Wilson School, Johnson showed an early talent for drawing, which prompted his teachers to encourage him to pursue an artistic career. For a while he entertained thoughts of becoming a cartoonist, but realized that his chances of succeeding were limited in smalltown Florence.

In 1918 Johnson moved to New York, where three years later he gained admission to the prestigious National Academy of Design (NAD). While there he won several awards and was encouraged by the artist Charles Webster Hawthorne (1872–1930), an instructor at NAD, with whom he also studied during the summers at the Cape Cod School of Art. The only black student at these summer classes, Johnson did odd jobs around the school in exchange for his tuition. Hawthorne recognized his student's talent and in 1926 helped raise funds for him to study in Paris, France, after he was refused a Pulitzer traveling scholarship on the grounds of race.

Developing a style
Paris was a vibrant center for artists and writers, and Johnson met Henry Ossawa Tanner, one of the most eminent black artists of the time, who had made Paris his home. Johnson embraced the modern styles he encountered in France. Many of his paintings from this time are landscapes and pastoral scenes and show the influence of painters such as Paul Cezanne (1839–1906). In 1927 Johnson moved to Cagnes-sur-Mer in the south of France, where he met the Danish textile artist Holcha Krake, the sister-in-law of German sculptor Chistoph Voll. Together with Krake, Voll, and Voll's sister Erna, Johnson traveled around Europe.

In 1929 Johnson briefly returned to New York, where he won a gold medal from the Harmon Foundation. He also met leading black intellectual Alain Locke, who became his mentor and promoted Johnson's work among his contacts in New York's literary and artistic society. A year later Johnson moved to Denmark and married Krake. In 1932 the couple visited Africa so that Johnson might be, as he put it, "a primitive and cultivated painter." They moved to New York on the eve of World War II (1939–1945). The Works Progress Administration's Federal Art Project gave Johnson teaching work at the Harlem Community Art Center, where he met artists such as Jacob Lawrence.

During this period Johnson's style changed and he began to paint scenes of black American life from his childhood in the rural South, as well as images of urban Harlem. He developed a flat, two-dimensional style, with simplified shapes and bold colors. After Krake's death in 1944 Johnson became mentally ill: From 1947 he was an inmate of the Central Islip State Hospital in New York, where he died in 1970.

See also: Lawrence, Jacob; Locke, Alain; Tanner, Henry Ossawa

Further reading: Powell, Richard J. *Homecoming: The Art and Life of William H. Johnson.* New York, NY: W. W. Norton and Company, 1993.
http://americanart.si.edu/education/guides/whj/index.cfm (Smithsonian American Art Museum site).

KEY DATES

1901	Born in Florence, South Carolina, on March 18.
1921	Begins studies at the National Academy of Design, New York.
1926	Moves to France.
1929	Returns to New York briefly; wins the Harmon Foundation's gold medal; marries Holcha Krake in Denmark.
1939	Joins the Works Progress Administration (WPA), through which he gets a job teaching in the Harlem Community Art Center.
1941	Has first solo exhibition in New York.
1944	Holcha Krake dies.
1947	Suffers a mental breakdown; spends the rest of his life in Central Islip State Hospital.
1970	Dies in Long Island, New York, on April 13.

JOHNSON-BROWN, Hazel W.
Army General, Nurse, Educator

In 1979 Hazel W. Johnson-Brown became the first African American woman appointed to the rank of brigadier general in the Army, as well as the first black chief of the Army Nurse Corps (ANC). Her high-profile achievements, as both a nurse and military leader, have helped pave the way toward greater numbers of African American women reaching the higher ranks of the Army. Born Hazel Winifred Johnson, she changed her surname to Johnson-Brown following her marriage to David B. Brown.

Early life
Johnson-Brown was born in Malvern, Pennsylvania, on October 10, 1927. The daughter of Clarence L. and Garnett Johnson, she grew up as part of a close family on a farm in West Chester, Pennsylvania. As a child she wanted to become a nurse and was eventually able to realize her dream. Johnson-Brown undertook her basic nursing training in New York City's Harlem Hospital: She graduated from there in 1950.

A changing profession
Johnson-Brown belonged to the first generation of African American nurses able to take advantage of the changing climate in the health profession (*see box on p. 38*). While many hospitals at the time were still segregated, particularly those in the South, and black American nurses often faced overt racial prejudice in the workplace, the profession was slowly becoming more inclusive and progressive. In 1951, for example, the American Nurses Association finally accepted African American nurses into its membership.

In 1955, after five years working as a civilian nurse, Johnson-Brown joined the Army. In many ways the military offered black American personnel of both genders a more egalitarian and integrated culture than they could ordinarily access in civilian life. African American nurses had served in the Reserve ANC since the end of World War I (1914–1918), and in 1948 President Harry S. Truman (1945–1953) signed an executive order calling for the integration of all people serving in the armed forces, regardless of race or sex. In March that same year, First Lieutenant Nancy C. Leftenant was the first black woman to become a member of the Regular Army Nurse Corps.

After becoming a second-lieutenant Johnson-Brown was also able to further her nursing education. In 1959 she earned a BA at Villanova University, Pennsylvania. Four years later she gained an MA in nursing education from Columbia University, New York City. While working toward her doctorate she was appointed director and assistant dean of the Walter Reed Army Institute of Nursing at the University of Maryland School of Nursing. In 1978 she gained a PhD in education administration from the Catholic University of America in Washington, D.C.

During this time Johnson-Brown was still on active duty and was stationed at various bases around the country, including in Washington, D.C., and Philadelphia. She also served abroad in Japan. By 1979 she was chief nurse of the Army Medical Command in Korea.

Rising through the ranks
During the Vietnam War (1964–1975), unprecedented numbers of African American men and women served in every area of the military, including in the ANC. Their outstanding record of achievement, together with the political and social changes that occurred as a result of the civil rights movement, resulted in the implementation of a more progressive culture within the armed forces. Simultaneously women's roles in the sector were also changing, and their importance to the service was being increasingly recognized and rewarded. In 1967, for instance, women became eligible for promotion to the rank of admiral or general for the first time.

Nevertheless, a disproportionately small number of African Americans was rising to the higher ranks in all the armed services. In 1977 newly elected president Jimmy Carter (1977–1981) took the advice of Clark M. Clifford, secretary of defense (1968–1969) in President Lyndon B. Johnson's administration (1963–1969), and undertook to increase the number of high-ranking African American personnel. Johnson-Brown was among those who benefited from the policy. In 1977 she was appointed a full colonel and in 1979 became a brigadier general, the highest rank ever achieved by an African American woman. On September 1 of that year, she was named the 16th chief of the ANC, one of the most challenging and prestigious posts within the Army. Johnson-Brown said that she hoped for the sake of the nursing corps that race had not been the criterion for her selection. Surgeon

INFLUENCES AND INSPIRATION

Hazel W. Johnson-Brown has often spoken of the huge debt that she owes to the many extraordinary women who struggled for the advancement of African American nurses, especially in the decades leading up to the civil rights movement.

Among those who helped pave the way for Johnson-Brown's achievements was Mabel Keaton Stauper (1890–1989), who campaigned tirelessly for the military to accept African American nurses into its ranks. M. Elizabeth Carnegie (1916–), the first black nurse appointed to the Florida Nurses Association, was also a huge influence.

Johnson-Brown said, "I'm just standing on their shoulders." She claimed, "I couldn't have done what I've done unless they had done what they did."

Johnson-Brown has herself helped blaze a trail for other African American nurses serving in the Army. In 1987 the black American Brigadier General Clara Adams-Ender (1939–) became the 18th chief of the ANC: Four year later she was in command of more than 20,000 U.S. nurses serving in the Persian Gulf War (1990–1991).

General, Lieutenant General Charles C. Pixley said that her achievement "was beset with obstacles and difficulties that could [only] be overcome by extraordinary dedication, enduring vitality, and great moral courage."

Making a real difference

As chief of the ANC, Johnson-Brown had under her command some 3,800 nurses on active duty, both at home and around the globe. During her four-year tenure Johnson worked hard to improve the training of the army's nursing personnel. In 1981, for example, she oversaw the publication of the first Army Nurse Corps Standards of nursing practice. She also campaigned for nursing to be included in the Reserve Officer Training Corp (ROTC) scholarship program and encouraged the writing of a history of the ANC. Johnson-Brown believed that education and training were important and established the first Nursing Research Symposium.

Johnson-Brown's period in office as head of the ANC also saw some major military and humanitarian operations: In 1980, for example, 54 ANC nurses took part in the evacuation and care of Cuban refugees during the so-called "Freedom Flotilla," the mass flight of some 125,000 Cuban refugees into the United States.

Return to civilian life

At the end of August 1983 Johnson-Brown completed her four-year term as chief of the ANC and retired from the Army. Although now in her late fifties, she continued to play an active role in nursing education, serving as an assistant professor in the nursing administration program at Georgetown University, and later as professor and director of the Center for Health Policy School of Nursing at George Mason University, Fairfax, Virginia, from which she retired in 1995. Johnson-Brown continued working as a consultant in health policy and health administration.

Throughout both her civilian and military careers Johnson-Brown has received many honors, including the Distinguished Service Medal, the Legion of Merit, the Army Commendation Medal with Oak Leaf Cluster, and the Meritorious Service Medal. In 1997 she attended the dedication of the Women in the Military Service for America (WIMSA) Memorial, at the gateway to Arlington National Cemetery in Washington, D.C.

KEY DATES	
1927	Born in Malvern, Pennsylvania, on October 10.
1950	Completes her nursing training at Harlem Hospital, New York City.
1955	Enlists in the Army Nurse Corps (ANC).
1959	Earns BA in nursing from Villanova University, Pennsylvania.
1977	Earns PhD in education administration from the Catholic University of America, Washington, D.C.
1979	Becomes the Army's first African American female brigadier general and the first black chief of the ANC.
1983	Retires from the Army.
1995	Retires from teaching.

See also: Military and African Americans; Stauper, Mabel

Further reading: Haskins, Jim. *African American Military Heroes (Black Stars).* New York, NY: John Wiley & Sons. Inc., 1998.
http://www.nurses.info/contemporary_hazel_johnson_brown.htm (Short biography).

JONES, Absalom
Abolitionist, Religious Leader

Committed to both his faith and the abolition of slavery, Absalom Jones played a central role in the establishment of the Free African Society and the African Episcopal Church of St. Thomas.

In 1804 Jones became the first African American to be ordained as an Episcopal priest in Philadelphia, a city with a large Quaker population. Jones endeavored to give black people greater control over their lives and their religious worship. By establishing their own religious institutions, he argued, African Americans could both worship God "in the way black people want to worship him" and create unity and social welfare within the black community.

Born in Sussex County, Delaware, on November 6, 1746, Jones was taken from the fields into his owner's house when he was very young. Working as a house slave afforded Jones the opportunity to learn to read. He later recalled, "I soon bought myself a primer and begged to be taught by anybody that I found able and willing to give me the least instruction." He used any money he had to buy books, including a copy of the Bible.

In 1762 Benjamin Wynkoop sold the rest of Jones's family to another slave owner and moved with Jones to Philadelphia. Jones worked in his grocery store from dawn to dusk. Wynkoop finally gave Jones permission to attend a night school for black people operated by the Quakers.

In 1770 Jones married Mary, the slave of one of his master's neighbors, and set about trying to gain her freedom with his extra earnings so that his children would not be born into slavery. He purchased Mary's freedom in 1778 and his own in 1784.

Episcopal Church and Allen

In the mid-1780s Jones began attending church at St. George's Methodist Episcopal Church and soon afterward began working as a lay preacher for the church. In 1787 he helped another lay preacher, Richard Allen, found the Free African Society, an organization that embraced abolitionism, raised money, and provided aid to both free blacks and ex-slaves living in Philadelphia. In the early 1790s Jones led the initiative to develop a separate black church for the community. On July 17, 1794, the St. Thomas Episcopal Church became the first black Episcopal Church in the nation. Bishop William White ordained Jones as the first black deacon on August 23, 1795, and as the first black priest in 1804. Jones died in 1818.

A

THANKSGIVING SERMON,

PREACHED JANUARY 1, 1808,

In St. Thomas's, or the African Episcopal, Church,
Philadelphia:

ON ACCOUNT OF

THE ABOLITION

OF THE

AFRICAN SLAVE TRADE,

ON THAT DAY,

BY THE CONGRESS OF THE UNITED STATES.

BY ABSALOM JONES,
RECTOR OF THE SAID CHURCH.

────

PHILADELPHIA:
PRINTED FOR THE USE OF THE CONGREGATION.
FRY AND KAMMERER, PRINTERS.
1808.

▲ *Absalom Jones's 1808 Thanksgiving sermon to celebrate the passing of a law by Congress prohibiting the import of slaves into America.*

KEY DATES	
1746	Born in Sussex County, Delaware, on November 6.
1787	Helps found the Free African Society.
1795	Ordained as deacon.
1804	Ordained as a priest.
1818	Dies in Philadelphia, Pennsylvania, on February 13.

See also: Allen, Richard; Slavery

Further reading: Nash, Gary B. *Forging Freedom: The Formation of Philadelphia's Black Community 1720–1840.* Cambridge, MA: Harvard University Press, 1988.
http://www.pbs.org/wgbh/aia/part3/3h85.html (PBS page and links).

JONES, Deacon
Football Player

Member of the Football Hall of Fame and considered by many to be the best defensive end in the history of the game, Deacon Jones struggled against racism throughout his childhood and early career.

Early life

Born in small-town Eatonville, central Florida, on December 9, 1938, David D. Jones grew up in a segregated community dogged by poverty and lack of opportunities. As he later commented, "I know what it's like to be a kid and to have no dreams." For Jones football was the only way out.

Jones started out in the sport in less than spectacular fashion: His college career was relatively obscure, consisting as it did of a year at South Carolina State University in 1958, a year out in 1959, and then a final season at Mississippi Vocational College. However, Jones's lucky break came in 1961 when two Los Angeles Rams scouts viewing films happened to spot him outrunning the players they were actually scouting.

Great defensive end

Although the Rams were initially unsure of where to play Jones, he soon proved himself as a fast, tough, and highly mobile defensive lineman. Teamed with tackle Merlin Olsen for most of the next decade, Jones worked his way up to becoming part of the "Fearsome Foursome," the most dominant defensive line in the football league of that time or since. During his time with the Rams, Jones also coined the now indispensable term "sack," meaning a tackle of the quarterback behind his line of scrimmage.

Jones won unanimous all-league honors six years in a row (1965–1970), played eight Pro Bowls, and was selected National Football League (NFL) Defensive Player of the Year in 1967 and 1968. After a season with the San Diego

▲ **Sports Illustrated** *called Jones "the greatest defensive end in modern football." He was inducted into the Hall of Fame in 1980.*

Chargers (1972–1973) and a brief spell with the Washington Redskins, Jones retired from professional football in 1974. He went on to have a radio and television career, where he became known for his knowledgeable commentaries, flamboyant humor, candor, and for his criticism of racism.

Successful too in the field of marketing and public relations, Jones has also received acclaim for his work with youth organizations. In 1997 he founded the Deacon Jones Foundation to assist young people through a program of education, mentoring, corporate internship, and community service.

Further reading: Klawitter, John, and Deacon Jones. *Headslap: The Life and Times of Deacon Jones.* New York, NY: Prometheus Books, 1996.
http://www.deaconjones.com (Deacon Jones Foundation site with information about the foundation and Jones).

KEY DATES	
1938	Born in Eatonville, Florida, on December 9.
1961	Begins playing for the Los Angeles Rams.
1974	Retires from professional football.
1980	Inducted into the Football Hall of Fame.

JONES, Edward P.
Writer

Writer Edward P. Jones first came to national attention with his powerful, unsettling novel *The Known World* (2003), which won the 2004 Pulitzer Prize for Fiction. He has been compared with leading African American novelist Toni Morrison for his imaginative and compassionate treatment of the theme of slavery.

A long apprenticeship

Born in Washington, D.C., in 1950, Edward P. Jones was raised by his single mother, who worked as a hotel maid to support her three children. Although unable to read or write herself, she encouraged her son's studies and eventually he won a scholarship to the Catholic College of the Holy Cross in Worcester, Massachusetts, where he took a degree in English.

After graduation, Jones moved back to Washington, D.C., and began writing short stories for publication in

▼ *Edward P. Jones has been praised for the strong, sympathetic characters in his fiction.*

magazines. He also earned an MA in creative writing from the University of Virginia. Unable to support himself solely through his writing, Jones earned his living for almost 19 years as an in-house business writer.

In 1993 Jones finally managed to publish a collection of short stories, *Lost in the City,* in which he portrayed the lives of ordinary working-class African Americans living in the nation's capital. The book gained Jones some acclaim, as well as two literary prizes, the Pen/Hemingway Award and the Lannan Foundation Grant. Despite receiving critical acclaim Jones was still unable to write full time. It was not until 2003 that he was able to publish his next work, the novel *The Known World.*

The Known World

In the novel Jones tells the story of a 19th-century black plantation and slave owner named Henry Townsend, who lives in a fictional southern county called Manchester. Jones first learned about the existence of black slave owners while at college and decided to write a novel on the subject because of the fresh perspective it offered on the historical institution of slavery. *The Known World* was widely hailed as a masterpiece, earning Jones a reputation as one of the most significant contemporary black novelists.

Jones has taught at several universities, including Princeton University, George Mason University, and the University of Maryland. In 2005 he was awarded the prestigious MacArthur Fellowship.

KEY DATES	
1950	Born in Washington, D.C.
1993	Publishes *Lost in the City.*
2003	Publishes of *The Known World;* wins several awards.
2005	Wins the MacArthur Fellowship.

See also: Morrison, Toni; Slavery

Further reading: Jones, Edward P. *The Known World.* New York, NY: Armistad, 2003.
www.harpercollins.com/authorintro/index.asp?authorid=5002 (Jones's official site).

JONES, Elaine R.
Lawyer, Civil Rights Activist

Outstanding lawyer and fearless crusader for civil rights, Elaine Ruth Jones stepped down on May 1, 2004, from her position as director-counsel of the National Association for the Advancement of Colored People's (NAACP) Legal Defense and Educational Fund, a post she had held for more than 10 years. Jones was the first woman to be appointed to the position, just one of the many education and career "firsts" that she has achieved.

Achieving early success

Born in Norfolk, Virginia, on February 3, 1944, Jones knew from early childhood that she wanted to be a lawyer and spend her life fighting for equality. After earning a degree in political science from Howard University, Washington,

▼ *Elaine R. Jones has achieved many firsts: She is an inspiration to black Americans, particularly women.*

D.C., in 1965 she joined the Peace Corps and became one of the first African Americans to serve in Turkey, where she taught English. On her return to the United States two years later Jones became the first African American woman to enroll in and graduate from the University of Virginia School of Law (UVL) at a time when Virginia's accepted policy was to pay for black students to attend college in other states rather than have them attend its all-white universities.

A matter of conscience

Before her graduation Jones was invited to join a prestigious law firm on Wall Street, New York, an offer that she initially accepted. After much deliberation, however, Jones eventually accepted a job for a much reduced salary at NAACP's Legal Defense and Educational Fund (LDF), effectively the legal arm of America's civil rights movement.

INFLUENCES AND INSPIRATION

Jones's parents were sources of inspiration: Her mother, a college-educated teacher, gave her a love of books and also made Jones understand the importance of education. Her father, a Pullman porter and member of the United States's first trade union, told her tales of inequality.

During a trip to Chicago, Illinois, at age seven, Jones and her family were turned away from hotels because of their race. This made her determined to become a lawyer so that she could right such wrongs. "From early childhood," she said, "I have always known

that the struggle for equality would be my life."

Jones's influence on civil rights has been acknowledged through various awards, including from the National Women's Law Center and the NAACP. In 2000 she also won the Eleanor Roosevelt Human Rights Award.

Jones's early years at LDF were spent in the South defending prisoners on death row, work she persisted with despite harassment from white supremacist groups such as the Ku Klux Klan. She also had to fight against the racism inherent in the legal system. In 1972, just two years after leaving law school, she became involved in her first landmark case when she acted as counsel of record in *Furman v. Georgia.* The Supreme Court ruling in that case overturned the sentences of 629 death row inmates on the grounds that racial bias had influenced the prisoners' sentencing; it also ultimately led to the abolition of the death penalty in 37 states over the next 12 years.

Jones left LDF in 1975 to act as special assistant to William T. Coleman, Jr., former LDF board chairman, when he was appointed secretary of transportation in Gerald Ford's administration (1974–1977). She returned to the LDF in 1979, spending the next 14 years at LDF's Washington, D.C., office, as the organization's legislative advocate. In this position Jones was key in securing the passage of many important laws, such as the Voting Rights Act Amendments of 1982, the Fair Housing Act of 1988, and the Civil Rights Act of 1991. During this period Jones also worked on many discrimination cases in the area of employment law, including launching class actions against powerful organizations such as American Tobacco Company and Monsanto.

KEY DATES

1944   Born in Norfolk, Virginia, on February 3.

1967   Becomes the first black woman to study at the University of Virginia School of Law; graduates in 1970.

1993   Acts as first woman director-counsel of the NAACP Legal Defense and Educational Fund.

2000   Receives Eleanor Roosevelt Human Rights Award.

2004   Retires from NAACP.

Making a difference

In 1989 Jones's work was recognized when she became the first black person to be elected to the American Bar Association's board of governors. She was also appointed the first woman director-counsel of LDF in 1993. In that role Jones pushed for equal access to health care and education, opposed racial discrimination, and continued to challenge the death penalty as being biased against minority groups.

In 1996 Jones took on the case of Kemba Smith, a young woman jailed for more than 24 years for her minor role in a northern Virginia drug ring. Jones campaigned personally on Smith's behalf and in doing so highlighted the draconian nature of federal mandatory sentencing guidelines. Although the court ruled against Smith, President Bill Clinton granted her clemency in 2000. Jones was also involved in a landmark affirmative action case involving the University of Michigan.

Toward the end of her career at the LDF Jones was involved in a controversy involving an exchange of memos with Senator Edward Kennedy. Conservative groups alleged that Jones had behaved unethically in seeking to delay Senate Judiciary Committee hearings on nominees to the U.S. Court of Appeals for the Sixth Circuit. Some commentators suggest the uncovering of these memos led Jones to announce her early retirement from LDF in 2004. Jones said "I am stepping down-—not retiring—confident that change is a good thing. Change is something we should all embrace. I am also convinced that more than one person can lead, and it is time for new leadership."

See also: Affirmative Action; Civil Rights; Supreme Court

Further reading: Smith, J. Clay, Jr. (ed.). *Rebels in Law: Voices in History of Black Women Lawyers.* Ann Arbor, MI: University of Michigan Press, 1998.
http://www.naacpldf.org (NAACP's LDF site, featuring Jones).

JONES, Eugene Kinckle
Social Welfare Reformer

A pioneering sociologist and civil rights campaigner, Eugene Kinckle Jones believed cooperation between races would enable African Americans to achieve equality and bring America true democracy.

Early life

The son of prominent professors Joseph Endom Jones and Rosa Daniel Kinckle, Jones was born into affluent circumstances in Richmond, Virginia, on July 30, 1855. Jones grew up observing his parents succeed at Virginia Union University, an integrated institution, and the experience encouraged his belief that positive interaction between races was possible. Jones also believed strongly that as an African American his only path to success was through education.

Gaining a BA in sociology from Virginia Union University in 1906, Jones continued his education at Cornell University, New York, where he earned an MA in social work in 1908. While at Cornell he helped found the Alpha Phi Alpha fraternity, although he was not recognized as a founding member until 1952. Jones also established fraternity chapters linking Cornell with Virginia Union, Howard University, and the University of Toronto, Ontario, as well as the Alumni Chapter at Louisville, Kentucky.

Moving on to the NUL

Jones found employment as a teacher at the State University and the Central High School in Louisville before joining the National Urban League (NUL) as field secretary in 1911. Appointed executive secretary seven years later, a post he held until 1941, Jones was the league's longest serving president. Under Jones's guidance the NUL campaigned against racial discrimination in employment, boycotted businesses, encouraged vocational education

▲ **Eugene Kinckle Jones helped develop the NUL into a serious political organization.**

provision, and pushed the government to include African Americans in its New Deal plans of the 1930s. Jones's importance as a sociologist was recognized when he was made an adviser on Negro Affairs to the Department of Commerce in 1933.

Jones, along with research director Charles S. Johnson, cofounded the NUL magazine *Opportunity*; it depicted "Negro life as it is with no exaggerations," and published the work of leading black writers and poets, including Jones's close friends Langston Hughes and Countee Cullen. As general secretary of the league from 1941 until his retirement in 1950, Jones helped establish the Schomburg Center for Research in Black Studies at the New York Public Library in Harlem. He died in 1954.

See also: Cullen, Countee; Hughes, Langston; Johnson, Charles S.; National Organizations

---

Further reading: Mason, Herman, Jr. *The Talented Tenth: The Founders and Presidents of Alpha.* Winter Park, FL: Four-G Publishers, 1999.
http://www.skipmason.com/hm/hm18.htm (Article on Jones's life).

KEY DATES	
1885	Born in Richmond, Virginia, on July 30.
1906	Enrolls at Cornell University's school of sociology.
1918	Becomes executive secretary of the National Urban League (NUL).
1941	Appointed general secretary of the NUL.
1954	Dies in New York City on January 11.

JONES, Frederick M.
Inventor

Frederick Mckinley Jones was a prolific inventor who is best known for devising the first reliable system for refrigerating trucks, an invention that transformed the transportation of perishable goods.

Early inventions

Jones was born in Cincinnati, Ohio, in 1892. He was orphaned when he was nine years old, and had to leave school after the sixth grade to earn a living. When the United States entered World War I (1914–1918) in 1917, Jones enlisted in the Army and fought in France. On his return he worked as an auto mechanic. At this time he developed a self-starting gasoline motor, an invention that he later patented in 1943.

In the 1920s Jones moved to Minneapolis, where he later got a job working for Joseph Numero, who owned a company that supplied equipment to the growing movie industry. In the late 1920s Jones invented a machine for

movie box offices that automatically dispensed tickets and change to customers (patented in 1939). More importantly, he invented a system that adapted silent movie projectors to play the new "talkie" movies that Hollywood studios were beginning to produce. However, Jones's inventions that had the most far-reaching effects were in quite a different area.

Refrigeration

After one of Numero's friends, a trucking executive, expressed frustration at the difficulty of transporting meat in hot weather without it spoiling, Jones set about devising a refrigeration system for trucks. Although mechanical refrigeration was used in commercial premises and households, blocks of ice remained the only method of keeping cargo cool in transit. In 1938 Numero and Jones developed a portable refrigeration unit. It was fitted under the trailer and could withstand the shock and vibrations of a vehicle in motion. The unit meant that perishable foods could now be transported thousands of miles. The pair set up a new company, Thermo King, to capitalize on their invention.

During World War II (1939–1945) the company made units exclusively for the Army for use in warehouses, vehicles, and shelters. After the war Jones continued to develop Thermo King's refrigeration units, including introducing units that operated over a wider temperature range, making it possible to transport anything from ice cream to fresh fruit and vegetables. Jones died in Minneapolis in 1961. Thirty years later, in 1991, he was awarded the National Medal of Technology.

▲ *Legend has it that Jones and Numero were inspired to invent the refrigerated truck after hearing about a load of spoiled chickens*

KEY DATES	
1892	Born in Cincinnati, Ohio, on May 17.
1938	Invents automatic refrigeration system for long-distance trucks.
1961	Dies in Minneapolis, Minnesota, on February 21.

Further reading: Webster, Raymond B. *African American Firsts in Science and Technology.* Belmont, CA: Thomson Gale, 2000. http://www.thetech.org/nmot/detail.cfm?ID=80&STORY=1&st= awardDate&qt=1991 (Story of Thermo King on the National Medal of Technology site).

JONES, Grace
Singer, Model

The singer, actor, and model Grace Jones was one of the best-known African American faces in the media in the 1970s and 1980s. Jones successfully made the transition from runway model to successful musician with hit songs like "La Vie en Rose." She also appeared in several films.

Super star

Jones was born Grace Mendoza in Spanish Town, Jamaica, on May 19, 1952. She moved as a teenager to Syracuse, New York, where she gained a reputation for wild behavior. After a period of studying drama Jones moved to New York City, where she started modeling. Her striking androgynous looks landed her assignments in Paris and the cover of such magazines as *Vogue* and *Elle*.

During her years in New York City Jones became a celebrity in the city's discos and gay nightclubs, such as Studio 54 and Le Jardin. In the mid-1970s, however, Jones began to tire of modeling and turned increasingly toward music. Her reputation as a flamboyant character was enough to land her a contract with Island Records, which released her debut double A-side single "Sorry"/"That's the Trouble" in late 1976. It was a huge hit in clubs and reached No. 71 in the *Billboard* Top 100 in February 1977. An album, *Portfolio,* followed in the same year but was not a huge mainstream success.

Over the next two years Jones recorded two more albums, *Fame* (1978) and *Muse* (1979), both of which had minor commercial success. For her next three albums, *Warm Leatherette* (1980), *Nightclubbing* (1981), and *Living My Life* (1982), Jones turned her back on the disco style that had marked her early recordings and instead started to work with acclaimed reggae musicians Sly Dunbar and

▲ *Grace Jones had a fiery temper and was known for her confrontations with talk-show hosts.*

Robbie Shakespeare. During this period singles such as "Private Life" (1980), "Pull Up to the Bumper" (1981), and "My Jamaican Guy" (1983) gained her an international cult following, although they had little effect on the U.S. charts. In 1984 Jones temporarily turned away from music, starring alongside Arnold Schwarzenegger in *Conan the Destroyer* before appearing as villain May Day in the James Bond film *A View to a Kill* the following year. In 1985 she also recorded the international hit single "Slave the Rhythm." After releasing the albums *Inside Story* in 1986 and *Bulletproof Heart* in 1989, Jones largely disappeared from public view, although she occasionally took cameo roles in films, such as Eddie Murphy's 1992 comedy *Boomerang.*

See also: Black Identity and Popular Culture; Murphy, Eddie

Further reading: http://www.andwedanced.com/ artists/grace.htm (Biography).

KEY DATES	
1952	Born in Spanish Town, Jamaica, on May 19.
1976	Releases debut single "Sorry"/"That's the Trouble."
1980	Releases first collaboration with reggae musicians Sly Dunbar and Robbie Shakespeare, *Warm Leatherette.*
1984	Stars with Arnold Schwarzenegger in *Conan the Destroyer.*

JONES, James Earl
Actor

James Earl Jones has one of the most recognizable faces and voices on stage, TV, radio, and the cinema screen. He has played a wide range of roles, from Shakespearean characters to providing the voice for Darth Vader in the *Star Wars* movies and Mufasa in *The Lion King* (1994).

Early life
Born Todd Jones in Arkabutia, Mississippi, on January 31, 1931, he was brought up by his grandparents on their farm after his parents separated. His father, Robert Earl Jones, was an actor who had been blacklisted as a result of his political activism. In 1936 Jones and his grandparents moved north to live on a farm in Dublin, Michigan, but the young Jones found the change so upsetting that he developed a severe stutter that made him stop speaking. He would only express himself through writing. Jones was helped by a teacher, who encouraged him to write poetry and to become more confident at expressing himself through public speaking and debating. Jones eventually won a scholarship to study medicine at the University of Michigan, but once there he became interested in drama.

Acting career
Following a period of military service, Jones moved to New York to pursue a career in acting and studied at the American Theater Wing while working as a janitor. In 1957 he made his theater debut, but his real break came when he was cast in Jean Genet's landmark 1961 production *The Blacks,* in which he starred alongside many future African American stars such as Cicely Tyson and Maya Angelou. Jones went on to star in several other productions, picking up awards for his performance in *Moon on a Rainbow Shawl* (1962). He won two Obies in 1965 for Bertolt Brecht's *Baal* and William Shakespeare's *Othello,* and received a Tony award for playing boxer Jack Jefferson in

▲ **James Earl Jones in 1991, when he won an Emmy for Best Actor in a Drama Series for his role in Gabriel's Fire.**

The Great White Hope (1968). Two years later Jones picked up an Oscar nomination for his performance in the film version of the play. He won a second Tony for August Wilson's play *Fences* in 1987.

Jones's career in film began in 1964 when he debuted in Stanley Kubrick's *Dr. Strangelove.* Since then Jones has worked constantly in both films and television. His finest performances include playing a reclusive writer in *Field of Dreams* (1989), Admiral Greer in three movies based on Tom Clancy novels in the 1990s, and his favorite, as the South African minister in *Cry, The Beloved Country* (1995). In 1996 he was awarded the National Medal of Arts.

See also: Angelou, Maya; Tyson, Cicely

Further reading: Jones, James Earl. *Voices and Silences.* New York, NY: Scribner, 1993.
http://www.achievement.org/autodoc/page/jon2bio-1 (Biography).

KEY DATES	
1931	Born in Arkabutia, Mississippi, on January 31.
1961	Appears in Jean Genet's *The Blacks.*
1968	Receives a Tony for *The Great White Hope.*
1977	Provides the voice of Darth Vader in the first *Star Wars* movie.
1993	Writes autobiography, *Voices and Silences.*

JONES, Lois Mailou
Artist, Teacher

Lois Mailou Jones was a prolific and successful artist who embraced many approaches to painting, from European-inspired impressionism and cubism to African and Haitian styles. She influenced generations of young African American artists through her teaching at Howard University in Washington, D.C.

Early life

Jones was born in Boston, Massachusetts, on November 3, 1905. Her parents were Thomas Vreeland Jones, a building inspector, and Carolyn Dorinda Adams, a beautician. Thomas Jones retrained, aged 40, to become a lawyer, and Jones later said that her father provided her with the early example that anyone can achieve anything if they want it badly enough.

A career in the arts

Jones majored in art at Boston's High School of Practical Arts before winning a scholarship to the Boston Museum School of Fine Arts, where she studied for six years. On graduating she worked as a freelance textile designer and was also employed to set up an art department at the Palmer Memorial Institute, a private African American boarding school in Sedalia, North Carolina.

In 1930 Jones began teaching design and watercolor painting at Howard University, where she worked for 47 years. All the time she continued to paint and draw, and in

▲ *Louis Mailou Jones at work in her studio. She was influenced by the bright colors and bold patterns of Haitian art.*

1937 she won a fellowship to spend a year studying in France, where she attended the Académie Julian. She was much influenced by the colorful, light-filled style of the impressionist painters, as well as by the angular style of cubism and by African art; her stylized painting of African masks, *Fetishes* (1938), draws on the two latter sources.

After marrying the Haitian artist Louis Vergniaud Pierre-Noël in 1953, Jones was inspired by Haitian life and culture and the brilliant light and color of the Caribbean. She moved between a colorful, realistic rendering of her subject matter and a more graphic, flatter, hard-edged style. Jones was increasingly influenced by African art after 1970, when she received a grant from Howard University to travel to Africa and document the work of artists there. Jones had more than 50 exhibitions during her career, and received many awards, including citations from both the Haitiian and U.S. governments, before her death in 1998.

Further reading: Benjamin, Tritobia Hayes, and Lois Mailou Jones. *The Life and Art of Lois Mailou Jones.* Petaluma, CA: Pomegranate, 1994.
http://americanart.si.edu/search/artist_bio.cfm?StartRow=1&ID=5658&showtext=1 (Smithsonian American Art Museum site).

KEY DATES	
1905	Born in Boston, Massachusetts, on November 3.
1927	Graduates from Boston Museum School of Fine Arts
1928	Sets up art department at the Palmer Memorial Institute in Sedalia, North Carolina.
1930	Joins faculty of the fine art department at Howard University.
1937	Spends a year in Paris, where she attends the Académie Julian.
1953	Marries Louis Vergniaud Pierre-Noël, a Haitian artist.
1970	Travels to Africa to document the work of African artists.
1977	Retires from Howard University.
1998	Dies in Washington, D.C., on June 9.

JONES, Marion
Athlete

Marion Jones dominated the world of female sprinting from 1997 to 2002, and made international news and sports history when she became the first woman to win five medals in a single Olympics, an honor shared only by male track and field greats Jesse Owens and Carl Lewis. Jones succeeded Jackie Joyner-Kersee as the United States's top female track and field athlete.

Early life

Jones was born in Los Angeles, California, on October 12, 1975, to Marion and George Jones. Her mother is originally from Belize, and Jones holds dual American-Belizean citizenship. She has an older half-brother, Albert Kelly, who is, in Jones's words, her "great and lasting hero." Her parents' marriage broke up soon after their daughter was born, and George left the family when Jones was three years old. Father and daughter remained estranged, despite Jones's efforts to reestablish contact.

Jones's mother worked two or three jobs to send her children to private schools. In 1983 she married Ira Toler, a retired postal worker, who became a stay-at-home father and was adored by Jones and her half-brother. When Ira died suddenly of a stroke in 1987, the family was devastated.

▼ *Marion Jones wins the 100-meter final at the 1999 World Championships held in Seville, Spain.*

Young talent

The young Jones was inspired by champion sprinters Florence Griffith-Joyner and Jackie Joyner-Kersee, who both provided her with positive role models. By age 14 she was well on the way to achieving her dream of competing at the Olympics. She had already gained recognition among the California track-and-field community. Invited to prestigious national meets, Jones competed against elite runners such as Evelyn Ashford and Gwen Torrence.

After her freshman year Jones never lost a high school track-and-field meet. She won numerous national athletic awards for her performance in both track and field and basketball. In 10th grade she ran the fastest 100 meters, 200 meters, and 400 meters in the United States and set a national high school record for the 200 meters, which still stands. At age 16 she competed in Olympic trials, placing fourth in the 200 meters, and missing a spot on the U.S. Olympic team by only 0.7 seconds. She was offered an alternate position for the 4 x 100-meter relay but turned it down, explaining later that if the team won gold in the event, which it did, she wanted to have earned it by running rather than by association.

Jones's basketball skills earned her a scholarship to the University of North Carolina, where she majored in communications and journalism. She played point guard for the Lady Tar Heels, leading them to the 1994 NCAA Championship and setting the freshman record for points and steals per game. Jones continued to excel in athletics, placing second in the long jump and sixth in the 200 meters at the NCAA Track-and-Field finals (after a mere month of training). She decided to forgo her junior year on the basketball team to focus on track and field and train

INFLUENCES AND INSPIRATION

Marion Jones owes her success to several people, including her stepfather, Ira Toler. Jones's father left the family when she was very young and Jones tried unsuccessfully to establish a relationship with him. When her mother married Toler, Jones quickly established a close relationship with him. Her half-brother Albert said, "Ira was always there for my sister. He talked to her, answered her questions, helped her with homework, took her to tee-ball games. Then he was gone."

Other inspirations included the legendary Florence Griffith-Joyner: Jones watched the athlete compete at the 1988 Seoul Olympics and was so inspired by the woman that she told everyone afterward, "I want to be an Olympic champion." She worked hard to achieve her dream and has provided great inspiration to many young black Americans.

Jones's reputation suffered, however, following allegations that her husband had used steroids. Many commentators believed that press reports promoted the idea that Jones was guilty of taking drugs herself. Jones has fought hard and vociferously to clear her name. Her supporters believe that Jones's confidence, charisma, persistence, and grace have rejuvenated women's track and field in the United States.

for the 1996 Olympics; however, she interrupted her summer track training to play for the U.S. basketball team at the World University Games, only to break her foot in practice. Her dreams for the 1996 Olympics were shattered.

During the year of rehabilitation Jones began dating C. J. Hunter, a champion shot-putter and assistant track coach at UNC. The North Carolina athletic community disapproved: Hunter was seven years older than Jones, had two children from a previous marriage, and had to retire from his position because of UNC's ban on coach–athlete dating. The couple eventually married in 1998.

A colossal career

After missing her chance for glory at the 1996 Olympics, Jones emerged faster than ever for the 1997 track-and-field season. She stunned the sports world by winning the 100-meter World Championship. In the 1997–1998 season she competed in 37 events on five continents, only losing once. She achieved the fastest 100-meter time by any woman other than Griffith-Joyner, and was ranked No. 1 in the world at the 100 meters and 200 meters by *Track and Field News*. At the 1998 National Championship Jones was the first woman in 50 years to win three separate events (100 meters, 200 meters, and long jump). Many expected her to surpass Joyner-Kersee and Griffith-Joyner in the record book and bring the sport back into the limelight.

Jones's celebrity status grew when she declared in 1998 that she would win five gold medals in the 2000 Sydney Olympics: She almost succeeded. After winning the 100-meter dash by 13 feet (3.96m), the second largest victory margin in Olympic history for men or women, Jones discovered that her husband, who had pulled out before

the games started with a knee injury, had failed four drug tests and was under investigation by the U.S. Doping Agency. For the remainder of the competitions, Jones was hounded by reporters. Despite the mental and emotional distractions, she won two more golds, in the 200 meters and the 4 x 400-meter relay, and two bronze medals in the long jump and the 4 x 100-meter relay. Hunter and Jones divorced a year later.

Jones continued to dominate after the Olympics: She won the 100-meter gold at the World Championships in 1999, the world title for the 200 meters in 2001, and achieved the top 10 times for 100 meters in the United States, holding four of the top five times for the event in the world. She completed her first undefeated season in 2002. Although she did not compete in 2003 owing to her pregnancy, Jones continued training afterward for the 2004 Summer Olympics; however, her performance was disappointing. Jones has never tested positive for drugs, but there have been allegations. Bob Weiner, a former White House antidrug campaigner, commented in 2004: "You can't target people who are innocent and try to make them guilty and with the specifics of the Marion Jones case that seems to be happening."

See also: Ashford, Evelyn; Griffith-Joyner, Florence; Joyner-Kersee, Jackie; Lewis, Carl; Owens, Jesse

Further reading: Jones, Marion, with Kate Sekules. *Marion Jones: Life in the Fast Lane.* New York, NY: Melcher Media/Time Warner Book Group, 2004.
http://www.usatf.org/athletes/bios/Jones_Marion.asp (Biography.)

JONES, Paul R.
Art Collector, Welfare Reformer

Paul R. Jones worked in community liaison during the implementation of civil rights legislation in the 1960s. More recently he has become well known as a pioneering collector of African American art.

Early life

Paul Raymond Jones was born in 1928 in the Muscoda mining camp near Bessemer, Alabama. He had four older sisters, who were all teachers. Despite his father's reservations, Jones's mother and sisters decided to send him to school in New York.

Jones returned to his hometown to attend high school and excelled in both his lessons and in sports. In his senior year Jones scored in the top 3 percent of all students in the state and earned a college scholarship. He was also awarded an athletic scholarship. Until he was given these opportunities, racism had rarely had much of an effect on Jones's life, but his time at college would change all that.

Jones took a scholarship at Alabama State University, Montgomery. He was an enthusiastic student, becoming president of the freshman class, president of his fraternity, halfback on the football team, and playing in the marching band. Two years later Jones opted to study law and approached the law school at the University of Alabama, Tuscaloosa. At first he was encouraged by the university and he went on to complete his undergraduate education at Howard University, Washington, D.C. Then the Alabama law school changed its mind and refused Jones a place on the grounds of race. Jones stayed at Howard for a year of graduate work before returning home.

Civil rights work

In Besemmer Jones began to work for the Birmingham Interracial Committee of the Jefferson County Coordinating Council for Social Forces. His work in the position made him a powerful figure in civil rights and welfare reform.

Jones later worked as a probation officer and then took a job at the Department of Justice. In this position, Jones helped ease the tensions during the civil rights struggle of the 1960s. Jones's reputation grew and he became recognized on a national scale for his work in the Department of Housing and Urban Development's Model Cities Program. The program aimed to revitalize urban communities. In 1970 Jones served with the Peace Corps in Thailand. In 1973 he became the regional director of the

KEY DATES

1928   Born in Bessemer, Alabama, on June 1.

1954   Works for Birmingham Interracial Committee of the Jefferson County Coordinating Council for Social Forces.

1968   Appointed director of the National Model Cities Association.

1971   Employed by Republican Party in run up to 1972 election to mobilize black voters in support of Richard Nixon.

1973   Becomes regional director of Atlanta branch of ACTION.

1978   Starts his own real estate company in Atlanta.

2001   Donates his collection of African American art to the University of Delaware.

Atlanta branch of ACTION, an umbrella agency for all federal volunteer programs. In 1978 he also started his own real estate company in Atlanta, Georgia.

Art collector

During the 1960s Jones had begun to collect art. His first acquisitions were three small prints—one each by European artists Toulouse-Lautrec, Edgar Degas, and Marc Chagall. However, Jones soon realized that the work of African American artists was not represented in the country's museums. Jones began to collect art on sale at annual exhibitions of African American art at Atlanta University. He also began to support the work of several young artists and soon many other artists came to him for help. Many of them were not able to exhibit their work and Jones dealt with them directly.

After 30 years Jones had amassed more than 1,500 paintings, sculptures, prints, and photographs. After years of collecting he could no longer store, let alone display, so many works and he arrived at a dilemma—to sell his collection and become a wealthy man, or to preserve it for the nation. In 2001 Jones donated his art to the University Museums of the University of Delaware.

Further reading: Amaki, Amalia K. *A Century of African American Art: The Paul R. Jones Collection.* Piscataway, NJ: Rutgers University Press, 2004.
http://www.museums.udel.edu/jones/jones-pages/about-jones.html (Biography).

JONES, Quincy
Musician, Producer, Activist

Quincy Jones, known as "Q" to his friends, is one of the giants of popular American music. The most nominated Grammy artist, with more than 75 nominations and 26 awards, Jones has worked with the most famous names in show business and has helped many of them establish their careers. Jones won an Emmy for the theme tune to Alex Haley's *Roots* (1977) and has received seven Oscar nominations. He has also been honored for his humanitarian work as a civil rights activist.

Early life
Quincy Delight Jones was born on March 14, 1933, on Chicago's South Side. In 1944 the Jones family went to live in Bremerton, a suburb of Seattle, Washington, moving to Seattle itself in 1948. Jones showed an early interest in music, trying out all the instruments in his school orchestra before settling on the trumpet. Jones also sang in a gospel quartet, where he met the singer Ray Charles. Three years Quincy's senior, Charles encouraged the

▼ *Quincy Jones toured in many European countries. Here he plays in Paris, France, in 1960.*

teenager to experiment with music. They formed a combo and began playing together in clubs and at local functions such as weddings.

A musical career
After graduating from high school, Jones studied briefly at Seattle University and then at Schillinger House, later the Berklee College of Music, in Boston. However, in 1951 he abandoned music school to join celebrated band leader Lionel Hampton (1908–2002) and his orchestra, going on tour with them two years later to Europe. On his return to America Jones settled in New York, working as an arranger and player for such musicians as Sarah Vaughan, Count Basie, Duke Ellington, and old friend Ray Charles. In 1956 Jones joined Dizzy Gillespie on a State Department-sponsored tour of the Middle East and South America.

Between 1957 and 1961 Jones lived in France. As record producer for Barclay Disques, the French subsidiary of Mercury Records, he worked with French stars Jacque Brel and Charles Aznavour. He also studied composition with the celebrated French musician and composer Nadia Boulanger (1887–1979). Jones became music director of

INFLUENCES AND INSPIRATION

Quincy Jones has worked with the greatest names in the music industry. He is also a well-known civil rights activist and philanthropist. He was a major supporter of Martin Luther King, Jr.'s Operation Breadbasket. Founded in 1962 the organization aimed at helping economically deprived black neighborhoods. It distributed food to communities in 12 cities.

The Reverend Jesse Jackson, who was one of the founders of Operation Breadbasket and its chair from 1967, later formed People United to Save Humanity (PUSH). Jones served on the board of directors of PUSH for many years. Jones was also the major force behind "We Are the World," the song made for U.S. LiveAid in 1985 to help the starving in Africa and America. In 1990 Jones established the Quincy Jones Listen-Up Foundation to carry out his charitable activities.

the Harold Arlen blues musical *Free and Easy*, touring Europe until the show closed in 1960. He then formed an 18-strong big band with members of the cast. Although the orchestra met with great reviews and good turnouts, they were not a financial success and Jones was left heavily in debt. Only the help of Mercury music director Irving Green saved him, and he returned to New York to work for the label there. By 1964 Jones had been made vice president, the first black musician to achieve such a high position in an established, predominantly white record company.

Despite his new responsibilities, Jones continued to work as a musician. He turned his attention to film scores with great success. His soundtrack for the 1964 movie *Pawnbroker* won him his first Grammy. Jones left Mercury Records a year later, moving to Los Angeles to concentrate on his career as a composer. He received an Oscar nomination for Best Original Soundtrack for *In Cold Blood* (1968) and composed the music for the cult hit *The Italian Job* (1969), among other notable films. He also composed the music for TV series, notably *Ironside* (1967) and *The Bill Cosby Show* (1974). Jones continued to record with jazz ensembles, but moved increasingly into the world of popular music, transferring some of the sounds traditionally associated with jazz to disco.

Making a mark

Between the end of the 1960s and early 1980s Jones recorded several Grammy-winning records, including *Walking in Space* (1969) and *You've Got It Bad, Girl* (1973). In 1974 Jones married actor Peggy Lipton. The couple had two daughters before divorcing in 1990. A brain aneurysm in 1974 disrupted Jones's career briefly, but before long he was back recording and producing.

Jones collaborated with several pop singers, including Michael Jackson. He produced the singer's first solo album, *Off the Wall* (1979), which made Jackson an international star and Jones the most sought-after record producer in the music industry. Jones and Jackson worked together again on *Thriller* (1984), which sold 30 million records and produced six Top 10 hits.

Between 1969 and 1981 Jones worked for A&M Records, but he decided to found his own record label, Qwest, in 1980. This was the first of many personal business ventures. In 1985 Jones ventured into film, coproducing the movie *The Color Purple*, directed by Steven Spielberg. Six years later he formed Quincy Jones Entertainment Co. as part of Time Warner Inc. The company produced *The Fresh Prince of Bel Air,* starring actor and rapper Will Smith. Jones also formed Qwest Broadcasting in 1993 with several partners, which became one of the largest minority-owned U.S. broadcasting companies. Quincy Jones/David Salzman Entertainment (QDE) expanded his interests into cable TV and radio. Jones's phenomenal success has made him one of the most powerful men in the media.

KEY DATES	
1933	Born in Chicago, Illinois, on March 14.
1951	Joins Lionel Hampton's band.
1961	Becomes musical director of Mercury Records.
1965	Moves to Los Angeles, California.
1980	Founds Qwest, his own record label.
1990	Founds the Quincy Jones Listen Up Foundation.

See also: Basie, Count; Charles, Ray; Ellington, Duke; Gillespie, Dizzy; Jackson, Jesse; Jackson, Michael; King, Martin Luther, Jr.; Smith, Will; Vaughan, Sarah

Further reading: Jones, Quincy. *Q: The Autobiography of Quincy Jones.* New York, NY: Doubleday, 2001.
http://www.imdb.com/name/nm0005065/ (IMDB page).

JONES, Roy, Jr.
Boxer

Roy Jones, Jr., overcame disappointment at the 1988 Olympics to become world heavyweight champion as a professional. Although James was considered in the 1990s to be the best boxer of his generation, his attitude toward the sport did not always endear him to boxing fans.

Amateur career

Jones was born in Pensacola, Florida, on January 16, 1969. Trained by his father, who introduced him to boxing, Jones was selected to represent the United States at the 1988 Olympics In Seoul, South Korea. Jones reached the final of the light-middleweight (156 lb.; 71kg) division, where he fought the home favorite Park Si Hun. Although Jones completely dominated the fight, the judges awarded the victory to the South Korean. The decision was so blatantly unfair that it provoked changes in the way amateur contests are scored. Much later one of the judges admitted that he had been bribed. Despite this Jones received the Val Barker award for the outstanding boxer of the games.

Professional career

Jones's first paid fight was a victory over Ricky Randall on May 6, 1989. Jones was both a skillful boxer and an extremely powerful puncher, and he won 20 of his first 21 fights by knockout. This string of victories earned him a shot against Bernard Hopkins for the International Boxing Federation (IBF) world middleweight (160 lb.; 73kg) title. The 1993 fight ended in a points victory for Jones.

For the remainder of the decade Jones established himself as one of the dominant figures in the sport of boxing, winning further world titles at supermiddleweight (168 lb.; 76kg) and light-heavyweight (175 lb.; 80kg). He lost only once, in a disqualification against Montell Griffin, but this defeat was quickly avenged. Most boxing experts agreed that Jones was the most talented fighter around, but he was criticized by some fans for a lack of

▲ **Roy Jones, Jr., at a news conference in May 2004 before his match with Antonio Tarver.**

commitment. He dallied with basketball, playing for minor league teams the Jacksonville Barracudas and the Brevard Blue Ducks, and talked about quitting boxing. Toward the end of the decade Jones was also attacked for the quality of the opposition that he faced.

In 2003 Jones stepped up in weight to beat John Ruiz for the World Boxing Association (WBA) heavyweight title. He was the first former middleweight to achieve the feat for over 100 years, although at the time most observers saw World Boxing Council (WBC) champion British boxer Lennox Lewis as the world's true top heavyweight. Jones dropped down to light-heavyweight again, but he lost his title to Antonio Tarver in 2004. Later that year a loss to Glen Johnson led some people to question whether Jones should retire. He also signed a multimillion deal to replace George Foreman as a commentator at HBO Sports.

See also: Foreman, George

Further reading Fleischer, Nat et al. *An Illustrated History of Boxing.* New York, NY: Citadel Press, 2002.
http://news.bbc.co.uk/sport1/hi/boxing/2962711.stm (Career).

KEY DATES

1969   Born in Pensacola, Florida, on January 16.

1993   Defeats Bernard Hopkins to win world middleweight title on May 22.

2003   Takes world heavyweight title by defeating John Ruiz on March 1.

JONES, Madame Sissieretta
Entertainer

One of the greatest black American opera singers of the 19th and early 20th centuries, Madame Sissieretta Jones was also known as "Black Patti" or Madame Jones. During her lifetime Jones performed before three U.S. presidents and for the Prince of Wales, heir to the British throne.

Born Matilda Sissieretta Joyner in Portsmouth, Virginia, on January 5, 1869, Jones was the daughter of Jeremiah Malachi Joyner, a Baptist minister, and Henrietta Beale, a talented soprano in the church choir. Jones began singing in public at a very early age at school functions and at her father's church. When she was seven years old her family moved to Providence, Rhode Island, and it was there that she began to further develop her unique, rich, soprano voice. At age 14 Jones began her first formal music training at the Providence Academy of Music; four years later she attended the New England Conservatory in Boston, Massachusetts.

Musical career

In 1887 Jones performed to 5,000 people at a benefit concert at Boston's Music Hall. Her performance attracted the attention of renowned concert managers Abbey, Schoffel, and Grau, who booked her to sing at the Wallack Theater in New York. Her debut there was such a success that she was invited on a concert tour of South America and the West Indies. The tour ran for two years; Jones was so popular with audiences that after her return to the United States in 1892, at age 23, she was asked to sing at New York's Madison Square Garden. Her performance led one newspaper to compare her to the famous Italian opera singer Adelina Patti (1843–1919); it also gave Jones the nickname "the Black Patti." Although Jones hated the name, it was to stay with her for the rest of her career.

▲ *The greatest black opera singer of her time, Madame Jones dedicated her later years to charity.*

Jones was considered for the lead role in at New York's Metropolitan Opera House (the Met), but racial prejudice kept her from appearing there. The Met's color barrier stayed intact until Marian Anderson became the first African American to sing a lead role there in 1955. Jones instead went on tour to Europe, visiting such places as Paris, France; London, England; and Milan, Italy. She was well received critically, her range and stage presence dazzling audiences and critics alike. After returning to the United States, Jones led the Black Patti Troubadours on tour at home and abroad. Although the group performed minstrel shows and musical skits, Jones ended the show singing spirituals and opera arias. In 1916 she retired, returning to Providence to live. She died of cancer in 1933.

See also: Anderson, Marian

Further reading: Story, Rosalyn M. *And So I Sing: African-American Divas of Opera and Concert.* Austin, TX: Amistad Press, 1993.
http://www.lkwdpl.org/wihohio/jone-sis.htm (Biography).

KEY DATES	
1869	Born in Portsmouth, Virginia, on January 5.
1892	Performs in New York's Madison Square Garden.
1893	Performs at the Chicago World Fair.
1916	Retires from performing.
1933	Dies in Providence, Rhode Island, in June.

JOPLIN, Scott
Musician

At the dawn of the 20th century Scott Joplin, the son of a former slave, rose to become one of America's finest composers and the uncontested "King of Ragtime." The style of music that Joplin helped popularize, which was also known as "rag," was syncopated and mixed elements of various styles to create a unique form of music. Joplin gave ragtime a formal structure made up of four 16-bar sections. His music drew on marches, quadrilles, jigs, and African bamboulas, as well as spirituals, the blues, minstrel songs, and what were known as "coon songs"—seemingly humorous songs written in what was meant to be black American colloquial speech—and was usually set to a 2/4 meter. His compositions are still popular today (*see box*).

Early life
Although it is unknown exactly where and when Joplin was born, U.S. Census data help narrow the possibilities. The June 1870 census lists Joplin as a two-year old living in northern Texas. Some accounts note a November 1868 birth, but if 1870 and 1880 census data are correct, it is more likely that Joplin was born in late 1867. After a short time in Texas, Joplin's parents moved with their six children to Texarkana, a city straddling the Texas–Arkansas border. While his mother worked as a domestic laborer in an affluent home, Joplin tagged along so he could teach himself to play the family's piano. This self-education continued until Julius Weiss, a local music teacher, noted the young musician's talent and took Joplin under his wing. Weiss, born in Germany, emphasized classical European musical training.

Sedalia and ragtime
In 1891 Joplin performed with a minstrel troupe in Texarkana, but he left for Chicago, Illinois, which was hosting the historic World Fair, where he played in local clubs. He eventually returned south to make his home in Sedalia, Missouri, the "Cradle of Ragtime." He began to gain a reputation as a composer of piano ragtime. He

▼ *Joplin's music has been used on the soundtracks of films as diverse as Louis Malle's* **Pretty Baby** *(1978) to Jet Li vehicle* **Danny the Dog** *(2005).*

INFLUENCES AND INSPIRATION

When Scott Joplin died, ragtime's widespread popularity was already in decline as early jazz became the dance music of choice. Joplin's music was integral to the development of 20th-century U.S. music, however: Compositions like *The Entertainer* and *Maple Leaf Rag* have inspired each new generation of musicians to explore the depths of Joplin's repertoire.

Some 25 years after Joplin's death jazz had moved beyond the big band sound, bringing some musicians back to ragtime, igniting a gradual revival of the music Joplin helped make popular. The 1970s was the crest of this revival. After new recordings of Joplin compositions broke sales records for the classical music labels that released them, his compositions were in demand and

his scores were reprinted, pleasing countless music lovers. Joplin's dream of producing his opera *Treemonisha* finally came true more than 50 years after his death, and George Roy Hill used Joplin's music for his classic film *The Sting*. Joplin's music is also celebrated each summer when thousands of ragtime fans descend on Sedalia for the Scott Joplin Ragtime Festival.

KEY DATES

1867	Born most probably in Texas at about this time.
1899	Publishes the American classic *Maple Leaf Rag.*
1908	Self-publishes his ragtime manual *School of Ragtime.*
1911	Completes the opera *Treemonisha.*
1917	Dies in Manhattan, New York, on April 1.
1976	Pulitzer Committee issues special award for Joplin's contributions to U.S. music.

also played cornet in a local group of black musicians called the Queen City Cornet Band. When not traveling with the band, Joplin returned home to Sedalia, where he was an active community member. In the town Joplin did more than play local venues like the Maple Leaf Club and the Black 400 Club; he also attended music classes at Sedalia's George R. Smith College, and taught local musicians. Eventually Joplin formed his own band and began touring outside his home territory.

Joplin started publishing his music in the 1890s, writing marches, waltzes, and rags. In 1898 he learned a hard lesson about the publishing world, however: He sold his very first piano piece, *Original Rags,* but was forced to share credit with an arranger who had nothing to do with the composition but happened to work at the company publishing the piece. Scores of African American musicians and composers suffered similar fates long into the 20th century, losing attribution rights and significant economic benefits. Joplin hired a lawyer to maintain control of his own intellectual property, a move that proved invaluable when his next rag took the world by storm. In 1899

Joplin published *Maple Leaf Rag* through Sedalia music store owner John Stark. Joplin and his new lawyer negotiated a deal that gave Joplin a one-cent royalty for every sale of the new rag. *Maple Leaf Rag* marked a new and highly successful period of Joplin's career. He also finished a piece for the stage called *The Ragtime Dance,* which featured the dancing and music popular at places like Sedalia's Maple Leaf Club.

Joplin moved to St. Louis, where he befriended fellow ragtime pioneer Tom Turpin, and met up again with John Stark, who had founded the publishing company House of Classic Rags. Joplin published several classic songs, including *The Entertainer,* and *The Strenuous Life*, a tribute to President Theodore Roosevelt for inviting Booker T. Washington to dine at the White House in 1901. Joplin also wrote an opera, *A Guest of Honor,* to commemorate the event, which he decided to take on the road in 1903. The tour folded when someone stole the box-office money; the company's resources, along with copies of the score, were seized to pay debts.

Joplin spent time in Chicago, Arkansas, and New York. In Arkansas he married Freddie Alexander, but she died of pneumonia less than three months later. After her death Joplin left Sedalia permanently. In 1907 he returned to New York, where he completed the opera *Treemonisha* (1911), but never realized his dream of seeing it on stage. Joplin continued to compose until his death in 1917.

See also: Washington, Booker T.

Further reading: Berlin, Edward A. *King of Ragtime: Scott Joplin and His Era.* New York, NY: Oxford University Press, 1995.
http://www.scottjoplin.org (Joplin site).

JORDAN, Barbara
Politician, Lawyer, Educator

Politician, lawyer, and educator Barbara Charline Jordan broke many accepted conventions during her lifetime. She was the first woman to preside over a legislative body in the United States and the first to deliver a keynote speech at a political convention. Jordan, who suffered from multiple sclerosis (MS), was also open about her lesbian relationship with longterm partner Nancy Earl despite being advised that it could ruin her political career. A well-respected woman, Jordan received praise from many leading politicians, including Bill Clinton who awarded her the Presidential Medal of Honor in 1994.

Road to success

Born in Houston, Texas, on February 21, 1936, Jordan was one of the three daughters of Benjamin and Arlyne Jordan. The family lived in the poor part of town. Jordan attended Roberson Elementary and Phillis Wheatley High School. She graduated magna cum laude from Texas Southern University in 1956, and earned a law degree from Boston University three years later, after which she taught at Tuskegee Institute, Alabama, for a year before going back to Houston to take her bar exams in 1960.

▼ **Barbara Jordan made history in 1972 when she presided over the Texas Senate.**

KEY DATES	
1936	Born in Houston, Texas, on February 21.
1966	Elected to U.S. Senate.
1972	Becomes first black woman to preside over a legislative body in the United States.
1976	Becomes the first black woman to deliver a keynote address at a political convention; retires three years later.
1996	Dies in Austin, Texas, on January 17.

Jordan was always interested in politics and she ran unsuccessfully for election to the Texas Senate in both 1962 and 1964 before being elected in 1966. She was the first ever female African American to be elected to the state senate and the first black American to win a seat since 1883. Jordan became the first black elected official to preside over the Texas Senate in 1967, and the first to chair a major committee, the Labor and Management Relations Committee. In 1972 she served as temporary president of the Texas Senate, becoming the first black woman in the nation to act as chief executive of a state. That same year she was elected to the House of Representatives, achieving yet another first as a black woman representing a previously Confederate state.

Jordan became a champion of ethnic minorities and the poor. She sponsored bills to help improve workers' rights and to improve voting registration for ethnic minorities. In 1974 Jordan was a member of the House Judiciary Committee during the Watergate hearings, the impeachment of President Richard M. Nixon, which resulted in his resignation. Her clear and commanding oratory led to her being chosen as a keynote speaker for the Democratic National Convention in 1976 and again in 1992. Ill health led Jordan to retire from Congress in 1979. She became professor of public affairs at the Lyndon Baines Johnson School of Public Affairs at the University of Texas at Austin, but continued to work as a political adviser. She died of pneumonia on January 17, 1996.

See also: Political Representation

Further reading: http://www.elf.net/bjordan/default.asp (Tribute with links).

JORDAN, June
Author, Activist, Teacher

June Jordan was one of the most prolific and widely published African American writers of the 20th century. From the late 1960s onward she challenged all forms of oppression through her writing and her work as a teacher and academic.

Early life

Jordan was born in Harlem, New York City, on July 9, 1936, and was brought up in Brooklyn. Her parents were Jamaican immigrants and Jordan was aware from an early age that they wanted her to succeed. Her father, Granville, was a postal worker and her mother, Mildred, was a nurse. Jordan later wrote about her parents' characters and difficult relationship in *His Own Where* (1971), a novel for young adults, and also in her autobiography *Soldier: A Poet's Childhood* (2000).

Jordan studied at Barnard College, New York, (1953–1955; 1956–1957) and the University of Chicago (1955–1956). During her time at Barnard she met and married a white Columbia University student, Michael Meyer, in 1955; the couple had a son in 1958, but the marriage ended in divorce seven years later.

A mover and shaker

In 1967 Jordan began her career teaching English and literature at the City College of New York; she later also taught at Sarah Lawrence College, New York, Yale University, Connecticut, and the State University of New York at Stony Brook. In 1989 she joined the department

▲ *June Jordan fought hard to get black English accepted in the education system.*

of African American studies at the University of California, Berkeley, where she became a professor. While there Jordan founded Poetry for the People, a program to encourage student activism and creativity. She also fought hard for black studies to be included in all university curricula.

At the same time Jordan established her reputation as a writer. Her collection of poetry, *Who Look at Me* (1969), was the first of 28 books, ranging from poems, novels, and plays to political essays. She became well-known for the direct, powerful style with which she tackled discrimination, often intertwining her own personal experiences with wider political struggles. Jordan was a well-known political essayist, publishing work on civil wars around the world and highlighting global injustices. The writer and activist Alice Walker wrote of her: "She is the bravest of us, the most outraged. She feels for all. She is the universal poet." Jordan died of breast cancer in 2002.

See also: Walker, Alice

Further reading: Jordan, June. *Some of Us Did Not Die: New and Selected Essays.* Philadelphia, PA: Basic Civitas Books, 2003. http://www.junejordan.com (Official site).

KEY DATES

1936   Born in Harlem, New York, on July 9.

1967   Begins teaching English at the City College of New York.

1969   Publishes her first poetry collection, *Who Look at Me.*

1981   Publishes her first collection of political essays, *Civil War.*

1989   Joins faculty of African American studies at the University of California, Berkeley.

2000   Publishes an autobiography of her early life, *Soldier: A Poet's Childhood.*

2002   Dies in Berkeley, California, on June 14.

JORDAN, Michael
Basketball Player

Michael Jordan is widely regarded as the best basketball player in the history of the game. He is also one of the highest-earning sports celebrities of all time and probably one of the most recognizable through his endorsement of products. Jordan's high-leaping style of play earned him the nickname "Air Jordan."

Early life

The fourth of five children, Michael Jeffrey Jordan was born on February 17, 1963, in Brooklyn, New York, but raised in Wilmington, North Carolina. His father, James, worked at an electric plant and his mother, Doloris, was a bankteller. A late developer—he did not make the basketball team at Emsley A. Laney High until the 12th grade—Jordan won a scholarship in basketball to the

▼ **Michael Jordan in a preseason game against the Seattle Supersonics in 1996.**

University of North Carolina (UNC) at Chapel Hill. By the time he enrolled there he had reached his full height of 6 feet 6 inches (1.98m).

The making of a star

For most of his freshman year at UNC Jordan was not outstanding on court, but he scored the winning basket in the 1982 National Collegiate Athletic Association (NCAA) championship game against the Hoyas of Georgetown. He was voted college player of the year by the NCAA in 1983 and 1984, and he was then selected to represent the United States at the 1984 Summer Olympics in Los Angeles, California. The so-called Dream Team took the men's basketball gold medal at the games, winning all eight of their matches by an average of 32.1 points.

Two months later Jordan was drafted by the Chicago Bulls: He was their third pick. Playing mainly as shooting guard but also sometimes as point guard or small forward, by the end of his first season he averaged over 28 points

INFLUENCES AND INSPIRATION

Michael Jordan was not the first African American to capitalize on sporting achievement, but he made more money out of it than anyone before him. In addition to his Nike and Wheaties advertising contracts, he endorsed a wide range of other products, including Gatorade sports drinks and Hanes underwear. That such high-profile firms were willing to pay vast sums to use him as their marketing spearhead and spokesman reflected a slow but significant change social and cultural attitudes: Advertisers could now use African Americans to promote their products to Americans of all ethnic backgrounds, not just fellow black people.

---

per game and was named National Basketball Association (NBA) Rookie of the Year. He topped the league in scoring for each of the next 10 seasons (a record), averaging more than 30 points per game. In 1988 he became the first NBA player to win both the Most Valuable Player (MVP) and the Defensive Player of the Year awards in the same season. At that point he signed a new contract with the Bulls, which was worth $25 million over the next eight years. He also additionally earned millions from advertising sponsorships with companies such as Nike (*see box*).

Between 1991 and 1993 Jordan helped the Bulls to three consecutive World Championships. On March 28, 1990, he scored a career-best 69 points in a match against Cleveland. At the end of the 1993 season Jordan retired from basketball. This was partly because the game had lost some of its former appeal, and partly because he was traumatized by the death of his father, who had been murdered in his car in North Carolina while returning from the funeral of a friend.

Jordan had always wanted to try baseball, and in February 1994 he joined the Birmingham Barons, a minor-league team affiliated to the Chicago White Sox, as an outfield player. That summer he batted .202 for them and then joined the Scottsdale Scorpions in the Arizona Fall League, for whom he batted .252. Disappointed, Jordan decided that baseball was not his game.

Making a comeback

In 1995 Jordan signed again with the Bulls. On his return he had to wear the number 45 jersey because the Bulls had previously honored him by retiring the number 23 jersey in which he had made his name. In June 1998 Jordan led the Bulls to their sixth NBA championship in eight years. He then announced his retirement again, only to make his third comeback in 2001 with the Washington Wizards. Over the next two seasons he rose to third place in the all-time scoring list. When Jordan retired forever in 2003, his career statistics were 32,292 points, 5,633 assists, and 6,672 rebounds; his scoring average was 30.1 points per game.

Other ventures

Jordan also ventured into acting: He costarred with Bugs Bunny in *Space Jam* in 1996. The movie was based loosely on Jordan's short and largely undistinguished baseball career, but with a comic plot that involved his kidnapping by Warner Brothers cartoon characters. He made another excursion onto the silver screen in *Like Mike* (2002), in which he played the owner of a pair of magic sneakers that turn a 14-year-old orphan into a professional basketball star.

Jordan also launched MVP.com, an Internet sportswear company, with Canadian ice hockey player Wayne Gretzky and Denver Broncos' quarterback John Elway, but the business was badly damaged in the dot.com crash of 1999 and was sold at a loss to CBS two years later. Jordan was among the celebrities who donated millions to help the victims of the September 11 terrorist attacks.

KEY DATES	
1963	Born in Brooklyn, New York, on February 17.
1982	Enrolls at the University of North Carolina (UNC).
1984	Is a member of gold-medal-winning team at Olympic Games; joins Chicago Bulls.
1988	Wins MVP and Defenseive Player of the Year.
1993	Retires from the court; turns to baseball.
1995	Returns to the Bulls; retires three years later.
2001	Joins the Washington Wizards.
2003	Retires permanently.

See also: Black Identity and Popular Culture

Further reading: Jordan, Michael. *For the Love of the Game: My Story.* New York, NY: Crown Publishers, 1998. www.ewsonline.com/sports/jordan/bio.html (Biography).

JORDAN, Vernon E.
Lawyer, Activist

Vernon Eulion Jordan, Jr., is sometimes called a "Renaissance man" for his range of abilities. A lawyer, activist, broadcaster, and businessman, Jordan has advised every president from Richard Nixon to Bill Clinton.

Early life
Born in Atlanta, Georgia, on August 15, 1935, Jordan was the son of a mail clerk in the Army. He grew up in Georgia, attending local schools. He went on to study political science at DePauw University, Indiana, graduating with a BA in 1957. He then studied law at Howard University, Washington D.C., receiving his JD in 1960. After graduation he went back to Georgia to enter private practice and became highly active in the civil rights movement.

Making a difference
In 1961 Jordan and two associates sued the University of Georgia for failing to admit African American students. He famously escorted Charlayne Hunter (now Hunter-Gault) and Hamp Holmes, the first black students to be admitted to the university, through the school gates. Jordan thought that the fight for equal rights was so important that he left private practice to devote all of his time to the cause.

In 1962 Jordan became the field director of the National Association for the Advancement of Colored People (NAACP), leading sit-ins and protests against segregation. He also pushed for greater black voter registration, becoming director of the Southern Regional Council's Voter Education Project. This helped add thousands of black people's names to the voting rolls. In 1970 Jordan became executive director of the United Negro College Fund (UNCF) for a year, before being appointed president of the National Urban League. Under Jordan the

▲ *In 1966 Vernon E. Jordan was a delegate to Lyndon B. Johnson's White House conference on civil rights.*

league gained corporate sponsors, more than tripling its budget, and began to publish the *Urban Review League.*

Such were Jordan's successes that he also attracted the attention of white supremacists. In 1980 he was shot in the back outside a motel in Fort Wayne, Indiana. Although Joseph Paul Franklin was subsequently arrested for the crime, he was acquitted; later he admitted the shooting.

After Jordan recovered, he went back into private practice with the Washington firm Akin, Gump, Strauss, Hauer, and Feld. From 2000 he also became senior managing director of Lazard Freres & Co, an investment banking firm and is on the boards of several companies, including American Express and Sara Lee. He has also sat on several presidential commissions.

See also: Civil Rights; Hunter-Gault, Charlayne

Further reading: Jordan, Vernon, E. *Vernon Can Read! A Memoir.* New York, NY: Public Affairs, 2001.
http://smithsonianassociates.org/programs/jordan/jordan.asp (Includes some audio transcripts of Jordan's memoirs).

KEY DATES	
1935	Born in Atlanta, Georgia, on August 15.
1957	Graduates from DePauw University, Indiana.
1960	Receives doctor of law (JD) from Howard University Law School.
1962	Becomes field director of the NAACP.
1971	Appointed executive director of the Urban League.
1980	Shot by Joseph Paul Franklin, a white supremacist.

JOYNER, Marjorie Stewart
Beautician, Inventor

In 1928 Marjorie Stewart Joyner became the first African American woman to receive a patent with a machine to set women's hair in a long-lasting curl. She called it the "permanent-wave machine."

Early life
Born in Monterey, Virginia, on October 24, 1896, Joyner was one of 15 children born to George Stewart, a teacher, and Annie Dougherty, a domestic worker. Following her parents' divorce, in 1912 the young Marjorie moved with her mother to Chicago, where she trained at A. B. Molar Beauty School, becoming its first African American graduate in 1916.

Madame C. J. Walker
That same year she married Robert E. Joyner, a chiropodist. Her mother-in-law encouraged her to study at one of Madame C. J. Walker's College's of Hair Culture. Walker was a well-known black businesswoman, who had founded a flourishing cosmetics company that employed several thousand African American women. Joyner began working for Walker and helped her open beauty colleges and salons; she recruited Walker agents, women who sold the company's products door-to-door. Joyner became vice president of the company in 1919, when Walker died. By the time of her death Walker employed 3,000 people at the factory, had more than 20,000 agents, and was believed to be the wealthiest black woman in the country.

The permanent-wave machine
In 1926, while still working for the Madame C. J. Walker Beauty Colleges, Joyner developed what she called her permanent-wave machine to make hairstyles last longer after they had been created. Her device consisted of a dome-shaped cover containing a scalp protector, curling irons, and clamping devices around which sections of hair could be wrapped. An electric current passed through the curlers and clamps, producing longer lasting curls and hairstyles than had previously been possible. Joyner was successful in patenting her invention in 1928, although all profits from the machine went to the Walker company, which owned the rights. In 1929 Joyner patented a scalp protector that made the procedure less painful. Unexpectedly the machine also found favor with white women who wanted to add curl to their hair.

A woman of influence
Joyner was an influential member in the black community in Chicago. During the Great Depression of the 1930s she worked with several of President Franklin D. Roosevelt's New Deal programs to help find young black people homes and work.

In 1945, together with educator and activist Mary Bethune McLeod, Joyner founded the United Beauty School Owners and Teachers Association, a national organization set up to create more opportunities for African American women to work and train in the beauty industry. Their "Pay While You Learn" policy, enabled thousands of African American women to train for a profitable career.

Bud Billiken Parade
When the influential black newspaper the *Chicago Defender* created the Chicago Defender Charities in 1945, Joyner worked with the organization to raise money for community projects, scholarship programs, and social and cultural events such as the Bud Billiken Parade, the largest African American parade in the nation, held since 1929 on the second Saturday in August. Joyner was president of the Charities for more than 50 years.

In 1973 Joyner earned a BS in psychology from Bethune-Cookman College, Florida. She died, at age 98, on December 27, 1994, in Chicago. Joyner once said, "There is nothing a woman can't do. Men might think they do things all by themselves—but a woman is always there guiding them or helping them."

KEY DATES	
1896	Born in Monterey, Virginia, on October 24.
1928	Receives a patent for her permanent-wave machine.
1994	Dies in Chicago, Illinois, on December 27.

See also: McLeod, Mary Bethune; Walker, Madame C. J.

Further reading: Casey, Susan. *Women Invent: Two Centuries of Discovery That Have Shaped Our World.* Chicago, IL: Chicago Review Press, 1997.
http://inventors.about.com/library/inventors/bljoyner.htm (Information on Joyner from a site about inventors).

JOYNER-KERSEE, Jackie
Athlete

In a career that spanned the 1980s and 1990s Jackie Joyner-Kersee emerged as one of the most outstanding all-round women athletes of the 20th century.

Born Jacqueline Joyner in a poor district in East St. Louis, Illinois, on March 3, 1962, she was not the only athlete in the family: Her older brother Al went on to become an Olympic triple-jump champion and to marry the sprinter Florence Griffith-Joyner. Early in high school Joyner proved herself to be both academically gifted and talented at sports. She competed on her school teams in volleyball, basketball, and track events, excelling in particular at long jump. She went on to win a basketball scholarship to the University of California, Los Angeles (UCLA), where she studied history.

The making of a great career

At UCLA Joyner initially concentrated on basketball and long jump. However, inspired by a program she saw about the great all-round sportswoman Mildred "Babe" Didrikson (1914–1956) and by track coach Bob Kersee, she began to train for the heptathlon, a two-day contest comprising seven events—100-meter hurdles, high jump, shot put, 200-meter sprint, long jump, javelin, and 800-meter race. She won many collegiate heptathlon competitions and went on to secure a silver medal in the event at the Los Angeles Olympics in 1984—narrowly missing out on gold owing to a hamstring injury, a problem, along with asthma, with which she battled for the rest of her career.

In 1986 Joyner married Bob Kersee. That same year she won the heptathlon at the Goodwill Games in Moscow with a world-record beating score of 7,148 points. At the 1988 Olympics in Seoul, South Korea, she scored 7,291

▲ *Jackie Joyner-Kersee takes the bronze medal for the long jump at the 1996 Atlanta Olympic Games.*

points to win the gold medal in the heptathlon, also winning gold at long jump. She again won gold in the heptathlon at the 1992 Barcelona Olympics and bronze in the long jump. Hamstring problems forced Joyner-Kersee to withdraw from the heptathlon in the 1996 Atlanta Olympics, although she overcame the injury to win a bronze in the long jump. That same year she started to play basketball for the Richmond Rage in the American Basketball League. Joyner-Kersee retired from athletics in 1998, after winning the heptathlon at the Goodwill Games in New York City.

See also: Griffith-Joyner, Florence

Further reading: Joyner-Kersee, Jackie. *A Kind of Grace: The Autobiography of the World's Greatest Female Athlete.* New York, NY: Warner Books, 1997.
http://www.galegroup.com/free_resources/bhm/bio/joyner_j.htm (Biography).

KEY DATES

1962   Born in East St. Louis, Illinois, on March 3.

1984   Wins silver medal in the heptathlon at the Los Angeles Olympics.

1986   Sets world record for heptathlon at Goodwill Games in Moscow with a score of 7,148 points.

1988   Wins gold medals in the heptathlon and long jump at the Seoul Olympics.

1992   Wins gold medal in the heptathlon and bronze in the long jump at the Barcelona Olympics.

JULIAN, Percy
Chemist

Percy Lavon Julian made many ground-breaking discoveries in chemistry that had wide-ranging applications, particularly in medicine.

Education

Julian was born in Montgomery, Alabama, in 1899. He overcame the limited schooling available to African Americans in Montgomery to earn a place studying chemistry at DePauw University, Indiana, from which he graduated with distinction in 1920. He went on to teach at Fisk University, Tennessee, and in 1922 won a fellowship to Harvard University, where he was awarded a master's degree in 1923. Unable to progress in his career at Harvard owing to racial prejudice, he left in 1926 to teach at the

KEY DATES

1899 Born in Montgomery, Alabama, on April 11.

1935 Synthesizes physostigmine.

1940s Leads research that results in large-scale production of the hormones progesterone and testosterone, and cortisone.

1975 Dies in Waukegan, Illinois, on April 9.

West Virginia State College for Negroes and then, in 1927, at Howard University in Washington, D.C. In 1929 Julian won a Rockefeller Fellowship that enabled him to study organic chemistry at the University of Vienna, Austria, from which he received a PhD in 1931.

Research work

Back in the United States Julian took up a position teaching organic science at DePauw University in 1933. There, with Josef Pikl, whom he had met in Vienna, Julian worked on making physostigmine, a substance used to treat the eye disease glaucoma. He was successful in 1935, but despite international acclaim was still unable to progress in his academic career. In 1936 he left academia to direct research at the Glidden Company in Chicago.

During his 17 years at Glidden Julian directed the development of a wide range of soy-based products, helping make soybeans an important national crop. Early products included a fire-retardant used by U.S. troops during World War II (1939–1945). Julian also developed a way of making artificial versions of the hormones progesterone and testosterone. This breakthrough made reproductive medicine and cancer treatments more widely available. At the end of the 1940s Julian created a synthetic version of cortisone, which is used to treat arthritis. In 1953 he set up his own company, the Julian Laboratories, which he sold eight years later to the pharmaceutical giant Smith, Kline, and French. Julian was awarded the NAACP's Spingarn Medal in 1947 and elected to the National Academy of Science in 1974. He died of cancer in 1975.

▲ *Percy Julian not only experienced racism in his academic career but also suffered when a mob threatened to burn down his Chicago home in 1950.*

Further reading: Krapp, Kristine M. *Notable Black American Scientists*. Detroit, MI: Thomson Gale, 1998.
http://www.chemheritage.org/scialive/julian/history/1.html
(Biography).

JUST, Ernest Everett
Scientist

Born in the segregationist post-Civil War South, Ernest Everett Just became one of the most highly respected scientists of his age. He is known for his research in a broad field of biological sciences and best remembered for his work in embryology and genetics.

Just was not only a distinguished scholar and scientist, his influence can also be widely seen in African American education. Perhaps more significantly, Just demonstrated that human accomplishment was possible regardless of race or color.

▲ *Ernest Everett Just was a prolific researcher. His work paved the way for fertility treatment and advances in genetic engineering.*

Early life

Just was born in Charleston, South Carolina, in 1883 to Charles Frazier and Mary Matthews Just. He prepared for college at Kimball Hall Academy, New Hampshire, where he completed the four-year course of study in only three years. Just won a place at Dartmouth College in Hanover, New Hampshire. In his first year at Dartmouth Just received the highest marks in the entire freshman class in Greek. He was then conferred as the Rufus Choate scholar for two years. In Dartmouth's class of 1907, Just was the only student to graduate magna cum laude. He won special honors in botany and history, with honors in sociology.

Career in science

In 1907 Just began to teach and do research at Howard University, the bastion of African American higher education, in Washington, D.C. In 1909 Just began research work at the Marine Biology Laboratory at Woods Hole, Massachusetts. His work there was the first opportunity for Just to gain recognition among the scientific community

Just went on to earn a PhD in zoology from the University of Chicago in 1916. Again he graduated magna cum laude following his work in experimental embryology, including a thesis on the mechanics of fertilization.

Throughout his career Just continued to make contributions to developmental biology—a field that investigates how animals grow from a single cell into a full-sized individual. He worked on the subjects of fertilization, experimental parthenogenesis, hydration, cell division, dehydration in living cells, and the effect of ultraviolet light in increasing the number of chromosomes in animal cells. He also investigated altering the organization of a cell with special reference to polarity— the direction in which a cell splits as the organism grows.

KEY DATES

1883 Born in Charleston, South Carolina, on August 14.

1907 Teaches at Howard University.

1916 Receives PhD from University of Chicago.

1941 Dies in Washington, D.C., on October 27.

INFLUENCES AND INSPIRATION

One key experience that played a major role in Ernest Just's life was his time at the Industrial School of State College in Orangeburg, South Carolina. Although the school was poorly funded, as most schools for African Americans were, the thoroughness and enthusiasm of the teachers inspired Just, gave him a good foundation, and showed him the direction for his future education. At the University of Chicago, where Just received his PhD, he studied under a prominent scientist, Frank Lillie (1870–1947), who proved to be another inspiration.

Just's period in Europe provided him with the working environment that was denied him by the segregation in the United States. It also gave him the opportunity to research the links between genetics and physiology, which was not considered important in the United States.

Collaborations

This broad range of research interests gave Just the opportunity to collaborate with some of the leading scientific figures of the time, including Jacques Loeb (1859–1924) and Frank R. Lillie (1870–1947), and to build on the work of E. G. Conklin (1863–1952) and other developmental biologists. Just's work helped establish principles of developmental biology and neuroscience that remain largely unchallenged today.

Just's collaborative work was not restricted to the United States. In 1924 he was selected from among the biologists of the world by a group of German researchers to contribute to a publication on fertilization, one of a series of monographs by specialists working on fundamental problems of the function and structure of the cell. He also contributed to a three-volume series on colloidal chemistry—the way in which large molecules that do not dissolve are mixed into liquids. Just published more than 50 scientific papers. In addition he wrote one of the most important science textbooks of the 20th century, *Biology of the Cell Surface,* in 1939.

Work in Europe

From 1920 to 1931 Just was the Julius Rosenwald Fellow in Biology of the National Research Council. Under the auspices of the program he was engaged as an adjunct researcher at the Kaiser Wilhelm Institute for Biology, in Berlin, Germany, working under Professor Max Hartmann (1876–1962). Just also worked at the marine biological laboratories in Naples and Sicily, Italy. In 1930 Just was invited to lecture at the Eleventh International Congress of Zoologists, held at Padua, Italy, where he reported on his work to date.

The way Just was accepted in the fascist state of Italy showed not only respect for his scientific achievements, but also his ability to work across national and racial boundaries. In 1933 Just settled in France.

Education legacy

As an educator, especially in "Negro Education," Just has a special significance: He founded the department of zoology at Howard University and developed the masters program in that subject, the first at any black college. The zoology department at Howard has produced more than 200 masters of science and is responsible for producing 12 percent of the nation's African American PhDs in the biological sciences.

Quiet man

In his work, Just showed all the traits of a true scholar. His imagination and industry were the basis for his success in the field of zoology. As a scholar he belonged to various scientific associations and was editor of key journals in his field, including *Protoplasm* (an international journal published in Berlin and devoted to the work done on the physical chemistry of the cell), and *Physiological Zoology*.

In 1915 Just was the first person to be awarded the Spingarn Medal. The honor was bestowed on him by the National Association for the Advancement of Colored People (NAACP).

Just left an indelible mark on the understanding of cells and other fields of biology. The insights he provided laid the basis for many of the advances that have been made today in genetic research and artificial fertilization. In addition Just was an inspiration to all African Americans, showing what could be achieved if they could work across the color barrier. When the Germans invaded France in 1940, Just returned to the United States. He died of pancreatic cancer in Washington, D.C., in 1941.

Further reading: Manning, Kenneth R. *Black Apollo of Science: The Life of Ernest Everett Just.* New York, NY: Oxford University Press, 1984.

http://www2.sjsu.edu/depts/Museum/ernest.html (Biography).

KARENGA, Maulana
Educator, Activist

Scholar activist, educator, and social theorist, Maulana Karenga was originally named Ronald Everett; he changed his name in 1965—"Maulana" means "master teacher" in Swahili. Karenga is professor of black studies at California State University, Long Beach, the director of the Kawaida Institute of Pan-African Studies in Los Angeles, and founder and national chairman of US, a cultural and social change organization. Karenga is also widely recognized as the creator of the African American holiday Kwanzaa.

An interest in learning
Born on a farm in Parsonsburg, Maryland, in 1941, Karenga was the 14th child of a Baptist minister. As a young boy Karenga found education and learning exciting; he was also involved as a student in civic activism. In the late 1950s he moved to Los Angeles, California, to attend Los Angeles Community College and later received his bachelors degree, an MA in political science and African studies, and two doctorates, one in political science from the United States International University and another in social ethics from the University of Southern California. Karenga later received an honorary doctorate from the University of Durban–Westville in South Africa.

Creating black consciousness
In the 1960s Karenga met the civil rights activist and religious leader Malcolm X and became involved in the black nationalist movement, which was involved in fighting for equal rights for African Americans.

In 1965 Karenga created the organization US to promote black consciousness. Through US and the philosophy Kawaida—based on the *Nguzo Saba*, or the Seven Principles of Unity, Self Determination, Collective Work and Responsibility, Cooperative Economics, Purpose, Creativity, and Faith—Karenga played a vanguard role in raising black consciousness and a belief in community and society. He played leading roles in the black arts movement, black studies, the black power movement, the Black Student Union movement, Afrocentricity, rites of passage programs, the study of ancient Egyptian culture as an essential part of black studies, the independent black school movement, African life-cycle ceremonies, the Simba Wachanga youth movement, and black theological and ethical discourse.

▲ *Maulana Karenga founded the organization US in 1965. Members were given a Swahili name, encouraged to wear African dress, and immersed in the group's doctrine and practices.*

As an effective public-policy advocacy group, among many other roles, US has engaged in the struggle for a realistic living wage for low-income workers that would provide them with adequate means to support themselves and their families, to rise above poverty level, and to live

KEY DATES	
1941	Born in Parsonsburg, Maryland, on July 14.
1965	Founds the organization US on September 7.
1966	Creates the holiday, Kwanzaa.

INFLUENCES AND INSPIRATION

As a cultural nationalist, Maulana Karenga has had a profound and far-reaching effect on black intellectual and political culture. He was inspired to engage in the struggle for equal rights and to push for a black cultural identity by several leading activists and educators. Karenga saw it as both important and possible to draw equally from the wisdom and accomplishments of both male and female elders and ancestors and to perpetuate their ideals. Among those people were Fannie Lou Hamer, who led the struggle for voting rights in

Mississippi and for significant black inclusiveness in the Democratic Party's decision-making process. Mary McLeod Bethune, who stood for the notion "We are heirs and custodians of a great legacy," was also an inspiration. Similarly, the accomplishments of intellectual W. E. B. DuBois, and activists Martin Luther King, Jr., and Frederick Douglass gave Karenga the strength to fight for what he believed in. The impetus to create the organization US came from the examples set by many such people.

The institution established the African American Cultural Center; the Mary McLeod Bethune Institute, an independent cultural school for children; the Kawaida Institute of Pan-African Studies, which sponsors an annual seminar in social theory and practice; and the University of Sankore Press.

The Black Panthers borrowed many civil rights techniques from Karenga's organization, such as an alert patrol, which followed the police around, confronting them in cases of harassment, taking their names, and giving legal counsel to victims of harassment.

a life of dignity and decency. The organization also engages in promoting interethnic community relations.

One of the things that Karenga is most famous for, however, is the creation of Kwanzaa, a week-long African American holiday first celebrated in California from December 26, 1966, to January 1, 1967. A cultural celebration, Kwanzaa takes its name from the Swahili *matunda ya kwanza*, meaning "first fruits" and draws on various African harvest festivals celebrated in the 10th month of each year. African Americans of all religious denominations celebrate Kwanzaa: In 2004 around 1.6 percent of the U.S. population took part in it.

Controversy

In 1967 and 1968 Karenga helped politician Adam Clayton Powell, Jr., to organize black power conferences, but he soon found himself at the center of controversy as his movement became increasingly associated with violence. In 1969 US followers were involved in a shootout with Black Panther members on the UCLA campus, which left two men dead. In 1970 matters came to a head when Karenga was accused of imprisoning and torturing Deborah Jones and Gail Davis. In 1971 he was convicted of two counts of felonious assault and one count of false imprisonment, and sentenced to serve one to ten years in prison.

After being released from prison in 1975 Karenga returned to his studies. By 1979 he was head of black studies at California State University in Long Beach. He

is also chair of the President's Task Force on Multicultural Education and Campus Diversity at California State University, Long Beach. He was a visiting professor in black politics at Stanford University and a distinguished visiting scholar in black studies at the University of Nebraska, Omaha.

Achievements

Karenga has written numerous articles and books, including *Introduction to Black Studies* (1982), *Kemet and the African Worldview: Research, Rescue and Restoration* (1986), *Kwanzaa: A Celebration of Family, Community and Culture* (1988), *Maat, the Moral Ideal in Ancient Egypt: A Study in Classical African Ethics* (1994), and *Kawaida Theory: An African Communitarian Philosophy* (2003). Karenga has received many awards, including the National Leadership Award for Outstanding Scholarly Achievements in Black Studies from the National Council for Black Studies.

See also: Bethune, Mary McLeod; Douglass, Frederick; DuBois, W. E. B.; Hamer, Fannie Lou; King, Martin Luther, Jr.; Malcolm X; Powell, Adam Clayton, Jr.

Further reading: Karenga, Maulana. *Kwanzaa: A Celebration of Family, Community and Culture.* Los Angeles, CA: University of Sankore Press, 1997.
http://www.officialkwanzaawebsite.org (Official site of Kwanzaa organization, including articles and links.).

KEITH, Damon J.
Lawyer

After forging a career as a distinguished attorney, Damon J. Keith became one of the first African American appeal court judges. He is known for several momentous decisions in support of civil rights.

Legal career

The son of a foundry worker at the Ford Motor Company's works at Rouge, Michigan, Damon Jerome Keith graduated from Northwestern High School in Detroit in 1939 and from West Virginia State College four years later. He served in the Army in World War II (1939–1945) and then earned a law degree from Howard Law School in 1949. In 1950 he entered practice as an attorney in Michigan.

From the start of his career Keith was active in civil rights, and in 1963 he was one of six Detroit lawyers invited to the White House by President John F. Kennedy to discuss the way forward for the movement.

In 1964 Keith was one of five African Americans who set up the law firm of Keith, Conyers, Anderson, Brown, and Wahls in the previously all-white legal district of Detroit. During the same period he also chaired the Michigan Civil Rights Commission and was president of the Detroit Housing Commission.

▲ *Judge Damon J. Keith has received a remarkable 37 honorary degrees in recognition of his work.*

Landmark rulings

In 1967 President Lyndon B. Johnson appointed Keith to the U.S. District Court for the Eastern District of Michigan, where he served as chief judge from 1975 until 1977. In that year President Jimmy Carter appointed him to the Court of Appeals for the Sixth Circuit.

Keith delivered several landmark rulings in civil rights and civil liberties cases: on school desegregation in *Davis v. School District of the City of Pontiac* (1970); on employment discrimination and affirmative action in *Stamps v. Detroit Edison Company* (1973) and *Baker v. City of Detroit* (1979). In *Garrett v. City of Hamtramck* (1971), Keith ruled that what civic authorities had proclaimed as urban renewal had in fact been a policy of "Negro removal," and ordered them to build new public housing.

Keith's most famous opinion came in *United States v. Sinclair* (1971), which found that the wiretapping of private residences without a court order was unconstitutional. The so-called "Keith Decision" was subsequently upheld by the U.S. Supreme Court and in 1974 contributed to the downfall of President Richard M. Nixon in the Watergate scandal.

Keith's tireless defense of the poor and ethnic minorities made him one of the most respected lawyers of the 20th century. Fellow U.S. Court of Appeals judge Peter Fay spoke for many when he remarked: "One cannot be around Damon for very long without sensing his commitment to all that is good about our country."

KEY DATES	
1922	Born in Detroit, Michigan, on July 4.
1943	Graduates from West Virginia State College.
1950	Starts practicing law.
1953	Marries Rachel Boone.
1964	Sets up law firm.
1967	Appointed judge of U.S. District Court, Eastern Michigan.
1977	Appointed to U.S. Court of Appeals.

Further reading: http://www.reuther.wayne.edu/keith_bio.html (Biography).

KELLEY, Robin
Academic, Writer, Intellectual

Robin D. G. Kelley is an award-winning author, respected academic, and a leading authority on African American studies. His teaching and research interests have focused on variety of subjects, from race, working-class radicalism, and the African diaspora to urban studies and cultural history, with a special emphasis on music.

From Harlem to Columbia

Born in Harlem, New York, on March 14, 1962, Kelley was brought up by his mother for the first nine years of his life in New York City's Washington Heights neighborhood. During a visit to Seattle in 1972 Kelley and his sister were kidnapped by their father, who refused to return them to their mother. In the end Kelley's mother chose to move to California to be near her children; Kelley ended up running away to Pasadena to be with her when he was 15.

In the early 1980s Kelley studied at California State University, Long Beach. He kept changing his major, finally graduating with a BA in history in 1983. While an undergraduate Kelley became involved in the Black Student Union. He was encouraged to undertake further study by two white left-wing professors, Jack Stuart and Leo Rifkin. Kelley gained an MA in African history in 1985, and a doctorate in 1987, both from UCLA.

Although Kelley originally intended to focus his PhD on South Africa, he was refused a visa to the country. He decided to research the Communist Party in Alabama instead, a subject of particular interest as Kelley was a member of the Communist Working Party. His subsequent book, *Hammer and Hoe: Alabama Communists During the Great Depression*, was published in 1990. Four years later Kelley wrote the award-winning *Race Rebels: Culture Politics and the Black Working Class*, which studied the contribution of black working-class people to the development of racial identity in the 20th century. In 1998 his book *Yo Mama's DisFunktional!* was selected as one of the Top 10 books of the year by the *Village Voice.*

The author of seven books and more than 100 essays and book reviews for such esteemed publications as the *Nation, New Politics*, and the *New York Times,* Kelley has also edited and coedited many works. He has been a consultant on film and TV projects, including *Jazz* (2001).

In 1994 Kelley became one of the youngest full professors in the country, teaching history and Africana studies at New York University until 2003, when he became a full professor in anthropology at Columbia University.

▼ *In 2005 Robin Kelley was writing a book on jazz musician Thelonious Monk.*

KEY DATES	
1962	Born in Harlem, New York, on March 14.
1985	Awarded MA in African history from UCLA.
1994	Becomes a full professor at New York University.
1998	Publishes *Yo Mama's DisFunktional!*.
2003	Joins Columbia University as a full professor in the anthropology department.

See also: Monk, Thelonious

Further reading: Kelley, Robin D. G. *Yo' Mama's DisFunktional!*. Boston, MA: Beacon Press, 1998.
http://www.columbia.edu/cu/news/03/06/robinKelley.html (Biography on Columbia University site).

KELLY, Leontine
Bishop

An inspirational religious leader, Leontine Kelly became the first African American woman to be elected a bishop by the United Methodist Church and, indeed, by any major Christian denomination. Her appointment paved the way for other women and African Americans to progress in the United Methodist Church.

Called to the ministry

The daughter of a Methodist minister, Kelly was born in Washington, D.C., in 1920. In 1940 she attended West Virginia State College, but quit after just one year in order to marry. In the early 1950s she divorced, and in 1956 she married the Methodist minister James Kelly. While raising her children, she took a BA at Virginia Union University and, after graduating in 1960, became a teacher while also working as a lay preacher for the United Methodist Church.

After her husband died in 1969 she decided to become a minister herself, and succeeded her husband in his post as minister of the Galilee Church. She gained an MA in divinity in 1976. The following year she became pastor of Asbury-Church Hill Church in Richmond, Virginia.

Becoming bishop

At the time, almost all the bishops in the United Methodist Church were men and the vast majority were white. There was only one female bishop—Marjorie Swank Matthews (1916–1985), who had been elected in 1980. It was much to Kelly's surprise and pleasure, therefore, when in 1984 she was elected a bishop and appointed resident bishop of the San Francisco Bay area. She held the post until her retirement in 1998.

Throughout her career Kelly has worked passionately for social justice. As a bishop she became well known for her progressive—and in some instances controversial—views. For example, she fought for the acceptance of gay and lesbian people within the Methodist Church and campaigned for nuclear disarmament.

Since 1998 Kelly has been a visiting professor at the Pacific School of Religion, Berkeley, California, and has continued to work for the United Methodist Church, becoming involved with its Initiative on Children and Poverty and playing a key role in the development of Africa University in Zimbabwe. She has been widely honored for her achievements, and in 2000 was inducted into the National Women's Hall of Fame in Seneca Falls, New York.

KEY DATES

1920   Born in Washington, D.C., on March 5.

1974   Ordained a minister in the United Methodist Church.

1984   Consecrated as the first African American female bishop of the United Methodist Church.

▲ *Leontine Kelly's appointment as bishop was controversial not only because of her race and sex but also because she was a divorced mother of four.*

Further reading: Craig, Judith. *The Leading Women: Stories of the First Women Bishops of the United Methodist Church.* Nashville, TN: Abingdon Press, 2004.
http://www.greatwomen.org/women.php?action=viewone&id=92 (Biography).

KELLY, Sharon Pratt
Lawyer, Politician

The first African American woman to become mayor of a major U.S. city, Sharon Pratt Kelly ultimately lost the position to the controversial politician Marion Barry.

Sharon Pratt was born in Washington, D.C., on January 30, 1944. Her mother died of breast cancer when she was two years old. As she grew up, she aspired to be many things. Her father gave her a law dictionary, but she also expressed a wish to be variously a cultural anthropologist, actor, and comedian. She graduated with a BA (1965) and a law degree (1968) from Howard University, before entering private practice as a lawyer in 1971. She went on to teach at Antioch Antioch School of Law from 1972 to 1976..

In 1977 Pratt became the first female member of the National Democratic Committee for the District of Columbia, later acting as party treasurer. In 1982 she married Democrat councillor Arrington Dixon, and that same year directed a failed Washington mayoral campaign for Patricia Robert Harris. In 1983 Pratt was made the first black vice president for community relations at Pepco, Washington's electric utility, and was awarded the Presidential Award by the NAACP.

Mayoral campaign

In 1988 Pratt launched her mayoral campaign for the 1990 election, challenging incumbent Marion Barry and three other councilmen. With promises to clean up the city and fire 2,000 mid-level managers, she secured the endorsement of the *Washington Post*. After winning the election easily when Barry dropped out after being charged with drug offenses, she was sworn in as mayor on January 2, 1991. Later that year she married James R. Kelly, III, and changed her name to Sharon Pratt Kelly. As mayor, Kelly was unsuccessful in convincing government employees of

▲ *Sharon Pratt Kelly has had a distinguished career in politics.*

the need to cut jobs. The city's high crime rate and continuing failure of many public services also contributed to her increasing unpopularity with citizens. Barry led a campaign in the second year of Kelly's term to have her recalled. Although the challenge failed, it was enough to weaken her administration, and Barry was reelected in the 1994 primaries. In 2002 Kelly became involved in homeland security and emergency preparedness through her company Pratt Consulting.

See also: Barry, Marion; Harris, Patricia Robert

Further reading: Haskins, James. *Distinguished African American Political and Governmental Leaders.* Phoenix, AZ: Oryx Press, 1999.

KEY DATES

1944	Born in Washington, D.C., on January 30.
1977	Becomes member of National Democratic Committee.
1983	Becomes vice president for Pepco; receives Presidential Award from NAACP.
1991	Elected mayor of Washington, D.C.
1994	Loses to Marion Barry in the Democratic primary.

KENNARD, William E.

Entrepreneur

Businessman William E. Kennard was the first African American chair of the Federal Communication Commission (FCC).

A native of Los Angeles, Kennard was born in 1957 to Robert, an architect, and Helen, an elementary school teacher. Kennard attended Hollywood High School in California, before graduating Phi Beta Kappa with a BA in communication from Stanford University in 1978. He went on to receive his law degree from Yale Law School in 1981. He was admitted to the bar in California and the District of Columbia.

Making a mark

Between 1981 and 1982 Kennard was the recipient of a legal fellowship from the National Association of Broadcasters. He served as the assistant general counsel for the association between 1983 and 1984. Kennard also

▼ **William E. Kennard in 2003 as chairman of the Federal Communications Commission.**

joined the legal firm Verner, Liipfert, Bernhard, McPherson & Hand, with which he served until 1993.

Kennard served as the FCC's general counsel from December 1993 to November 1997, after which he was appointed chair and served until January 2001. During his tenure Kennard implemented policies that helped to create an explosion of new wireless phones, brought the Internet to a majority of households, and made digital-age technologies more available to schools, libraries, low-income Americans, and people with disabilities. His mission and objective simply stated: "We need to make technology cool in our communities. And that involves a change in culture."

Kennard recognized that the "digital divide," created by a lack of access to new technology owing to poverty or an inefficient communication infrastructure, was a problem. He advocated investment in education: By the end of his tenure close to $6 billion had been invested in wiring schools across the country to the Internet. This project of reaching out to communities was tailored especially toward downtown schools and low-income areas.

On leaving the FCC Kennard joined the Carlyle Group in May 2001 as a managing director in the Global Telecommunications and Media group. Kennard played key roles in investments in Dex Media, Inc., and Casema Holding, BV. Kennard has also sat on the boards of several companies, including Nextel Communications, Inc., the New York Times Company, Dex Media, Inc., and eAccess, Ltd. He has received honorary degrees from Howard, Gallaudet, and Long Island universities.

KEY DATES

1957 Born in Los Angeles, California.

1983 Becomes assistant general counsel to the National Association of Broadcasters.

1993 Becomes general counsel for the Federal Communications Commission (FCC).

1997 Is nominated by President Bill Clinton as chair of the FCC; stays in this position until 2001.

2001 Joins the Carlyle Group.

Further reading: http://www.techlawjournal.com/people/kennard.htm (Tech Law Journal official site)

KENNEDY, Annie Brown
Lawyer, Politician

Annie Brown Kennedy is a leading North Carolina attorney. She was the first African American woman to serve in the state House of Representatives in Raleigh. Her law firm, which she established with her husband, Harold Lillard Kennedy, Jr. (1926–2005), has provided over 50 years of service to the people of Forsyth County and is the oldest existing African American practice in North Carolina.

Many members of Kennedy's family have distinguished themselves in the law and in public life. Her husband also served in the House of Representatives (1977–1978) and was an active civic and religious leader. Two of the Kennedys' sons are partners in their parents' law firm Kennedy, Kennedy, Kennedy and Kennedy, L.L.P.

Early life
Annie E. Brown was born in Atlanta, Georgia, in 1924. She graduated from Spelman College, the city's prestigious black women's college, in 1945. She went on to gain a doctor of law (JD) from Howard University School of Law in Washington, D.C. There she met fellow student Harold L. Kennedy, Jr. They married in 1951. In 1952 Annie Kennedy was licensed to practice law in Georgia.

A husband-and-wife team
In 1953 the Kennedys settled in North Carolina; a year later she passed the state bar and they set up a law practice in Winston-Salem, Forsyth County, where Harold Kennedy had largely grown up. He was the grandson of Francis Marion Kennedy, Sr., the third president (1910–1913) of the historically black Winston-Salem

State University. Annie Kennedy was the first African American woman attorney in the county and only the second in the state.

The Kennedys' practice flourished, and Kennedy and her husband became leading figures in the Forsyth community. During the 1960s Harold Kennedy helped found the multiracial St. Anne's Episcopal Church. They were also both active members of the local chapter of the National Association for the Advancement of Colored People (NAACP). The Kennedys were also generous patrons of the arts and of education: Together they set up the Harold and Annie Brown Kennedy Scholarship fund at Howard University School of Law.

In the House of Representatives
Both the Kennedys were politically active, supporting the Democratic Party. In 1979 Kennedy was appointed by Governor James. B. Hunt, Jr. (1976–1984, and 1992–2001) to serve in the North Carolina House as the representative for Forsyth County.

Although Kennedy missed the 1981–1982 session, in the latter year she became the first African American woman to be elected to the House. Alfreda Johnson Webb (1923–) was the first African American woman appointed to the House in 1971, but she lost her seat in an election shortly afterward without even serving. Kennedy continued to serve in the General Assembly until 1994. During her time in office she served on several committees on subjects such as the judiciary, ethics, and labor. She was only one of nine females in the United States to serve on a judiciary committee in a state legislature at the time.

In 1987 Kennedy was the first woman to be elected president of the Forsyth County Bar Association and in 1996 was the first African American attorney to be inducted into the North Carolina Bar Association's General Practice Section Hall of Fame. In 2002 Kennedy was inducted into the Hall of Fame of the North Carolina Association of Black Lawyers. Two years later Dominion, one of the largest energy companies in the nation, listed Kennedy as one of nine prominent African Americans in their 14th "Strong Men and Women: Excellence in Leadership" ceremony.

KEY DATES

1924   Born in Atlanta, Georgia, on October 13.

1945   Graduates with a bachelor's degree from Spelman College, Atlanta.

1952   Is first licensed to practice law.

1955   Founds a legal practice with her husband in Winston-Salem, North Carolina.

1979   Appointed to serve in the North Carolina House of Representatives.

1982   Elected to serve in the North Carolina House of Representatives.

Further reading: www.dom.com/about/education/strong/2004/kennedy.jsp (Short biography).

KEYES, Alan L.
Politician, Diplomat, Broadcaster

Former diplomat and the first black Republican presidential candidate of the 20th century, Alan Lee Keyes is one of the United States's most influential conservative leaders. He is also a forceful, outspoken, and charismatic speaker for the Christian Right.

Early life
Born on Long Island, New York, on August 7, 1950, Keyes was the son of an army sergeant and a teacher. As a result of his father's tours of duty, Keyes lived in many places throughout the United States as a child and also spent time overseas in Italy. He was brought up to be a devout Catholic. He enrolled at Cornell University, New York, but his bitter criticism of local protests in favor of civil rights and in opposition to the Vietnam War (1964–1973) led to death threats and he was forced to leave. He transferred to Harvard University, Massachusetts, and graduated with a BA (1972) and then a PhD in government studies (1979).

In 1978 Keyes began working for the State Department as a foreign service officer. His skill at debate brought him to the attention of former United Nations ambassador Jeane Kirkpatrick (1926–), who said that Keyes was "one of the most dramatically articulate people I've ever known in my life." Keyes's work took him to India and Zimbabwe before he received an appointment as ambassador to the UN Economic and Social Council in 1983 and as assistant secretary of state for international organization affairs under President Ronald Reagan (1981–1989) two years later. In 1987 he resigned from the State Department.

Staunch conservative
The late 1980s saw Keyes increasingly active in politics. His conservative views and fiery rhetoric led to his securing the Republican nomination for the U.S. Senate

▲ **Alan L. Keyes believes that the country's most pressing problems, such as crime, can be traced to lack of respect for moral principle.**

in Maryland in 1988 and 1992. He was defeated on both occasions, but went on to become a Republican presidential candidate in 1996 and then again in 2000.

The author of two books, *Masters of the Dream: The Strength and Betrayal of Black America* (1995) and *Our Character, Our Future: Reclaiming America's Moral Destiny* (1996), Keyes is also known for his radio talk show, "America's Wake-Up Call: The Alan Keyes Show," which aired on WCBM in Baltimore from 1994 to 1999, and a television commentary show, *Alan Keyes is Making Sense*, broadcast in 2002 on MSNBC.

In 2004 Keyes failed in his third Senatorial bid, standing for the Republican Party of Illinois. He made the headlines early in 2005 owing to a family rift following his daughter Maya's public announcement that she was gay.

Further reading: Keyes, Alan L. *Our Character, Our Future: Reclaiming America's Moral Destiny.* New York, NY: Zondervan, 1996.
http://www.renewamerica.us/keyes/ (Keyes's site).

KEY DATES

1950 Born on Long Island, New York, on August 7.

1972 Receives BA from Harvard University; receives doctorate seven years later.

1978 Serves in the State Department until 1987.

1996 Becomes first black Republican presidential candidate of the 20th century.

KEYS, Alicia
Songwriter, Musician, Producer

Award-winning musician Alicia Keys is a critically acclaimed songwriter, pianist, singer, and producer. Her distinctive sound has made her popular with international audiences.

Early promise
Born in New York on January 25, 1981, Keyes was raised from age two by her mother in the notorious Hell's Kitchen neighborhood of the city. It was evident early on that Keys was a musical prodigy. At age four she performed on stage in *The Wizard of Oz*; a year later she was studying music. At age seven, Keys began to play the piano, playing and learning classical music by composers such as Beethoven, and Chopin.

Aged 12 Keys enrolled in the Professional Performance Arts School, a public high school in Manhattan, to study voice, dance, and classical and jazz piano. She chose to major in choir, which gave her the opportunity to develop her vocal range. She wrote her first song, "Butterflyz," which featured on her debut album, at age 14.

Keys graduated as valedictorian from the Professional Performing Arts School at age 16. "I was so deeply involved in music, I had already outgrown all the pressure of high school cliques and gossip," she later said.

Making an impression
After briefly attending Columbia University on a scholarship, Keys left to devote herself to a full-time musical career. In 1998 she came to the attention of a number of record labels, and several of the majors attempted to outbid each other to sign her. Clive Davis, president of Artista Records, signed Keys, becoming her mentor. When Davis left the company to form his own record label J Records in 1999, Keys went with him. She continued the process of writing, producing, and recording

▲ *Alicia Keys toured extensively in 2004, first in the United States and then worldwide.*

the debut she had begun working on at age 14. In 2001 the 19-year-old released her first album, *Songs In A Minor*. The title was a reference to both her classical aspirations and to the fact that she wrote most of the songs while still very young. The album, which was a mix of rhythm and blues (R&B), hip-hop, classical, and jazz, sold more than 50,000 copies on the day of its release, and debuted at No. 1 in the *Billboard* Album Chart. The album went multi-platinum and earned Keys five Grammys at the 2002 awards, including Song of the Year for "Fallin'," Best R&B Album, and Best New Artist.

In December 2003 Keys released her second album, *The Diary of Alicia Keys*, which immediately went to No. 1 in the *Billboard* chart. In 2005 she won Grammys for Best R&B Album and Best Female R&B Vocal Performance and was voted the second most powerful artist in the pop industry in the *Los Angeles Times*.

KEY DATES	
1981	Born in New York City, on January 25.
1997	Graduates as valedictorian from the Professional Performing Arts School at age 16.
2001	Releases her first album, *Songs In A Minor*.
2002	Wins five Grammys for her debut album.

Further reading: Bankston, John. *Alicia Keys.* New York, NY: Mitchell Lane Publishers, 2002.
http://www.aliciakeys.net/ (Official site).

KINCAID, Jamaica
Writer

Known for her autobiographical novels and regular nonfiction contributions to the *New Yorker*, Jamaica Kincaid has managed to rise above an impoverished background, an interrupted education, and family indifference to become a celebrated writer and feminist.

Early life

Born as Elaine Potter Richardson on May 25, 1949, in Antigua, then part of the British West Indies, she was raised by her mother and her political activist stepfather, who was also a carpenter. The relationship that Kincaid had with her mother forms a central theme in many of her books. Although initially a close bond, this changed following the birth of Kincaid's three brothers: The young girl began to feel neglected, emotionally, materially, and in terms of her education. An intelligent child who learned to read at age three, Kincaid was taken out of school after the arrival of her third brother as her family could no longer afford school fees. Her mother sent her to work as an au pair in New York when she was 16, but Kincaid refused to send money home. Depressed, lonely, and resentful, she exiled herself from her family as well as from the island on which she grew up.

Writing career

After several uninspiring jobs, Kincaid completed her high school education and won a scholarship to study photography in New Hampshire, but she returned to New York after just two years. She began writing, initially a series of articles for *Ingenue* magazine under the name Jamaica Kincaid for fear that her family would disapprove of her new career. She became friends with *New Yorker* columnist George W. S. Trow, who began to feature Kincaid's writing in the magazine's "Talk of the Town"

▲ *Jamaica Kincaid's books often explore themes central to her childhood in Antigua.*

section. In 1976 Kincaid became a staff writer for the magazine, a job she remained in for nearly 20 years.

In 1983 Kincaid published her first book, a collection of short stories called *At the Bottom of the River*. Subsequent novels were characterized by simple, lyrical prose, and evocative, often angry, and heavily autobiographical descriptions of the lives and relationships of women born into tropical poverty. Kincaid returned to Antigua in 1985, a visit that inspired the nonfiction *A Small Place* (1988). Another nonfiction piece, *My Brother* (1997), is an account of her brother's death from AIDS.

The winner of several writing awards, Kincaid is married to composer Allen Shawn, son of famed *New Yorker* editor, William Shawn. They live in Vermont, where she teaches and continues to write.

Further reading: John, Annie. *Jamaica Kincaid.* New York, NY: New American Library, 1984.
http://www.missourireview.org/index.php?genre=Interviews&title=An+Interview+with+Jamaica+Kincaid (Interview with Kincaid by journalist Kay Bonetti).

KEY DATES	
1949	Born in St. John's, Antigua, on May 25.
1965	Travels to New York to work as an au pair.
1973	Changes name to Jamaica Kincaid.
1976	Becomes staff writer at the *New Yorker* magazine.
1983	Publishes first book, *At the Bottom of the River.*

KING, B. B.
Singer, Musician

Often called the "King of the Blues," legendary musician B. B King has recorded more than 50 albums and received numerous awards, including 13 Grammys in a long and illustrious career. King remained a true blues artist, making soulful haunting music with Lucille, his trademark Gibson guitar.

Early life
Born near Itta Bena, Mississippi, on September 16, 1925, Riley B. King, was the son of Albert King and Noral Ella Pully. At age five, he went to live with his mother in Kilmichael, after his parents separated in 1930. His uncle, Archie Fair, who preached in the Church of God in Christ, first taught King to play the guitar. His early musical influences, the spirituals he heard in church and the musicians whom he heard played at his Aunt Mimi's house, such as Blind Lemon Jefferson, remained a lifelong

▼ *B. B. King calls his Gibsons "Lucille," prompted by a club brawl in which two customers fought over a woman of that name; the fight almost cost King his guitar when the club went up in flames.*

inspiration. When King was 10 his mother died and he lived alone until the plantation owner for whom he worked loaned him the money to buy a guitar.

Music is my family
King moved to Indianola, where he went to school, playing with the Famous St. John Gospel Singers and working in local fields. When King heard the striking blues guitar of T. Bone Walker, however, he dropped out of school and began to study the techniques of local blues musicians, including Bessie Smith and Ma Rainey.

After serving in the Army in World War II (1939–1945), King concentrated on playing the blues. He received his big break in 1948, singing with Sonny Boy Williamson on KWEM radio. He was later given his own radio show, "Sepia Swing Club," on WDIA. As B. B. King, the name he adopted as a DJ, he recorded "Take a Swing with Me" for WDIA in 1949. Two years later he released "Three O'Clock Blues," which topped *Billboard's* R&B chart for three months. King's success grew through sheer hard work as well as a huge amount of talent. He played around 3,000 concerts a year and had a string of moderate hits. In 1966 he was nominated for the first of 13 Grammys with "The Thrill is Gone." King's stirring music also appealed to white audiences and he once expressed disappointment that "my people don't appreciate me like whites."

KEY DATES	
1925	Born near Itta Bena, Mississippi, on September 16.
1948	Sings with Sonny Boy Williamson on KWEM radio.
1949	Records first record, "Take a Swing with Me."
1966	Wins first Grammy for "The Thrill is Gone."
1984	Inducted into Blues Foundation Hall of Fame.
1987	Inducted into Rock and Roll Hall of Fame.

See also: Rainey, Ma; Smith, Bessie; Williamson, John Lee

Further reading: King, B. B., and David Ritz. *Blues All around Me: The Autobiography of B. B. King.* New York, NY:Harper Paperbacks, 1999.
http://www.bbking.com/ (Official site).

KING, Coretta Scott
Civil Rights Leader

Influential humanitarian leader Coretta Scott King devoted her life to securing universal peace and social justice through nonviolent means, and to honoring the memory of her late husband, Martin Luther King, Jr.

Early life

Born in Heiberger, near Marion, Alabama, on April 27, 1927, Coretta Scott was the daughter of Bernice McMurray and Obadiah Scott. Her father was relatively well off: He owned his own farm and sawmill, which was destroyed by a fire that the Scotts put down to racism.

Obadiah and Bernice emphasized the importance of education to their children Coretta, Edythe, and Obie, who all went to college. Coretta graduated valedictorian of Lincoln High School in 1943, winning a scholarship to Antioch College in Yellow Springs, Ohio, where she earned a BA in music and education. She joined the local branch

▼ *Coretta Scott King, pictured here in front of a portrait of Martin Luther King, Jr., fought hard to get a national holiday dedicated to the civil rights leader.*

of the National Association for the Advancement of Colored People and Antioch College's Race Relations Committee, and performed with actor and activist Paul Robeson.

Martin Luther King, Jr.

In 1951 Scott won a scholarship to the New England Conservatory of Music, Boston. While studying for a degree in voice and violin she met Martin Luther King, Jr. The couple married in June 1953 and moved to Montgomery, Alabama in September 1954, where King served as pastor of the Dexter Avenue Baptist Church.

Balancing her responsibilities as a mother of four children with her activism, Coretta King took part in the Montgomery bus boycott of 1955, delivered speeches, organized and performed in fundraising Freedom Concerts, and accompanied her husband on his campaigns.

After her husband's assassination in 1968, King continued to campaign against poverty and social injustice and founded the Martin Luther King, Jr., Center for Nonviolent Social Change. Twice named "Woman of the Year," King led international goodwill missions and spoke at numerous peace and justice assemblies. She suffered from declining health in the early years of the 21st century. She suffered a heart attack and stroke in 2005, and died in a clinic in Mexico in January 2006.

KEY DATES	
1927	Born near Marion, Alabama, on April 27.
1951	Enrolls at the New England Conservatory of Music, Boston, Massachusetts.
1953	Marries Martin Luther King, Jr., in June.
1968	Martin Luther King is assassinated on April 4.
1981	Founds the Martin Luther King, Jr., Center for NonViolent Social Change.
2006	Dies in Mexico on January 30.

See also: Civil Rights; King, Martin Luther, Jr.; Robeson, Paul

Further reading: Shelf Medearis, Angela. *Dare to Dream: Coretta Scott King and the Civil Rights Movement.* New York, NY: Puffin, 1999.
http://www.thekingcenter.org/csk/bio.html (Biography).

KING, Dexter
Activist

Dexter King is the youngest son of the revered civil rights leader Martin Luther King, Jr., and Coretta Scott King. In 2005 he was acting chief operating officer of the Martin Luther King, Jr., Center for Nonviolent Social Change in Atlanta. King was also chief executive officer (CEO) of Intellectual Properties Management (IPM), which licenses Martin Luther King, Jr.'s images and words.

Early life
Born in Atlanta, Georgia, on January 30, 1961, Dexter Scott King and his siblings were aware from an early age that their parents were involved in something important. King also said that they knew that "danger was always lurking." Their fears were realized when Martin Luther King, Jr., was assassinated on April 4, 1968. The murder was traumatizing for the King family, and the young Dexter grew up under pressure to follow in his father's footsteps.

On graduating from Atlanta's Frederick Douglass High, King turned down a scholarship from the University of Southern California and enrolled instead at Morehouse College, where his father had received his BA. He dropped out of college to pursue an interest in music video.

Becoming involved
In 1986, when the first Martin Luther King, Jr., national holiday was observed, Dexter King collaborated with Philip Jones to produce his first video commemorating the occasion. It was followed by a music album dedicated to King's father, featuring several leading musicians including Whitney Houston, Prince, and Run-DMC.

In 1989 King became president of the Martin Luther King, Jr., Center for Nonviolent Social Change in Atlanta; Coretta Scott King was the CEO. King resigned after four

▲ Dexter King at a press conference in Atlanta in 1999 after a civil trial convicted Lloyd Jowers of hiring a hit man to kill Martin Luther King, Jr.

months, but when his mother retired on October 21, 1994, the board of directors voted him in as CEO.

King held the position from January 1995 until 2004, when his brother Martin Luther King, III, became president and CEO. During his time there King helped resolve the dispute between his family and the National Park Service: The Kings wanted the center to be a museum, with exhibitions and programs for children, but the Park Service wanted it to be a visitor's center. King got the Service to agree to the family's wishes. In 1997 King met James Earl Ray, the man convicted of murdering his father. Convinced that Ray was not guilty King worked hard for his release, but in 1998 Ray died of liver disease in prison. King continues to speak on civil rights issues and to promote nonviolent action.

See also: Houston, Whitney; King, Coretta Scott; King, Martin Luther, Jr.; Prince

Further reading: King, Dexter Scott. *Growing Up King: An Intimate Memoir*. New York, NY: Warner, 2003.
http://slate.msn.com/id/1816/ (Article on King).

KEY DATES

1961	Born in Atlanta, Georgia, on January 30.
1979	Enrolls at Morehouse College.
1989	Becomes president of the Martin Luther King, Jr., Center for Nonviolent Social Change.
1995	Appointed CEO of the center.
1997	Meets with James Earl Ray, the man convicted of Martin Luther King, Jr.'s murder in 1968.

KING, Don
Boxing Promoter

Don King is a boxing promoter whose extravagantly frizzed hair and flamboyant, publicity-seeking manner have made him one of the most recognizable personalities in sports. He is extremely successful and is reputed to be worth more than $100 million, but King has also made many enemies and has been accused by former clients of behaving less than honorably. For some commentators, however, King, who was formerly in prison for manslaughter, is an example of the American Dream come true. He has been named the "Greatest Promoter in History" by the WBC, WBA, and IBA, boxing's three major sanctioning bodies.

Early life
King was born in Cleveland, Ohio, on August 20, 1931. His father Clarence was killed in a steel plant explosion when King was 10. King's mother, Hattie, used the insurance payout to move her six children from the Cleveland ghetto in which they had been living to a middle-class neighborhood of the city. Hattie King made a living baking pies and selling roasted peanuts.

King spent a year at Case Western Reserve University, but he dropped out after becoming involved in gambling. Before long King was running a numbers racket himself.

Changing lanes
In 1954 King was tried for the murder of a man who had been shot while attempting to rob one of King's gambling houses, but the court returned a verdict of justifiable homicide and the defendant walked free. In 1967, however, his luck changed when he was convicted of the second-degree murder of a gambling associate who owed him $600. Although the charge was later reduced to manslaughter, King served 3 years and 11 months in Ohio's Marion Correctional Institution.

On his release from jail in September 1971 King moved into fight promotion. He was soon associating with some of the biggest names in heavyweight boxing. In 1972 he persuaded Muhammad Ali to appear in an exhibition bout to raise funds for a hospital that was threatened with closure: The event grossed $80,000. In 1974 he set up Don King Productions. One of his first undertakings was the so-called "Rumble in the Jungle," the historic fight in Kinshasa, Zaire, in which Ali recaptured his world crown from George Foreman. King saw off stiff competition from other promoters by guaranteeing the fighters $5 million each. The success of the event spawned a year later the so-called "Thriller in Manila," the third fight between Ali and Frazier, which King staged in the Philippines for tax reasons. With profits from the sale of tickets, broadcasting rights, and merchandise for these events King became the world's leading fight promoter: Every aspiring boxer, particularly African Americans, wanted to be part of the King stable.

King was naturally reluctant to remind the public about his shady past, and in the late 1970s it was mostly overlooked or at least dismissed as the easily pardonable indiscretions of a young man who had seen the error of his ways and cleaned up his act. King could not avoid conflict, however. When Ali claimed to have been paid $1.2 million less than King had promised him for his

▼ **Don King's flamboyant personality has made him a popular guest on shows such as the Howard Stern Radio Show.**

INFLUENCES AND INSPIRATION

Don King was the biggest fight promoter of the last quarter of the 20th century. As an African American he appealed particularly to black boxers, who figured that he would represent their interests better and be more sympathetic than white impresarios.

Yet although King is widely credited with making almost 100 fighters into millionaires, including Muhammad Ali, not all of them have thanked him for his work on their behalf. Several accused him of swindling them: Mike Tyson, himself a controversial figure, went from calling King "a surrogate father" to denouncing him for doing "more bad to black fighters than any white promoter ever in the history of boxing." Tyson also sued King for $100 million.

Allegations of tax evasion and fight fixing and other misdeeds remain unsubstantiated, however, and many people view King as changing the face of international boxing. King has been honored with awards for his achievements. He was inducted into the International Boxing Hall of Fame in 1997. The *New York Times* also listed him among the top 100 African Americans who helped shape the United States's history during the 20th century.

1980 comeback fight against Larry Holmes, the former champion ended up suing King. They eventually settled out of court for $50,000.

The American dream

The King bandwagon gathered even greater momentum in the 1980s. In 1981 King became the first promoter in history to guarantee a boxer $10 million: The lucky recipient was Sugar Ray Leonard for the "Brawl in Montreal," his first light-heavyweight world title fight against Roberto Duran of Panama.

Four years later King was back in the news for different reasons: He was charged with tax evasion. Although King was subsequently cleared, his secretary was sent to prison for four months. The trouble was not over for King, however: Larry Holmes and several other leading boxers claimed to have been swindled by the promoter. One of

them, Tim Witherspoon, took action and, although again the case was settled privately, the former world heavyweight champion is thought to have been paid more than $1 million. The bad publicity did nothing to reduce King's pull as a promoter: In 1993 he staged a fight in Mexico City between his client Julio Cesar Chavez and Greg Haugen. The fight drew an audience of 132,000. In 1994 King promoted 47 world championship bouts, a record number in a single year.

King's reputation could not stand up to endless allegations of wrongdoing. In 1995 the promoter was widely condemned for overhyping a fight between former No. 1 star Mike Tyson, who had just finished a jail sentence for rape, and Peter McNeeley, a relatively unknown boxer. King's detractors claimed that the promoter distorted the ratings to make McNeeley look like a Top 10 boxer. He clearly was not, as shown when Tyson knocked him out in the second minute of the first round. Undeterred, King then put on two hugely successful fights between Tyson and Evander Holyfield: The 1996 confrontation was watched by a pay-per-view television audience of 1.6 million. A year later the rematch, in which Tyson was disqualified for biting off part of his opponent's ear, earned gate receipts of $14.3 million. King continued to promote boxing events into the 21st century. In 2002 the World Boxing Association named him Promoter of the Decade.

See also: Ali, Muhammad; Foreman, George; Holyfield, Evander; Leonard, Sugar Ray; Tyson, Mike

Further reading: Newfield, Jack. *Only in America: The Life and Crimes of Don King.* New York, NY: William Morrow, 1995. http://www.donking.com/ (Official site).

KEY DATES

1931	Born in Cleveland, Ohio, on August 20.
1954	Kills man who tried to rob him.
1967	Jailed for four years for manslaughter.
1974	Sets up Don King Productions; organizes Muhammad Ali–George Foreman "Rumble in the Jungle" fight.
1975	Organizes the "Thriller in Manila," a Muhammad Ali–Joe Frazier rematch.
1985	Is charged with tax evasion, but acquitted.
2001	Inducted into World Boxing Hall of Fame.

KING, Martin Luther, Jr.
Civil Rights Activist, Religious Leader

Martin Luther King, Jr., was one of the most famous civil rights leaders of the 20th century. Not only did he highlight the inequalities suffered by African Americans in the United States, but he inspired millions of black Americans to rise up and protest the discrimination and indignities that they suffered on a daily basis. A brilliant public speaker, King emphasized the importance of nonviolent protest to achieve social change. His speeches and ideas are studied in courses in schools and universities around the world.

The road to the ministry
Born Michael Luther King, Jr., in Atlanta, Georgia, on January 15, 1929, he was the first son and the middle child of the Reverend Michael Luther King and Alberta Williams King, a teacher and daughter of the founder of Ebenezer Baptist, the church of which both King, Sr. and Jr. were pastors. Both Michael, Sr., and Michael, Jr., changed their names to Martin in honor of the German Lutheran leader Martin Luther (1483–1546).

King's father and grandfather were leaders of the local chapter of the National Association for the Advancement of Colored People (NAACP), and King was aware of the civil rights struggle from an early age. He also suffered the indignities of racism when he was growing up: A prize-

▼ **Martin Luther King made his famous speech "I Have a Dream" on August 28, 1963.**

KEY DATES	
1929	Born in Atlanta, Georgia, on January 15.
1948	Earns a BA from Morehouse College at age 19.
1953	Marries Coretta Scott; a year later moves to Montgomery, Alabama, to become pastor of Dexter Street Baptist Church.
1955	Mounts the year-long Montgomery bus boycott.
1957	Becomes head of the Southern Christian Leadership Conference (SCLC).
1963	Organizes the March on Washington on August 28.
1964	Awarded the Nobel Prize for Peace in Oslo, Norway.
1968	Assassinated on the balcony of the Lorraine Hotel, Memphis, Tennessee, on April 4.

winning high school orator, King was angered when he and other members of the debating team were forced to give up their bus seats to white passengers.

A talented student, King performed so well in his college entrance examinations that he was able to enter Morehouse College at age 15. Impressed with the philosophy of theology professor George Kelsey, and following the example set by President Benjamin Mays, King chose to enter the ministry. He graduated in 1948 after majoring in sociology, and completed his undergraduate divinity studies at Crozer Theological Center. After doing postgraduate work at Harvard and Boston universities, King received a PhD in systematic theology in 1955. During this time he was also ordained and named assistant pastor at Ebenezer Baptist Church. In 1953 he married Coretta Scott; in 1954 he became pastor of Dexter Avenue Baptist Church in Montgomery, Alabama.

Nonviolent protest
In December 1955 Rosa Parks, who had worked as secretary of the NAACP in Montgomery, refused to give up her bus seat to a white male passenger. She was arrested and charged with violating segregation laws. Montgomery NAACP president E. D. Nixon contacted King and suggested a bus boycott. King became president of the Montgomery Improvement Association (MIA), the organization that planned the protest that led African Americans to stop

INFLUENCES AND INSPIRATION

The life of Martin Luther King, Jr., is an example of how influences help shape and prepare individuals for their future contribution to society. As the son and grandson of Baptist ministers Michael King and Adam Daniel Williams, King felt the powerful attraction of a career in the ministry. Even as a young child, he was impressed with what persuasive oratory could achieve. Both King's father and grandfather were leaders of the local chapters of the NAACP, which gave the young King early exposure to civil rights issues.

It was not until his junior year in college that King, impressed by the intellect and engagement of Morehouse president and Baptist minister, Benjamin Mays, made the decision to go into the ministry. As a young divinity student, King struggled with the philosophies of social gospelist Walter Rauschenbasch, and the socialism of Karl Marx and Rhienhold Niebuhr, who all approached the resolution of social problems from different perspectives. He was also exposed to the nonviolent resistance of the Indian civil rights leader

Mohandas K. Gandhi (1869–1948) when he attended a lecture given at the University of Pennsylvania by Mordecai Johnson, president of Howard University. Gandhi's philosophy of Satyagraha, or unwavering search for truth through nonviolent means, provided King with the basis for the civil disobedience strategies used in the civil rights movement. King was also inspired by Ghana's president Kwame Nkrumah (1909–1972). He admired Nkrumah's statement, "I prefer self-government with danger to servitude with tranquility."

using public buses for 382 days. They patronized black-owned taxis, used car pools, or walked to their destinations instead. The protest proved that nonviolence could work as a formal strategy of civil disobedience. It also helped King become known as a leading and brilliant civil rights activist.

In November 1956 the U.S. Supreme Court affirmed that Alabama's bus segregation laws were unconstitutional and a federal order mandating integration of the buses reached Montgomery in December. African Americans returned to use the buses, but many white Americans were not pleased with the outcome: Churches, homes, and bus passengers were attacked. In spite of the violence, protests against inequality continued. In 1957 President Eisenhower signed the first civil rights legislation in 75 years and sent federal troops to Little Rock, Arkansas, to enforce school desegregation. In that same year King became the founding president of the Southern Christian Leadership Leadership Conference (SCLC), an organization that coordinated civil rights action in the South. King eventually moved the center of operations to Atlanta in 1960. He also became copastor with his father of the Ebenezer Baptist Church, a position he retained until his death.

As his reputation grew, King was recognized by the international community as a leading orator and civil rights activist, but he also came under increasing personal threat. In September 1958 a mentally-ill woman stabbed King in the chest during a book signing in Harlem, New York City. Undeterred, he returned to actively promote civil

rights following his recovery. In 1959 he visited India with his family, where he learned more about the work of Mahatma Gandhi, whom he admired greatly (*see box*). At home King and the SCLC assisted in or mounted peaceful protest actions in Albany, Georgia, Birmingham and Selma, Alabama, and throughout the state of Mississippi.

Arrested and jailed on numerous occasions, King narrowly escaped serious injury several times. In May 1963 he wrote "Letter from a Birmingham Jail" from a prison cell in Alabama, arguing that it was right for human beings to protest unjust laws. In August he delivered the much celebrated "I Have a Dream" speech to 250,000 protesters from the steps of the Lincoln Memorial; it was the closing address of the March on Washington. The speech shows King's oratorical skills at their very best. King and the SCLC also worked to promote voter registration among African Americans in the South. He planned the Poor People's Campaign for economic justice throughout 1966 and 1967. As his successes grew, friends and family became increasingly worried about King's personal safety. Their fears were proved right when King was shot dead on April 4, 1968, in Memphis, Tennessee.

See also: Civil Rights; King, Coretta Scott; Mays, Benjamin E.; Nixon, E. D.; Parks, Rosa

Further reading: Carson, Clayton (ed.). *The Autobiography of Martin Luther King, Jr.* New York, NY: Warner Books, 1998. http://www.kingian.net/king_flash.htm (Interactive site).

KINGSLEY, Anna
Plantation Owner

The Senegalese-born Anna Kingsley is one of the most remarkable figures in the 19th-century history of Florida. A freed slave and the common-law wife of a wealthy white plantation owner, she became a land and slave-owner in her own right. Her story, set during one of the most tumultuous periods of Florida's history, conveys the full complexity of the interracial relations of the times. What scholars know of Kingsley's life is largely derived from legal documents such as wills and property deeds. Kingsley left no personal papers, such as diaries or letters, and there is no known surviving portrait or photograph of her. Nevertheless, a picture emerges of a strong, proud, and resourceful woman who managed to flourish in an increasingly racist society.

The Wolof princess
Anna Kingsley was born Anta Majigeen Ndaiye, probably in 1793. She was a high-status member—a "princess"—of the Wolof, a Muslim people living in the area that is now Senegal and Gambia in West Africa.

During the late 18th century the Wolof themselves became victims of African slave raiders. In 1805 raiders burned down Anta's village, murdered her father, and took her into slavery. The 12-year-old Kingsley was taken to the island of Gorée, a major slave trading post in Senegal, and sold to European slave traders. With some 120 other African captives, Kingsley undertook the perilous Atlantic crossing—the "Middle Passage"—packed into the hot, cramped hold of a Danish ship. In 1806 the ship landed in Cuba and Kingsley was taken to a slave market in Havana, where she was sold to the plantation owner and trader Zephaniah Kingsley.

KEY DATES

1793	Born in Senegal at about this time.
1806	Sold as a slave to Zachariah Kingsley of Florida and becomes his common-law wife.
1811	Is given her freedom and later sets up her own plantation.
1824	The Kingsleys settle on Fort George Island.
1821	Florida becomes part of U.S. territory.
1838	Settles in Haiti.
1870	Dies near Jacksonville, Florida, in July.

Zephaniah Kingsley took Anna back to his plantation, called Laurel Grove, in East Florida, close to St. Augustine. There she became his common-law wife and took the name Anna Kingsley. Eventually the couple would have four children—George (born 1807), Martha (born 1809), Mary (born 1811), and John Maxwell (born 1824). Zephaniah Kingsley had other black mistresses, too, but it seems that Anna quickly established herself as the chief "wife," holding much the same status that she might have done in the polygamous households of the Wolof.

A mixed-race household
At the time Florida was a Spanish colony, its inhabitants included Spanish and U.S. American settlers, Native Americans, and enslaved and freed blacks. In general, while the Spanish rulers accepted the institution of slavery as necessary to the running of the profitable plantation system, they promoted a greater degree of racial assimilation than was usually found in the southern United States. Interracial common-law marriages, like that between Anna and Zephaniah Kingsley, were common. The manumission (or legal freeing) of long-serving slaves was encouraged, as was the practice of self-purchase in which slaves bought their own freedom.

In 1811 Zephaniah Kingsley granted the 18-year-old Anna and her children their freedom. "Ma'am Anna," as she was known, had already taken over much of the management of her husband's estate, especially during his long absences on business. In 1813, however, Kingsley decided to set up her own plantation, just across the St. John River from Laurel Grove, and also bought 12 of her own slaves.

Fort George Island
Only a few months after Kingsley set up her estate, Spanish Florida came under attack from U.S. soldiers and armed civilians from the neighboring states. Plantations were looted and burned, and their inhabitants wounded or even killed. During one such raid Zephaniah Kingsley was kidnapped and held to ransom, and Laurel Grove was destroyed. Rather than allow her own estate to fall into the hands of the raiders, Kingsley set it alight. As soon as Zephaniah was freed, he, Kingsley, and their household of slaves and freedmen left for the safety of Fort George Island, at the mouth of the St. John River.

INFLUENCES AND INSPIRATION

Some historians argue that as a former slave who herself became a slave owner, Anna Kingsley most probably had complex attitudes toward slavery.

Brought up in a slave-owning society, Kingsley then became a victim of the slave trade. As a plantation owner she enjoyed the prosperity bought to her by the slave system, but became increasingly aware that Florida's draconian slave laws threatened her own family. This contradictory attitude toward slavery mirrored that of her husband, whose own standpoint was affected by his marriage to a black woman and his parenting of mixed-race children. Although Zephaniah Kingsley, Jr. (1765–1843) did not enter the slave trade until 1802, he quickly prospered by it, coming to own eight ships as well as his 200-acre (81-ha) estate on the St. John River. He treated his slaves well, allowing them a day and a half every week to tend to their own crops and giving many their freedom. By adopting this attitude toward his slaves, he believed that he could assure his plantation's peace and prosperity.

This complacency was challenged after 1821, however, when the new American rulers of Florida began to press through discriminatory laws that threatened the freedom of the territory's free blacks, including that of his own family. During the 1820s Kingsley became politically active as he attempted to protect the status of Florida's blacks. In 1829 he published *A Treatise on the Patriarchal System of Society*, in which he proposed a social system that discriminated not between black and white but between those who were free and those who were not. A class of free blacks, he argued, would help maintain a racially harmonious society, while slavery would continue to insure its prosperity. By the 1830s, however, Kingsley must have realized that no real compromise was possible between a society that exploited slaves and one that promoted racial equality, and he prepared to resettle his family in the free republic of Haiti.

There they set up a new plantation and home—much of which still survives. The arrangement of the main buildings reflects the finely balanced social position that Kingsley held. On one side is the main house, in which Zephaniah lived, and on the other side, connected by a brick walkway, is a second, smaller house, which included the kitchens as well as Anna's own apartment. It is an arrangement that suggests not only the independent spirit of the Wolof "princess," but also her slightly inferior status as the black wife of a white husband.

Whatever the ambiguities of Kingsley's social position, both of her daughters were able to marry into wealthy local white families. In 1821 Spain ceded Florida to the United States, and the status of the region's many freed blacks was put in jeopardy. Many resisted the changes by fighting alongside the Seminoles, who were fighting white settlers and the American government.

In 1823 Zephaniah Kingsley was appointed a member of Florida's legislative assembly, but despite his efforts to maintain the status quo, new laws came into force that discriminated against the state's black population, whether freed or slave. By 1837 conditions had became so oppressive that Kingsley, along with her sons George and John, left Florida for Haiti, which in 1804 had become the first free black republic in the Americas.

Haitian haven

Once again Kingsley set up a new family plantation—Mayorasgo De Koka—on Haiti's northern coast. Both she and Zephaniah Kingsley, who spent long periods there, enjoyed their new home.

In compliance with Haitian law, the Kingsleys freed their slaves, and they planned to set up a school for the estate workers' children. Kingsley was at long last able to enjoy the freedom and equality that had been denied her on the mainland.

Her husband did not have long to enjoy his new life, however: He died in 1843, leaving Kingsley and their children moderately wealthy. In 1860 Kingsley moved back to the St. John River area to be close to her two daughters. The following year the Civil War (1861–1865) broke out, and Florida joined the side of the Confederacy. Kingsley's sons-in-law supported the Union, and she had to seek refuge in Philadelphia and New York City. After the war Kingsley settled back in Florida, where she died in 1870.

Further reading: Schafer, Daniel L.: *Anna Kingsley.* St. Augustine, FL: St. Augustine Historical Society, 1994. www.oah.org/pubs/magazine/women/tilford.htm ("*Anna Kingsley: A Free Woman.*" Article by Kathy Tilford from *Organization of American Historians* magazine).

KITT, Eartha
Singer, Actor

Eartha Kitt was one of the most glamorous entertainers of the 20th century. The actor and director Orson Welles once called Kitt "the most exciting girl in the world." Kitt's trademark was her distinctive throaty, feline voice.

Early life
Born in North, South Carolina, on January 17, 1927, Kitt and her half-sister were abandoned first by their white father and then by their part-black, part-Cherokee mother at a young age. Sent to Harlem, New York, to live with an aunt, Kitt enjoyed greater prospects. She learned to sing and play the piano, showing great talent. After winning a place at the Metropolitan High School (now the High School for the Performing Arts), Kitt was forced to leave school, aged 14, after her aunt threw her out.

Kitt took on a variety of jobs in order to survive. Her first break came at 16, when she auditioned for Katherine Dunham's dance school and won a scholarship. The experience opened up the chance to tour in Europe, where her provocative dance style and singing were enjoyed by American troops during World War II (1939–1945).

After the war ended, Kitt stayed in Paris, France, singing in nightclubs. She came to the attention of actor and director Orson Welles, who in 1950 cast her as Helen of Troy in his *Time Runs*. It was a success, and Kitt returned to the United States, where she sang in New York clubs. She so impressed producer Leonard Stillman that in 1952 he revived his musical revue *New Faces* especially for her. Two years later she appeared in the film version.

Career takes off
In the early 1950s RCA Victor signed Kitt to the label: *RCA Victor Presents Eartha Kitt* was released to critical acclaim in 1953, reaching the Top 5 on the album charts. Kitt had a

▲ **Eartha Kitt was the focus of both FBI and CIA investigations in the late 1960s.**

Top 10 hit with "C'est Si Bon (It's So Good)," which became her signature song, and another massive hit at the end of 1953 with "Santa Baby." Kitt carried on singing in nightclubs. Her wit, overt sexiness, and playfulness, combined with a great talent, made her popular with audiences and critics alike. A Tony nomination for the Broadway drama *Mrs. Patterson* confirmed her success.

Kitt appeared in many movies, including *The Accused* (1958), starring Sidney Poitier, and in the title role of *Anna Lucasta*, with Sammy Davis, Jr., and Nat King Cole, for which she received an Oscar nomination. In the 1960s Kitt appeared in TV shows such as *I Spy*, but for many fans her best performance during this time was as the villain Catwoman in the *Batman* TV series.

Kitt's career suffered when she criticized the Vietnam War (1964–1973) and its effect on minorities at a celebrity women's lunch hosted by President Lyndon Johnson and Lady Bird Johnson at the White House. She was blacklisted and moved to Europe. In the 1970s the revelation that Kitt had been investigated by the FBI and CIA brought her sympathy and she performed and toured in America again.

See also: Cole, Nat King; Davis, Sammy, Jr.; Poitier, Sidney

Further reading: http://www.imdb.com/name/nm0457755/ (Biography).

KEY DATES

1927   Born in North, South Carolina, on January 17.

1950   Orson Welles casts her in *Time Runs*.

1968   Criticizes Vietnam War during White House party; is blacklisted.

1970s   Press reveals that Kitt was the focus of an FBI and CIA investigation; her career takes off again.

KNIGHT, Gladys
Singer

Legendary soul and rhythm and blues (R&B) singer Gladys Knight has been performing for more than 50 years. She is best known for fronting the band Gladys Knight and the Pips. One of the most popular R&B and soul bands of the 1960s and 1970s, the group had a string of hits such as the million-copy selling record "Midnight Train to Georgia" (1973).

Early life

Knight was born in Atlanta, Georgia, on May 28, 1944. She made her public singing debut at age four at the Mount Moriah Baptist Church, where her parents sang in the choir. By age five Knight was performing in churches across Atlanta and had toured in Florida and Alabama with the Morris Brown Choir. In 1952, at age eight, Knight won the first prize of $2,000 on Ted Mack's popular *Original Amateur Hour* national TV show.

Gladys Knight and the Pips

In 1952 Knight became a member of a band called the Pips along with her brother "Bubba" (Merald), sister Brenda, and cousins William and Elenor Guest; they were named for their cousin and first manager James "Pip" Woods. In

▼ *Gladys Knight and the Pips had 24 Top 40 hits in the 1960s and 1970s.*

1959 Brenda and Elenor left the band; they were replaced by Edward Patten, another cousin, and Lanston George, a friend. Renamed Gladys Knight and the Pips, the band quickly established itself on the R&B circuit. Its first recording, "Every Beat of my Heart" (1961) reached the Top 10 pop charts and was No. 1 on the R&B chart.

In 1965 the band became part of Berry Gordy's famous Motown stable. Although never a Motown A-list band, Gladys Knight and the Pips had several big hits, including the original version of "I Heard It Through the Grapevine" (1967), later a hit for Marvin Gaye, and "Neither One of Us" (1973). During her time at Motown Knight came across a young talented band whom she brought to Gordy's attention; he eventually signed them up as the Jackson 5.

In 1973 Knight and the Pips moved to the New York label Buddah Records; they released over the next year a series of popular hit songs, including "Midnight Train to Georgia," their only No. 1 pop chart hit, and "You're the Best Thing That Ever Happened to Me." The group also won two Grammy awards in 1974. Its other hits include "Save the Overtime" (1983) and "Love Overboard" (1987), both No. 1 on the R&B chart. In 1989 the Pips retired, and Knight launched a solo career. She has released several hit records to critical acclaim and won a Grammy for the album *Many Different Loads* (2001). Knight has received many honors, including a BET Lifetime Achievement Award and induction into the Rock and Roll Hall of Fame.

KEY DATES	
1944	Born in Atlanta, Georgia, on May 28.
1952	Forms the Pips with other family members; renamed Gladys Knight and the Pips seven years later.
1973	Has No. 1 pop chart hit with "Midnight Train to Georgia."
1996	Inducted into Rock and Roll Hall of Fame.
2005	Receives BET Lifetime Achievement Award.

See also: Gaye, Marvin; Gordy, Berry; Jackson 5

Further reading: Knight, Gladys. *Gladys. Between Each Line of Pain and Glory, My Life Story.* New York, NY: Hyperion, 1997.
www.soultracks.com/gladysknight.htm (Short biography).

KNIGHT, Suge
Music Entrepreneur

Suge Knight's life has been the focus of much attention. The founder of Death Row Records and promoter of gangsta rap, Knight has been vilified in the press for his alleged drug connections, rap feuds, and violence. Physically imposing at 6 feet 2 inches (1.9m) and 320 pounds (145kg), Knight was also implicated in the murders of Tupac Shakur and the Notorious BIG. Following several parole violations he was imprisoned, but subsequently released.

Early life
Born in Compton, a suburb of Los Angeles, on April 19, 1965, Marion Knight was the son of Marion, Sr., and Maxine Knight. He was educated at Lynwood High School in Lynwood, California, where he ran with a gang called

▼ **Suge Knight was once the bodyguard of musician Bobby Brown, who gave him valuable advice.**

the Mob Piru Bloods. He then went on to study at El Camino Community College, Torrance, before being awarded a sports scholarship to study at the University of Nevada at Las Vegas. He proved himself an excellent student and a talented athlete, and after graduation was taken on as a replacement player with the Oakland Raiders during the 1980s National Football League strike, but decided to retire from football.

Moving on
Knight went to work as a music promoter and bodyguard to celebrities. He once said that he learned a lot from one of his charges, the musician Bobby Brown, who taught him that the key to artistic and financial freedom was ownership of the master tapes.

In 1987 Knight was arrested for auto theft, carrying a concealed weapon, and attempted murder. He was placed on probation. Two years later he set up a music publishing

INFLUENCES AND INSPIRATION

Former engineer and founder of Interscope Records, Jimmy Lovine provided the financing for Death Row Records. In 1990 Lovine cofounded Interscope Records with Ted Fields. Atlantic Records helped finance the label and as a result owned a 50 percent share in the company. Although Lovine successfully built up a stable of independent rock artists such as Nine Inch Nails, in 1992 he decided to help finance Death Row Records, founded by Knight and Dr. Dre. Interscope acted as distributor for the new label. Death Row quickly established itself as a force to be reckoned with. The label capitalized on the popularity of gangsta rap, which had emerged in Compton in south-central Los Angeles in the late 1980s. The label's first six releases became double-platinum albums. Between 1992 and 2005 the company sold about 40 million records, through heavyweight stars such as Snoop Dogg, Tupac Shakur, M. C. Hammer, and Lil Bow Wow. The company's success was not without its downside, however. Death Row was rumored to have strong links to the drug trade and was investigated by the FBI in the mid-1990s. It was also involved in an East Coast–West Coast rap feud that began in the mid-1990s and resulted in the deaths of stars Tupac Shakur and and the Notorious BIG. In 1997 Interscope severed all ties with Death Row.

---

company and is said to have made a lot of money from the rapper Vanilla Ice. One of Knight's friends claimed to have written the rapper's hit single "Ice, Ice Baby." Vanilla Ice is said to have signed over royalties to Knight after being dangled out of the window of a high-rise building. Ice later denied the story.

Death Row

In 1992 Knight, funded by Interscope Records (*see box*), formed Death Row Records with Dr. Dre, who had formerly been with Ruthless Records. Death Row was a success from the beginning, with stars such as N. W. A. and Snoop Dogg, Dr. Dre's protégé, signed up from the start. Rumors began to circulate about Knight's business practices, however, and his alleged bullyboy techniques. There were also accusations of drug links and money laundering. Knight was accused of assault in 1990 and 1992, and in 1994 he was convicted of robbery and assault.

The East Coast–West Coast feud

In the mid-1990s a feud between East-Coast and West-Coast rappers became public, focused mainly around Sean Combs's Bad Boy Records, established in 1993, and Death Row Records. It began to spiral out of control following an incident at the August 1995 Source awards in which Knight publicly mocked Combs. Although Combs apparently tried to diffuse the situation over the next few years, the disagreement became increasingly more violent, including a shooting incident at Snoop Dogg's trailer while he was filming a video. Finally rapper Tupac Shakur, who had signed with Death Row Records in 1996, was shot while Knight was driving him back from a Las Vegas boxing match. He later died. Less than a year later the Notorious BIG was also murdered. Shakur's mother sued Death Row for unpaid royalties, and others followed suit. It seemed that the label was over, especially when Knight was jailed for violating parole. He only served half his term; released in 2001, he started a new label called Tha Row. On December 23, 2002, he was arrested for another violation, serving 61 days in prison. On June 21, 2003, Knight was jailed for assaulting a parking lot attendant in Los Angeles, a second parole violation. He was released in April 2004.

KEY DATES

1965   Born in Compton, Los Angeles, on April 19.

1987   Arrested for carrying a concealed weapon and attempted murder.

1992   Forms Death Row Records.

1996   Is injured in drive-by shooting that ends in Tupac Shakur's death.

2001   *Rolling Stone* article implicates Knight in death of Notorious BIG; starts Tha Row.

See also: Brown, Bobby; Combs, Sean; Dr. Dre; M. C. Hammer; Notorious B.I.G.; Shakur, Tupac; Snoop Dogg

---

Further reading: Brown, Jake. *Suge Knight: The Rise and Fall of Death Row Records*. Phoenix, AZ: Amber Books, 2001.
http://www.pbs.org/wgbh/pages/frontline/shows/lapd/race/deathrow.html (Article about Knight's life).
www.sixshot.com/az/suge_knight/suge_knight.asp (Biography).

KOUNTZ, Samuel
Surgeon

One of the finest surgeons of the 20th century, Samuel Kountz was a pioneer in the field of kidney transplantation. During his career he performed more than 500 kidney transplants and sought to raise public awareness of the need for organ donation. In 1974 Kountz became the first black president of the Society of University Surgeons.

An uncertain beginning

Samuel Lee Kountz, Jr., was born in Lexa, Arkansas, on January 23, 1930. Kountz and his two brothers were the sons of a minister in the local Baptist Church; their grandfather had been a slave. Both of Kountz's parents were determined to give their children a good education, emphasizing that this was the only way forward.

After graduating from Morris Brooker College High School at age 14, Kountz went on to study at the black Arkansas Baptist Academy in the state capital, Little Rock, with the intention of eventually becoming a minister like his father. His education at the academy failed to prepare him adequately for his entrance exam to the Arkansas Agricultural, Mechanical, and Normal College at Pine Bluff, however, and it was only after the intervention of former teachers and other well-wishers that he was granted a place. By that time he had changed his career plans and had decided to become a physician. He wrote on his admission application that, "I hope to be one of the best doctors in the world in my day and time. I believe that it is my calling and highest ambition."

KEY DATES

1930   Born in Lexa, Arkansas, on January 23.

1958   Awarded an MD (doctor of medicine) by the University of Arkansas.

1959   Becomes a research student under Roy Cohn at Stanford University School of Medicine, California.

1961   With Cohn carries out the first successful mother-to-child kidney transplant.

1967   Becomes full professor at the University of California in San Francisco.

1972   Appointed chairperson of the department of surgery at the Downstate Medical Center, New York City.

1981   Dies in Kings Point, New York, on February 23.

Kountz quickly proved himself a hard-working and committed student, and in 1952 he graduated with a BS in biological science.

Fierce competition

Education at all levels during the 1950s was still largely segregated and there were very few black medical schools. Competition among African American students who wanted to study medicine was extremely fierce. Kountz had already been turned down by two black medical schools when Arkansas's senator William Fulbright (1905–1995), met him during a visit to the college and suggested that he take a higher degree in biochemistry as a way of improving his chances.

With Fulbright's help, Kountz was able to win a place at the largely white University of Arkansas in Fayetteville, studying there for the next four years while also working as a teaching assistant in the university's chemistry laboratories. He graduated with an MS in biochemistry in 1956, having already secured himself a place at the university's medical school at Little Rock. He was one of the first black American students ever to earn this distinction.

Years of study

Kountz graduated with an MD from the University of Arkansas for Medical Sciences in the summer of 1958 and went to San Francisco County Hospital to complete his compulsory one-year internship. Kountz wanted to carry out research as well as to become a practicing surgeon, and in 1959 he gained a place on the prestigious surgical resident program at Stanford University School of Medicine in California, where he would be able to do both.

Transplants

By the late 1950s doctors around the world were already carrying out the first kidney transplants. However, such operations had been successful only in cases in which the donor and recipient were identical twins and there was a high likelihood of tissue compatibility. In other cases, the recipient's immune system usually rapidly rejected the transplanted kidney as a foreign body. Thus far, fewer than 5 percent of patients undergoing a kidney transplant had survived more than two years. While at Stanford, Kountz came to the attention

INFLUENCES AND INSPIRATION

Samuel Kountz's relationship with the Stanford professor of surgery, Roy. B. Cohn (1910–1999), must count among the longest-lasting and most fruitful collaborations in U.S. medical history. It was all the more remarkable because it crossed the existing racial boundaries; it also encouraged many other black Americans to enter the medical profession.

A native of Portland, Oregon, Cohn first joined the Stanford faculty in 1938, and in the decades following World War II (1939–1945) established himself as one of the world's leading experts on transplantation. He was also good at spotting talented students: On encountering Kountz, however, Cohn had to work hard to overcome resistance from

fellow faculty members, wary of accepting African Americans, even brilliant ones, into their ranks. Cohn was successful and took Kountz on as his student. For nine years, the two doctors collaborated and were almost like father and son. They were able to make important advances in their field. Cohn retired from Stanford in 1989, after a 50-year career there.

of Roy Cohn, a pioneer in the field of organ transplants (*see box*), who fought hard on Kountz's behalf in the face of faculty racism to get him accepted as his student.

During the 1960s Cohn and Kountz, working in one of the great collaborations of 20th-century medical history, developed procedures that would enable doctors to temporarily suppress the recipient's immune system long enough for the new organ to be accepted.

Working with Donald Laub they began to experiment using dogs to work out the immunological problem. They transplanted kidneys from one dog to another, monitoring the response of the native kidney with those in the grafted kidney. The team saw that the rate of blood flow through the transplanted organ declined and when Kountz examined a tissue sample, he recognized the first stages of rejection: The immature blood cells were attacking the cells lining the small blood vessels of the grafted kidney. This showed him that the blood vessels of the kidney would die from being starved of blood and oxygen. These experiments were vital in showing Kountz and the Stanford team that they could predict if rejection was going to occur by monitoring the blood flow, therefore allowing them time to stop this with immunosuppressive drugs.

In 1961 Cohn and Kountz undertook the first successful transplant of a kidney between mother and child and over the following years were able to extend such procedures to transplants between unrelated donors and recipients by carefully monitoring a patient's reaction to the transplanted organ and administering immunosuppressive drugs at carefully calculated intervals. As Cohn commented in *Stanford Today*: "Some aspects of our first human case suggested that part of the immunological problem showed itself in the circulatory system."

Achievements

In 1963 Kountz's groundbreaking work won him an instructorship at Stanford, and the following year he was awarded both a $1,000 Investigator Award from the American College of Cardiology and a Fulbright Scholarship, which he used to fund several research trips to Egypt. In 1965 Kountz was appointed associate professor of surgery at Stanford University and in 1967 he became a full professor at the University of California in San Francisco, which developed into the largest kidney transplant research center in the United States. While at the University of California Kountz also helped develop the Belzer Kidney perfusion machine, used to preserve a kidney after its removal from a donor's body.

In 1972 Kountz moved to New York City to take up a new position as chair of the department of surgery at the Downstate Medical Center, part of the State University of New York. Kountz continued to research ways of improving transplantation surgery as well as using his reputation to publicize the need for more kidney donors. Four years later he performed a kidney transplant operation on NBC's *Today Show*, resulting in about 20,000 people phoning in to become donors. In 1977 Kountz went to South Africa to help train surgeons at the University of Cape Town. Soon after his return, Kountz fell seriously ill with a rare nerve disease, which rendered him unable to speak: He died in 1981. Kountz's contribution to medical science has been recognized through a number of awards and honors.

Further reading: Organ, Claude H. Jr., and Margaret M. Kosiba (eds.). *A Century of Black Surgeons: The USA Experience.* 2 vols. Norman, OK: Transcript Press, 1987. www.princeton.edu/~mcbrown/display/kountz.html (Biography).

KYLES, Samuel
Civil Rights Activist

As an eyewitness to the assassination of Martin Luther King, Jr., Samuel "Billy" Kyles was, in 2005, the only surviving person to have been with King during his final hours. A civil rights activist, Kyles has been pastor of Monumental Baptist Church, Memphis, since 1959.

Early life
Born in Mississippi in 1934, Kyles spent most of his childhood in Chicago before returning to the South to participate in the burgeoning civil rights movement. "When I got to Memphis everything was segregated from the cradle to the grave," Kyles observed. "I never could understand why cemeteries had to be segregated—dead people should be able to get along."

Civil rights
Kyles became a Baptist minister and was active in the desegregation struggles in the South during the 1950s and 1960s. He soon rose to leadership within the civil rights movement. In February 1968 Memphis garbage workers went on strike, protesting working conditions and low wages. Kyles invited Martin Luther King, Jr., to support them by leading a march, but it ended in violence. King pledged to return to Memphis to attend another, more peaceful rally. This he did on April 3. That evening he addressed a rally organized by Kyles. King's speech became known as the "Mountaintop" speech; it seemed prophetically fatalistic. Kyles recalled King's frequent mentions of death and observed, "I am so certain he knew he wouldn't get to the 'Promised Land' with us."

A dreadful day
The next day Kyles went to meet King at the Lorraine Motel to take him and his entourage to his home for a meal. As he left his room, King was struck by a sniper's

▲ *Samuel Kyles arranged the civil rights events that brought Martin Luther King, Jr., to Memphis on the day of his assassination.*

bullet shortly after walking out onto the balcony. He spent the last hour of his life in the room with Kyles and Ralph Abernathy. James Earl Ray (1929–1998) was later jailed for the crime, but later recanted his confession. New evidence suggests Ray might have been telling the truth, and the identity of King's murder has remained a matter of controversy. The debate has even touched on Kyles's own role and the truthfulness of his and other witnesses' statements in recent years.

Later life
A member of many civic and professional organizations, Kyles also worked on Jesse Jackson's presidential campaigns of 1984 and 1988 and was a panelist at the 1998 White House conference on hate crimes. He has received numerous honors and awards, and remains a speaker against civil rights abuses.

See also: Abernathy, Ralph; Civil Rights; Jackson, Jesse; King, Martin Luther, Jr.

Further reading: Frady, Marshall. *Martin Luther King, Jr.* New York, NY: Viking Penguin Inc., 2002.
http://www.hilltoptimes.com/story.asp?edition=84&storyid=2252 (Kyles's account of King's assassination).

KEY DATES	
1934	Born in Shelby, Mississippi, on September 26.
1959	Becomes pastor of the Monumental Baptist Church, Memphis, Tennessee.
1968	King is assassinated by James Earl Ray at the Lorraine Motel, Memphis, on April 4.
1992	Receives Tennessee Living Legend Award.

LABELLE, Patti
Singer, Actor

Award-winning singer Patti LaBelle has worked with the biggest names in show business. Known to millions of Americans as Adele Wayne on NBC's hit series *A Different World* (1990–1993), LaBelle has also established a successful career as an actor.

Road to success

Born in Philadelphia, Pennsylvania, on May 24, 1944, Patricia Louise Holt grew up singing in her local Baptist Church. In 1960 she formed a group called the Ordettes with her friend Cindy Birdsong. Soon afterward Nona Hendryx and Sarah Dash joined them and the group renamed themselves the Blue Belles. In 1962 they had a Top 20 rhythm and blues (R&B) and pop chart hit with the single "I Sold My Heart to the Junkman." By 1967 the group had achieved two more chart hits and were known as Patti LaBelle and the BlueBelles; Birdsong quit to join the Supremes, featuring Diana Ross.

By 1970 the group, now called LaBelle, had a new manager and had taken on a more soul/rock image. Their songs were often about racism, sexism, and political issues. After releasing their self-titled debut album, they began to tour, singing with rock acts such as the Who. In 1974 they became the first African American act ever to appear at New York's Metropolitan Opera House. Later that year they released the album *Nightbirds*, and the single "Lady Marmalade," which in 1975 became a No.1 hit on the R&B and pop charts and became a great international success. A year later, following the release of two more albums, the group split up.

In 1977 LaBelle released her self-titled solo debut to moderate success, although her next three releases, *Tasty* (1979), *It's All Right with Me* (1979), and *Released* (1980), all failed to crack the Top 100. Deciding to venture into new territory, she costarred in a 1982 Broadway revival of *Your Arms too Short to Box with God*, for which she

▲ *Patti LaBelle performed "Way Up There" at the 2003 memorial service for the NASA astronauts killed in the* Challenger *shuttle disaster.*

received critical praise. She also made her TV debut in the movie *Working* that same year.

At the end of 1983 LaBelle released the album *I'm in Love Again*, which went gold; she achieved her second No. 1 R&B hit, "If Only You Knew," in early 1984. She also reached the Top 20 in the pop charts with "New Attitude," which was featured on the soundtrack of *Beverly Hills Cop* (1984), starring comedian Eddie Murphy. In 1986 LaBelle released the platinum-selling *Winner in You*.

In 1990 LaBelle was cast in the successful TV show *A Different World*. The following year her gold-selling album *Burnin'* won LaBelle a Grammy for Best Female R&B Vocal Performance. A popular artist, LaBelle was awarded an American Music Award for Favorite R&B Female Artist and was honored with a star on Hollywood Boulevard's Walk of Fame in 1993. She picked up a second Grammy for Best Traditional R&B Vocal Performance for *Live! One Night Only* in 1999. In 2004 LaBelle released the popular album *Timeless Journey*. She has also written a cookbook, *LaBelle Cuisine: Recipes to Sing About*.

See also: Murphy, Eddie; Ross, Diana

Further reading: www.pattilabelle.com (LaBelle site).

KEY DATES

1944   Born in Philadelphia, Pennsylvania, on May 24.

1975   The single "Lady Marmalade" becomes a No. 1 hit on both the U.S. R&B and pop charts, and an international smash.

1993   Wins an American Music Award for Favorite R&B Female Artist.

LANGSTON, Charles Henry
Educator, Abolitionist

Charles Henry Langston was an active force in the antislavery movement in Ohio and Kansas in the mid-19th century. Like his brother John Mercer Langston, he played a leading role in the struggle to attain racial equality for African Americans in the decades immediately before and after the Civil War (1861–1865).

Early life

Langston was born on a plantation in Fredericksburg, Virginia, in 1817. He was the third child of Captain Ralph Quarles, the white owner of the plantation, and Lucy Jane Langston, who was part Native American and part African American. Lucy was a former slave whom Quarles had emancipated, along with their first child Maria, in 1806. Quarles treated his sons well and gave them their early schooling, instilling in them the importance of education. When both Quarles and Lucy died in 1834, their sons Gideon, Charles, and John became the sole heirs of Quarles's estate.

Leaving executors to handle the sale of the plantation, the brothers moved to the free state of Ohio. Shortly afterward Langston and Gideon enrolled to study in the preparatory department of Oberlin College, which was one of the first colleges to accept African American and female students. Around this time Langston also helped set up and then taught at a school for colored children in a black settlement near Chillicothe—children for whose eduction the government made no provision. He was not yet 16.

When he turned 21 Langston received the legacy left to him in his father's will. He is recorded as owning a farm of 11,000 acres (4,451ha) in Jackson county with a white tenant.

Campaigning for reform

With the financial security that his father's legacy afforded him, Langston, like his brother John, devoted increasing amounts of time to the reform movement. In the early 1840s he was involved with the short-lived abolitionist newspaper *Palladium of Liberty*, and in 1848 he was appointed as the western representative of the Sons of Temperance. He was active in specifically African American organizations, including the Ohio Black State Convention, of which he was president in 1849. He also began campaigning to secure African Americans the vote. In the 1850s he served as executive secretary of the Ohio State Anti-Slavery Society, of which John was president.

Oberlin-Wellington Rescue

Oberlin was an important stop on the Underground Railroad, the secret network that assisted escaped slaves reach freedom in the North. Langston helped fugitive slaves find refuge in the town or assisted them in their journey northward to safety in Canada. In 1858 he received widespread publicity for the role he played in the rescue of one such fugitive, John Price, whom slave catchers and federal marshals had captured in Oberlin (*see box*).

A federal grand jury indicted 37 of the people who freed Price. Only two of the people indicted, Simeon M. Bushnell and Charles Langston, were singled out as ringleaders of the rescue and went to trial. Langston used his trial in 1859 to speak eloquently against the inequalities and injustices suffered by African Americans. He was rousingly applauded and the judge responded by saying: "This Court does not make laws; that belongs to another tribunal. We sit here under the obligations of an oath to execute them, and whether they be good, it is not for us to say." Bushnell received a sentence of 60 days in jail. Langston, as a result of his speech, was sentenced to 20 days' imprisonment and fined $100 for his role in what became known as the Oberlin-Wellington Rescue.

Eventually the men from Kentucky and Columbus who had captured Price were arrested and charged with kidnapping. In return for the charges against them being

INFLUENCES AND INSPIRATION

Charles Langston's work as a teacher, antislavery campaigner, and underground railroad operative touched the lives of countless African Americans, most famously the fugitive slave John Price. Price had escaped from a Kentucky slave owner and by 1858 was living in Oberlin, Ohio, in the home of a black laborer. Under the Fugitive Slave Law of 1850, the federal government was required to assist slaveholders in reclaiming their runaway slaves. On the morning of September 13 a number of federal marshals and slave catchers joined forces to seize the 18-year-old Price. They bundled him into a carriage and took him to Wellington, intending to transport him back South on the railroad. Langston was among the crowd of about 500 Oberlin residents who rushed to Wellington to free Price. When Langston was unsuccessful in negotiating Price's release, the crowd stormed the building where the young man was being held and rescued him. Price was hidden in safe houses in Oberlin and later escorted to Canada. Langston made his trial for involvement in the rescue a rallying call for black rights. John Mercer Langston later described Price's rescue as "at once the darkest and the brightest day in the calendar of Oberlin."

dropped, they decided to drop the charges against the rest of the rescuers, who were released in July 1859. With the exception of Bushnell, who was still serving his sentence, they returned to Oberlin and were greeted with jubilant celebrations. The rescue prompted a surge of support for the abolitionist cause.

On October 16, 1859 white abolitionist John Brown led a raid on the federal arsenal at Harpers Ferry, Virginia. He and his followers were killed or captured and Brown was sentenced to die on December 2. On that day black leaders conducted ceremonies throughout Ohio. In Cleveland Langston was the chief speaker and addressed about 2,000 black and white mourners.

The Civil War

Following the outbreak of the Civil War in 1861 Langston went to Quincy, Illinois, where he recruited African Americans to join the Union Army. The following year he moved to Kansas, where he settled in Leavenworth, a town whose population was swelling rapidly with the arrival of slaves fleeing from the South. Langston continued to recruit for the Union Army. He also set up and taught at a school for the town's growing black community and became a leading figure in numerous charitable organizations to provide for the welfare of the new arrivals. Langston was a leading figure in the Kansas Emancipation League and continued to campaign relentlessly for the African American right to vote; in 1865 he was elected president of the Leavenworth Suffrage Club.

In 1868 Langston returned to Ohio, where the following year he married Mary Patterson Leary, the widow of Lewis Sheridan Leary, a free man who had been killed while taking part in Brown's raid.

Back to Kansas

The Langstons moved to Kansas, where they settled on a farm near Lawrence and had three children. Their youngest child was Carolina Mercer Langston, who later became the mother of the famous writer Langston Hughes. Until he was 12 years old, Langston Hughes lived in Lawrence with his grandmother, Mary Langston.

In 1870 Langston was at long last able to stop campaigning for the vote, when the Fifteenth Amendment to the Constitution affirmed the right of citizens to vote without restrictions based on race or color. In the 1870s Langston became increasingly involved in the Kansas Republican Party.

In the 1880s, while the Langston family lived in Lawrence, Charles was active in community organizations, including the Lawrence Colored Benevolent Society and the *Historic Times*, a local black newspaper. Langston died at his home on Alabama Street, Lawrence, in 1895, aged 75. He was buried in Oak Hill Cemetery. Mary Langston died in 1915.

See also: Hughes, Langston; Langston, John Mercer

Further reading: Sheridan, Richard B. *Freedom's Crucible: The Underground Railroad in Lawrence and Douglas County, Kansas, 1854–1865.* Lawrence, Kansas: University of Kansas, 1998.
http://www.kshs.org/publicat/history/1999winter_sheridan.htm (Study on Langston published by Kansas State Historical Society).
http://www.oberlin.edu/external/EOG/Oberlin-Wellington_Rescue/rescuemain2.htm (Account of the rescue with links, including Langston's court speech).

LANGSTON, John Mercer
Activist, Congressman

Civil rights activist, educator, and diplomat John Mercer Langston gave his life to official service at a time when other black people were struggling to achieve equality.

Born in Louisa County, Virginia, on December 14, 1829, Mercer was the son of plantation owner Captain Ralph Quarles and his former slave Lucy Langston. Quarles freed Lucy and Langston; his two brothers and his sister were born free. In 1834 both of Langston's parents died of a sudden illness, and the children were taken into the guardianship of William Gooch, a friend of Quarles who lived in Chillicothe, Ohio. Quarles's estate passed to his sons Gideon, Charles, and John. When Gooch moved to Missouri, a slave state, Langston moved to Cincinnati, where he came across the community of freedmen who lived there.

At age 14 Langston enrolled in the preparatory department of Oberlin College in Ohio, graduating from the collegiate department in 1849, the fifth African American to do so. He went on to take an MA in theology. In the 1840s Langston also became active in the antislavery movement. Encouraged by former slave Frederick Douglass, he made

▼ *John Mercer Langston served as a diplomat in Haiti and the Dominican Republic.*

a speech at the first National Black Convention in Cleveland in 1848 in which he called for people to shelter runaway slaves.

Langston's goal was to work in the law, but his skin color kept him out of most law schools. Eventually, Judge Philemon Bliss (1813–1889) personally tutored Langston, who passed the bar exam in 1854, becoming the first black lawyer in Ohio. Langston had a successful practice, and began to run for local government. He served on the city council of Brownhelm, Ohio, between 1855 and 1860, and became town clerk—making him possibly the first African American to take public office through election.

Making a difference

During the Civil War (1861–1865) Langston contributed to the Union cause by raising the first black regiment in U.S. military history, the Massachusetts 54th. After the war Langston took a succession of public positions, including president of the National Equal Rights League, education inspector of the Freedmen's Bureau, dean of Howard University Law School, and U.S. consul general to Haiti. In 1889 Langston became the elected congressman for Virginia, although a legal battle over the election result meant that he was unable to take office for 18 months. He retired from political life in 1894, dying three years later.

KEY DATES	
1829	Born in Louisa County, Virginia, on December 14.
1841	Attends Oberlin College.
1854	Passes the bar exam and becomes a lawyer.
1860	Becomes the elected town clerk of Brownhelm, Ohio.
1889	Elected congressman for Virginia.
1897	Dies in Washington, D.C., on November 15.

See also: Douglass, Frederick; Langston, Charles Henry

Further reading: Cheek, William, and Aimee Lee Cheek. *John Mercer Langston and the Fight for Black Freedom, 1829–1865.* Urbana, IL: University of Illinois Press, 1989. http://www.oberlin.edu/external/EOG/OYTT-images/JMLangston.html (Profile on Oberlin College site).

LARSEN, Nella
Writer

Nella Larsen was a novelist and short-story writer who was part of the Harlem Renaissance, the literary flowering of African American authors in New York City in the 1920s. Her promising literary career was brought to an abrupt end when she was accused of plagiarism. Although she was cleared of the charges, Larsen abandoned writing.

Early life

Nella Walker was born in Chicago, Illinois, on April 13, 1891, to a Danish mother and an African American father. Following her parents' separation, she was raised by her mother and white stepfather, Peter Larson. She took her stepfather's name, making it her own by changing the spelling slightly.

Highly intelligent, Larsen completed high school at the Normal School of Fisk University in Nashville, Tennessee, and is also believed to have studied at the University of Copenhagen between 1909 and 1912, although this is difficult to verify. In 1912 Larsen embarked on a three-year nursing course at New York City's Lincoln Hospital. She worked briefly in Alabama before returning to New York.

Writing career

In May 1919 Larsen married Samuel Elmer Imes, a prominent African American physicist. She quit nursing in 1921 to work as a librarian at the New York Public Library in January 1922. She worked there until 1926, spending her free time writing fiction. Her first novel, *Quicksand*, appeared in 1928 and won both critical acclaim and the Harmon Foundation's Bronze Medal for Literature. Larsen was heralded as a key member of the Harlem Renaissance.

Passing, her second novel, followed in 1929, and Larsen was awarded a Guggenheim Fellowship in 1930, the first African American woman to be given that honor. She used it to travel to Spain to work on her next novel.

▲ *Nella Larsen became the first woman to win a Guggenheim Fellowship in 1930.*

Unfortunate events

On her return to New York City 18 months later, Larsen faced scandal. She was accused of plagiarizing "Sanctuary," a short story first published in 1930, from a story written by Sheila Kaye-Smith and published in January 1922. Although Larsen's editors at *Forum* magazine cleared her of all charges, she did not recover from the accusation and gave up writing without finishing the novel she had begun in Spain.

Larsen suffered a further blow when she learned of her husband's infidelity and the couple subsequently divorced. Larsen moved to the Lower East Side and resumed her nursing career, continuing to work well past retirement age.

Larsen lived alone; she was found dead in her apartment on March 30, 1964. Since the 1970s her literary work has been reexamined and her reputation as an author of some repute has been restored.

See also: Harlem Renaissance; Imes, Samuel

Further reading: Davis, Thadious M. *Nella Larsen. Novelist of the Harlem Renaissance*. Baton Rouge, LA: University of Louisiana State Press, 1996.
www.library.csi.cuny.edu/dept/history/lavender/386/nlarsen.html (Comprehensive biography).

KEY DATES	
1891	Born in Chicago, Illinois, on April 13.
1928	Publishes first novel, *Quicksand*.
1929	Publishes second novel, *Passing*.
1930	Received a Guggenheim Fellowship; accused of plagiarism, but cleared; gives up writing.
1964	Found dead.

LA SALLE, Eriq
Actor

A talented and enigmatic actor, Eriq La Salle is also becoming increasingly renowned as a screenwriter, director, and producer.

Early life
Eriq Ki La Salle was born in Hartford, Connecticut, on July 23, 1962. Raised in the state, La Salle showed an interest in acting from an early age. He went on to study at the prestigious Julliard School of Drama in New York City for two years. By the time he graduated from New York University in 1984 with a bachelor of fine arts degree in theater, La Salle had already won roles in several Shakespeare in the Park productions. He soon found steady work on and off Broadway. La Salle was also cast in a number of television shows, including *One Life to Live*, in which he had a regular spot as the reporter Mike Rivers.

Career highlights
Moving to California in 1991, La Salle starred briefly in the television series *The Human Factor* and guest-starred in several successful programs, including *LA Law, Quantum Leap,* and *A Different World.* La Salle also appeared in movies, winning supporting roles in *Coming to America* (1988) and *The Color of Night* (1994). However, it was as gifted surgeon Dr. Peter Benton in the internationally successful TV show *ER* that La Salle gained universal acclaim. During his eight years as Dr. Benton, La Salle was awarded two NAACP Image Awards for Outstanding Actor in a Drama Series and nominated for three Emmys and a Golden Globe. Benton's relationship with Dr. Elizabeth Corday (Alex Kingston) also hit the headlines as one of the first successful interracial relationships on televison. La Salle eventually insisted that the relationship be written

▲ *In 2002 Eriq La Salle said, "Art should offend people because art should challenge people."*

out of the plot, arguing that his character should have a healthy relationship with a black woman instead. Upon signing his final three-year contract with the show, La Salle became one of the highest-paid actors in television history.

La Salle made his directorial debut in 1996 with the TV movie *Rebound.* That same year he wrote, directed, and starred in the short film *Psalms from the Underground.* In 1997 he set up the production company Humble Journey. His short films have won awards at the Worldfest Houston film competition and the USA Film Festival. In 2002 La Salle produced *The Salton Sea* and cowrote, produced, directed, and starred in his first feature film, *Crazy as Hell*, for which he won a Black Reel Award for Best Independent Actor. In 2005 he starred in the thriller *Inside Out.*

KEY DATES	
1962	Born in Hartford, Connecticut, on July 23.
1984	Plays Mike Rivers in *One Life to Live.*
1994	Cast as Dr. Peter Benton in *ER.*
1996	Makes his directorial debut, *Rebound.*
1997	Founds production company Humble Journey Films.
2002	Directs, produces, and stars in *Crazy as Hell.*

Further reading: Halliwell, Leslie. *Halliwell's Who's Who in the Movies.* New York, NY: HarperResource, 2003. http://www.imdb.com/name/nm0005113/ (IMDB entry on La Salle).

LAST POETS
Musicians

The Last Poets have been hailed as the godfathers of rap, described as the rappers of the civil rights era, and credited for paving the way for hip-hop. Since its inception the group's line-up has varied greatly, and at various times members have included: Umar bin Hassan, Abiodun Oyewole, David Nelson, Gylan Kain, Felipe Luciano, Jalal Nuriddin, Suliaman El Hadi, and Nilajah.

Origins
The group was founded by Jalal Mansur Nuriddin, an Army paratrooper who chose to go to jail rather than fight in the Vietnam War (1964–1973). While in prison, he converted to Islam and learned how to "spiel," an early form of rapping. Nuriddin also became friends with Umar Bin Hassan and Abiodun Oyewole.

After the three men were released, they settled in Harlem, New York City, where they joined the East Wind poetry workshop and developed a musical style that combined spiels with a musical backing. The trio began performing on local street corners.

Formation
The Last Poets officially formed in Marcus Garvey Park shortly after the death of Martin Luther King, Jr., and on the anniversary of Malcolm X's birthday, on May 19, 1968. The group took its name from a poem by the South African poet Keorapetse Kgositsile (1938–), also known as Little Willie Copaseely, who wrote about the necessity of putting away poetry in the face of revolution. Kgositsile wrote: "When the moment hatches in time's womb there will be no art talk/The only poem you will hear will be the

▲ *The Last Poets have inspired many musicians, including the poet Gil Scott-Heron.*

spearpoint pivoted in the punctured marrow of the villain…. Therefore we are the last poets of the world."

The Poets took their inspiration from writers such as Amiri Baraka, musicians such as Sun Ra, and political organizations such as the Black Panthers and the Nation of Islam, and their poems reflected the radicalism of the time. They chose African-flavored jazz rhythms as their musical background, consciously rejecting the rhythm-and-blues sound that was popular at the time.

Success
After seeing a performance by the Poets on a local television program, Alan Douglas, a well-known jazz producer, signed the group. They released their debut album, *The Last Poets*, in 1970. The album included tracks that attacked racists and the government and condemned white oppression ("White Man's Got a God Complex") and political apathy in the African American community ("Niggas Are Scared of Revolution"). The album was a commercial success, selling over a million copies, and put rap music firmly on the musical map. However, before the group could build on its success and take off on a planned tour, Oyewole was arrested for robbery and served four years in a North Carolina prison. He was replaced by Nilajah, who was a percussionist.

KEY DATES

1968   The Last Poets form on May 19.

1970   Release their debut album, *The Last Poets;* Oyewole leaves and is replaced by Nilajah.

1971   Release their second album, *This Is Madness;* Hassan leaves and is replaced by Suliaman El Hadi.

1980s   Hugely influential on rap music; bands such as Public Enemy sample their work.

1995   Band splits leading to fight over the band name: Oyewole and Hassan win the right to use the Last Poets.

The next album, *This Is Madness,* released in 1971, was even more politically outspoken than the first and made the Poets a target of the FBI's counter-intelligence program, which focused on forces that its director, Edgar J. Hoover, believed were politically dangerous. Following the release of the album, Hassan left the group to join a religious sect. He was replaced by Suliaman El Hadi.

In 1972 the group released the album *Chastisement*, which introduced a sound the Poets called "jazzoetry," a mix of jazz and funk with poetry. In 1974 the Poets released *At Last*, a free-form jazz album. After its release Nilajah left the group, and with the exception of *Delights of the Garden* in 1977, the group did not release any material for some time.

Regeneration

The 1980s saw the popularity of rap music reach new heights and the work of the Last Poets became popular with a new generation of hip-hop and rap fans. Their earlier records became collectors' items and rap groups such as the highly influential Public Enemy began to use samples of the Last Poets' work in their recordings.

The group began collaborating with various performers, including the British punk band the Pop Group, before returning to recording in their own right. In 1984 they released the album *Oh My People*, which was followed in 1988 by *Freedom Express*. After these releases the group went quiet once more. Hassan released a solo LP in 1993 entitled *Be Bop or Be Dead*, while Nuriddin became a mentor of a British acid jazz collective called Galliano.

The real Last Poets

Hassan and Nuriddin worked on several projects until 1995, when the group began to fight each other and split into two splinter groups, which each laid claim to the Last Poets name. Nuriddin and El Hadi were known as the Last Poets and released the single "Scatterrap." Abiodun Oyewole and Umar Bin Hassan released the album *Holy Terror*, and were billed as "Formerly of the Last Poets." After a legal dispute Oyewole and Hassan won the right to the name.

Over the course of the Last Poets' more than 30-year history, members of the group have collaborated in various combinations to produce more than a dozen albums. They performed in the inaugural season of HBO's *Def Poetry Jam* and were cast in the movie *Poetic Justice* (1993). In 1994 they toured with Lollapalooza and performed in venues around the world. The Last Poets have been a major influence on hip-hop, linking poetry with its roots in an oral tradition that dates back to the griot storyteller. Their work is a vital part of hip-hop, rap, and African American history.

See also: Baraka, Amiri; King, Martin Luther Jr.; Malcolm X; Scott-Heron, Gil

Further reading: Oyewole, Abiodun, and Kim Green. *On a Mission: Selected Poems and a History of the Last Poets.* New York, NY: Henry Holt & Company, 1996.
http://www.math.buffalo.edu/~sww/LAST-POETS/last_poets0.html (Biography, poems, and links).

LATIMER, Lewis H.
Inventor, Draftsman

Considered one of the most significant African American inventors of the late 19th century, Lewis Howard Latimer secured a great number of patents for his many inventions during his lifetime. A former assistant to the inventor Alexander Graham Bell (1847–1922) and the only black American member of Thomas Alva Edison's (1847–1941) renowned group of research scientists, Latimer was key in the development of the electric light bulb: He developed the process for manufacturing the all-important carbon filaments.

Early life

Latimer was born in Boston, Massachusetts, in 1848, the youngest child of George and Rebecca Latimer. His parents were fugitive slaves who had fled from servitude in Virginia to raise a family in the relative freedom of the North. Latimer grew up in poverty: His father struggled to earn enough money to support his family. Latimer attended school until the fifth grade, showing a talent for drawing and reading, but he also had to help provide for his family, especially after the disappearance of his father in about 1857.

Following the outbreak of war between the Union states of the North and the Confederate states of the South in 1861, Latimer's elder brothers enlisted in the Union Army. When he turned 16, Latimer joined the Union Navy. He served on the gunboat USS *Massasoit*, and saw action blockading Confederate ships on the James River.

A career in drafting and patents

At the end of the Civil War (1861–1865) Latimer returned to Boston, where a couple of years later he got a job as an office boy for Crosby and Gould, a patent law firm in the city. The position marked the beginning of Latimer's career. He studied the work of the company's draftsmen, bought tools and second-hand books on mechanical drawing, and taught himself to become a draftsman. After demonstrating his newly acquired skills, he was promoted, and in 11 years his salary increased from $3 to $20 a week. Surrounded by designs for new and improved machines and processes, Latimer also began work on his own inventions. In 1874 he received his first patent for a design for a toilet for railroad cars.

In 1873 Latimer married Mary Wilson Lewis; six years later the couple moved to Bridgeport, Connecticut, where other members of the Latimer family lived. Bridgeport was a booming industrial city, and Latimer found it filled with men constantly trying to make technological advances.

▲ **Lewis Howard Latimer was a man of many talents: As well as being an inventor, Latimer was a poet, musician, and author.**

KEY DATES	
1848	Born in Boston, Massachusetts, on September 4.
1864	Joins Union Navy and fights in Civil War.
1868	Begins work at Crosby and Gould, a patent law firm.
1874	Receives his first patent, for a toilet for railroad cars.
1880	Becomes a draftsman for Hiram Maxim's U.S. Electric Lighting Company.
1884	Starts to work for Thomas Edison as a patent expert at about this time.
1928	Dies in New York on December 11.

INFLUENCES AND INSPIRATION

Lewis Latimer's desire for self-improvement and social betterment was shaped by the example of other self-made Americans, such as the inventors with whom he worked, but most of all by his parents and their determination to raise their children free from slavery. In 1842 George and Rebecca Latimer escaped from their lives as slaves in Norfolk, Virginia, and made their way north by pretending that George, who had a pale complexion, was a plantation owner and that Rebecca was his slave. Shortly after the couple arrived in Boston, slave catchers recognized and captured George. His case became a major focus for the antislavery debate. When a judge ruled that Latimer still belonged to the man from whom he had escaped, an African American minister paid $400 for his release.

Some 15 years later George Latimer went missing. His disappearance came shortly after the Supreme Court ruled in *Dred Scott v. Sandford* (1857) that blacks—free men as well as slaves—were not and could never become citizens of the United States. The decision was a major setback in the abolitionist campaign to secure rights for African Americans.

Some historians speculate that because George Latimer had no official papers to prove his status as a free man, he disappeared to avoid being recaptured and sent back to his former owner in Virginia.

In 1880 Latimer got a job with Hiram Maxim at the U.S. Electric Lighting Company, in an industry that was beginning to transform the way people lived. Latimer immediately began studying the new technology of electric lighting. Within a short amount of time he was contributing his own ideas for improvements to the design and manufacture of lighting systems; three such patents were filed in Latimer's name. Latimer moved with the U.S. Electric Lighting Company to New York, and also traveled to Philadelphia, Montreal, and London, England, to supervise the installation of lighting systems.

Making a difference

Returning from London in 1882, Latimer found himself without a job when the U.S. Electric Lighting Company was restructured. He went on to work for a number of other electrical companies before being employed by the Edison Electric Light Company, which had become the leader in its field. Later in his life Latimer recalled that he first worked with Thomas Edison on the inventor's patent applications for the telephone, which were made between 1875 and 1880.

In about 1884 Latimer was employed by the Edison Electric Light Company for his expertise in the design, manufacture, and patenting of electric lighting. He worked first in the engineering department and from 1889 in the legal department, which protected Edison's patents from rival companies. He also wrote a book about the Edison system of incandescent lighting in 1890. Following another company restructure in 1911, Latimer again lost his job. From that time onward he worked as a patent consultant for an old friend and colleague, New York engineer and patent solicitor Edwin W. Hammer.

Latimer believed in the American dream of social and economic betterment through hard work. After serving, like many other black Americans, in the Civil War, he also believed that black people should attain full social equality and integration in postwar America. Although he faced prejudice, Latimer worked toward these goals in both his professional and private life. He became an officer of the Grand Army of the Republic, an association of Civil War veterans, and was a founding member of the Edison Pioneers, an elite group of men who had been associated with Thomas Edison. Latimer was also involved in his local community and with African American issues. He maintained close relationships with prominent African Americans such as the inventor and businessman Samuel Scottron and the lawyer and political activist Richard Greener. He helped found the Unitarian Church in Flushing, a predominantly white suburb in Queens, New York, where he lived, and supported charities such as the White Rose Mission in Harlem. He died in 1928.

See also: Greener, Richard; Slavery

Further reading: Fouché, Rayvon. *Black Inventors in the Age of Segregation: Granville T. Woods, Lewis H. Latimer, and Shelby J. Davidson.* Baltimore, MD: John Hopkins University Press, 2003.
http://edison.rutgers.edu/latimer/blueprnt.htm (Biography).

LAW, Oliver
Labor Organizer, Soldier

Today Oliver Law is chiefly remembered for his participation in the Spanish Civil War (1936–1939), when as a battalion commander he became the first African American to command U.S. citizens in a racially integrated military unit. Prior to the Spanish Civil War, however, Law was also a leading figure in the Chicago labor movement during the Great Depression that hit the United States in the 1930s and spread across Europe.

The struggle to survive

Oliver Law was born on a Texas ranch in 1899. Although little is known of his early years he served as a ordinary soldier in World War I (1914–1918). After the war Law eventually settled in Chicago, Illinois, where he worked in several different jobs, including as a stevedore and a taxi driver. In 1929 the United States suffered a devastating economic downturn that plunged millions of people into long-term unemployment, poverty, and destitution.

Like many other working people, both African American and white, Law joined the Communist Party in order to achieve better rights and social conditions for ordinary Americans. African Americans made up about 10 percent of the U.S. Communist Party membership. During the 1930s Law helped organize a series of mass demonstrations in Chicago and became known for his oratory and rousing speeches. Law was often arrested, however, and, after the International Unemployment Demonstration in Chicago on March 6, 1930, he was beaten badly by the police.

Spanish Civil War

In 1936 civil war broke out between Spain's Republican government and extreme right-wing fascist insurgents called the Nationalists, led by General Francisco Franco (1892–1975). Left-wing parties and labor unions around the world took up the cause of the Republicans, and many volunteers went to Spain to fight on the side of the antifascist forces as part of the International Brigades.

In the United States African American support for the Spanish Republicans was widespread, in part because the fight against fascism was considered to be closely allied with the struggle against racism. Black American musicians like Count Basie held benefit concerts, and there were black pro-Republican rallies in Harlem, New York City. Some 80 black volunteers, including Law, joined the Abraham Lincoln Brigade, the U.S. contingent of about 3,000 volunteers who fought in Spain from 1936. The majority of the brigade were communists, although some Americans came from the Socialist Labor Party and the Socialist Party of America.

Making a mark

Law arrived in Spain in January 1937 and proved himself a courageous and skillful soldier. He was promoted to commander of the machine-gun company. When Robert Merriman (1908–1938), the brigade's leader, was wounded during the Battle of Jarama Valley on February 11, 1937, Law was rapidly promoted to battalion commander. It was the first time in U.S. history that an integrated military force had been led by an African American officer.

Eslande Goode (1896–1965), the wife of actor and communist Paul Robeson, recounted the story of an old southern colonel who commented on the fact that Law was wearing a captain's uniform. "Law replied with dignity, 'Yes, I am, because I am a Captain. In America, in your army, I could only rise as high as corporal, but here people feel differently about race and I can rise according to my worth, not according to my color.'" In July, however, Law was killed while leading an attack on Mosquito Ridge during the Battle of Brunete. Claims that he had been killed because of his color were dismissed. Paul Robeson later tried unsuccessfully to get a film made of Law's life.

KEY DATES	
1899	Born in Texas.
1929	Joins the Communist Party.
1937	Arrives in Spain in January as part of the Abraham Lincoln Brigade to fight in the Spanish Civil War ; becomes battalion commander; dies at Mosquito Ridge, Spain, on July 9.

See also: Basie, Count; Robeson, Paul

Further reading: Carroll, Peter N. *The Odyssey of the American Lincoln Brigade: Americans in the Spanish Civil War.* Stanford, CA: Stanford University Press, 1994.
http://www.spartacus.schoolnet.co.uk/SPlawO.htm (Biography).

LAWRENCE, Jacob
Artist, Educator

Jacob Armstead Lawrence is one of the best known and most influential African American artists. His ideas were shaped by African American teachers and intellectuals in a New York City that was still influenced by the Harlem Renaissance of the 1920s. He made the Harlem district of the city and African American life and history the main subjects of his work, portraying the quest of black people for freedom, social justice, and human dignity. Lawrence developed a highly individual style, using vivid colors, dark tones, flat shapes, and dynamic arrangements, and he often created narrative series of paintings to tell a story.

Lawrence was born in Atlantic City, New Jersey, on September 7, 1917, to Jacob Lawrence and Rose Lee

▼ **Between 1940 and 1941, when this picture was taken, Jacob Lawrence produced 60 panel paintings entitled The Migration of the Negro.**

KEY DATES

1917   Born in Atlantic City, New Jersey, on September 7.

1930   Moves to Harlem, New York.

1941   Completes The Migration of the Negro, which is exhibited at Edith Halpert's New York gallery to critical acclaim.

1942   Paints Life in Harlem series.

1970   Awarded the Spingarn Medal by the National Association for the Advancement of Colored People.

1971   Becomes professor of art at the University of Washington in Seattle.

2000   Dies in Seattle, Washington, on June 9.

Armistead. His parents separated in 1924, and his mother moved Lawrence and his siblings to Philadelphia, where she placed them in foster homes while she found work in Harlem. Lawrence joined his mother there in 1930.

He showed an early talent for art in the free classes that he attended at the Harlem Art Workshop, where he was taught by Charles Alston (1907–1977) at his studio "306." By the middle of the 1930s Lawrence had met many of the key figures of the Harlem Renaissance at Alston's studio, including Alain Locke, Langston Hughes, Ralph Ellison, Claude McKay, Countee Cullen, and the artists Romare Bearden, Aaron Douglas, and Augusta Savage (*see box*). Lawrence's relationship with such people and his experiences of living in Harlem helped shape his development as an artist.

The Harlem experience

By the late 1930s Lawrence had already established the themes and approaches that came to characterize his distinctive work. Many of his early pictures featured scenes of everyday life in Harlem, which he rendered in bold colors and shapes using cheap poster paints. He also began to focus on African American history and culture, and in 1937 created the first of his narrative series of paintings, a sequence chronicling the life of the Haitian former slave and general Toussaint L'Ouverture (1744–1803). Lawrence followed it with similar narrative series about the lives of abolitionists Frederick Douglass, Harriet Tubman, and John Brown.

INFLUENCES AND INSPIRATION

Jacob Lawrence was profoundly influenced by the many intellectuals, writers, and artists of the Harlem Renaissance.

Three individuals in particular shaped his outlook during his formative years as teenager. The first was the young African American artist Charles H. Alston (1907–1977), who taught Lawrence at the Utopia Children's House community center and later at the Harlem Art Workshop. He also gave Lawrence workspace in his studio, affectionately known as "306," which became a gathering place for other artists, writers, and intellectuals, including Ralph Ellison, Richard Wright, and Alain Locke.

The African American educator and sculptor Augusta Savage (1892–1962) also played an important part in Lawrence's career. She gave him art lessons in 1936, helping him to win a scholarship to study at the progressive American Artists School in New York from 1937 to 1939. She also helped Lawrence secure employment as a painter with the government's Works Administration Project in 1940.

Lawrence was also much influenced by the black historian Charles Seifert (1871–1949). Seifert's lectures on black culture and history, delivered at his home on 137th Street in Harlem, opened Lawrence's eyes to the history and lives of African Americans.

The Migration of the Negro

Lawrence's greatest success, however, came with The Migration of the Negro (1940–1941). This series of 60 paintings, accompanied by captions, told the story of the Great Migration, in which hundreds of thousands of African Americans moved from the rural South to the cities of the North during World War I (1914–1918) and the 1920s.

Set in bleak landscapes, the first pictures of the series show scenes of poverty, prejudice, and violence suffered by African Americans in the South. This is followed by images of their flight northward, and then by depictions of the buildings, industry, and people of the urban North. The final paintings illustrate aspects of life, both positive and negative, in the new black American communities of the North. The Migration of the Negro established Johnson's reputation as a great artist not only in the black community but in the wider art world. The paintings were exhibited at a leading New York gallery and then at museums throughout the country. They were jointly purchased by the Museum of Modern Art, New York, and the Phillips Collection, Washington, D.C.

Later themes and series

Lawrence continued to address social themes in his next series of paintings, Life in Harlem (1942). In 1942, after the United States entered World War II (1939–1945), Lawrence was drafted into the Army; two years later he worked as a war artist on board a troopship. Although the paintings he created during this period have been lost, when Lawrence was discharged from the Army in 1946, the Guggenheim Foundation awarded him a fellowship that he used to record his wartime experiences: He completed the resulting War Series in 1947. At the same time Lawrence was also invited to teach at Black Mountain College in North Carolina, known to be one of the most experimental centers of arts education. In 1949, however, Lawrence entered Hillside Hospital in Queens, New York, to seek treatment for depression, an experience that he again recorded in his paintings. In the following decade his paintings became much more complex. The use of light and shadow is much more evident in his work and he also used masks to represent questions of identity

During the 1960s Lawrence addressed the struggle for desegregation in his work. In 1964 he spent nine months in Nigeria, where he painted scenes of local life. On his return to the United States Lawrence began a series of pictures on the theme of the builder, many of which include black and white Americans working together. He also produced book illustrations and public murals. From 1971 to 1986 he was professor of art at the University of Washington in Seattle. Before his death in 2000 Lawrence illustrated many children's books.

See also: Bearden, Romare; Cullen, Countee; Douglas, Aaron; Douglass, Frederick; Ellison, Ralph; Great Migration; Locke, Alain; Savage, Augusta; Tubman, Harriet; Wright, Richard

---

Further reading: Nesbett, Peter T., and Michelle Dubois (eds.). *Over the Line: The Art and Life of Jacob Lawrence.* Seattle, WA: University of Washington Press, 2001.
http://www.whitney.org/jacoblawrence/ (Excellent site on Lawrence by the Whitney Museum of American Art).

LAWRENCE, Martin
Actor, Comedian, Producer

Martin Lawrence is a comedian, actor, and producer, best known for his roles in such films as *Bad Boys*, also starring the actor Will Smith.

Born in 1965, in Frankfurt, Germany, where his father was stationed with the Air Force, Lawrence moved back to the United States at age six. His family settled in the suburban town of Landover, Maryland. Soon afterward his father left the family and Lawrence later said that when his mother would come home from work tired, "I would lie on the end of her bed trying to make her laugh. I knew when I made my mother laugh, I had something."

Lawrence attended Eleanor Roosevelt High School in Landover, where he preferred clowning around to studying. One of his teachers finally made a deal with him: If he behaved during class he could try out his comedy routine for the last few minutes of the period. He was a hit, and he became determined to make a living from comedy.

After graduating from high school in 1984, Lawrence began to perform in comedy clubs in Washington, D.C.,

KEY DATES

1965 Born in Frankfurt, Germany, on April 16.

1989 Makes first film appearance in *Do the Right Thing*.

1994 Receives an Image Award for best comic actor for his role in *Martin*.

while holding down a day job as a janitor. After moving to New York he appeared on *Star Search*, a show that allowed unknown performers to compete for prizes. Although Lawrence was not one of the winners, a Hollywood producer contacted him a few months later and asked him for a screen test at Columbia Pictures in California.

Making the big time

Lawrence got his first regular TV work in the comedy series *What's Happening Now!* He also became more successful as a stand-up comedian, appearing in Los Angeles comedy clubs and on cable television comedy shows. Director Spike Lee spotted Lawrence and gave him a small role in the 1989 movie *Do the Right Thing*. That same year he also became host of HBO's *Def Comedy Jam*.

In 1990 Lawrence appeared in *House Party*. He had his first starring role in the film *Talking Dirty After Dark* and in 1992 he starred with comedian Eddie Murphy in the movie *Boomerang*. Lawrence also appeared in his own hugely successful sitcom, *Martin*, which won a NAACP Image Award for outstanding television series. In 1994 Lawrence released the concert film *You So Crazy*, which became one of the highest-grossing concert films of all time.

Between 1995 and 1999 Lawrence's reputation as an actor was cemented with a series of successful films, including *Bad Boys*. In 1996 he made his directorial debut with the film *A Thin Line Between Love and Hate*. Lawrence's life has not been without controversy, however: In 1996 he was arrested at an airport for having a loaded gun in his suitcase and in 1997 he was arrested for assault. More recent projects include films such as *Black Knight* (2001), *Badboys 2* (2003), and *Badboys 3* (2006).

See also: Lee, Spike; Murphy, Eddie; Smith, Will

Further reading: http://www.imdb.com/name/nm0001454 (Biography).

▲ **Comedian Martin Lawrence won the NAACP Image Award in 1994.**

LEE, Malcolm D.
Filmmaker

Writer–director Malcolm D. Lee was inspired to go into movies by his cousin Spike Lee. Although some people might have been put off by having such a prestigious director in the family, Lee gained his first experience in movies working on his cousin's films. Known for the comedies *The Best Man* and *Undercover Brother,* Lee has established himself as a director and writer of some distinction. He told CNN: "I'm not trying to follow in Spike's footsteps. I'm just trying to be my own filmmaker.... Hopefully, you won't be able to pigeonhole me and say, 'This is the Malcolm Lee style,' because I want to make different kinds of movies."

Early life
Born in New York on January 11, 1970, Lee was raised in a middle-class family and neighborhood. He attended a predominantly white prep school and for many years was the only black student in his class. When Lee was growing up, his cousin Spike was establishing a

▼ **Malcolm D. Lee gained his first film experience working on his cousin Spike's movies.**

formidable reputation as a director. When he was 17 Lee went to work as a production assistant on Spike's movie *School Daze* (released 1988). He later worked on *Malcolm X* (1992) and *Clockers* (1995).

Making a career in movies
After graduating from Georgetown University in 1992 with a BA in English and fine arts, Lee was awarded a one-year fellowship in screenwriting by Disney. During that time Lee completed two screenplays, one of which was developed into the short film *Morningside Rep* (1996). Based on Lee's own experiences, the film follows the experiences of two black students in a predominantly white school: The film was even shot at Lee's old school. *Morningside Rep* was critically acclaimed and won a number of awards, including two from the Black Filmmakers' Hall of Fame.

Lee returned to New York and, following in his cousin's footsteps, began to study filmmaking at the New York University Tisch School of Arts. In 1999 Lee graduated to full-length movies with his comedy *The Best Man.* Produced by Spike Lee's company 40 Acres and a Mule, Lee's film focused on a group of middle-class black American friends who gather together for a wedding. The film was a hit, reaching No. 1 at the box office in October 1999 and crossing over to appeal to mainstream audiences. It also helped establish the careers of several black actors, including Nia Long and Taye Diggs. Lee's second film, *Undercover Brother* (2002), was an adaptation of John Ridley's Web comic of the same name. It was a moderate success at the box office.

See also: Lee, Spike; Long, Nia

Further reading: http://www.imdb.com/name/nm0002700/ (IMDB entry).

LEE, Spike
Director, Filmmaker

Award-winning filmmaker Spike Lee is one of the most influential directors in Hollywood. Lee's often controversial films, including *Do the Right Thing* and *Jungle Fever*, have launched the careers of many African American stars, including Halle Berry and Samuel L. Jackson.

Early life

The eldest of four children, Shelton Jackson Lee was born in Atlanta, Georgia, on March 20, 1957, to William "Bill" Lee, a jazz composer and bassist, and Jacqueline Shelton Lee, an art teacher. Nicknamed "Spike" by his mother when he was a child, Lee moved with his family in 1959 to Brooklyn, New York, where they lived in several racially integrated areas, including Crown Heights. Lee grew up experiencing the rich diversity of New York life, since his parents made sure that all of their children were taken to galleries, museums, movies, plays, and to hear music, including the jazz that his father played at venues such as the Blue Note.

After graduating from John Dewey High School in Brooklyn, Lee went to Morehouse College in Atlanta, his father's alma mater, from which he graduated in mass communications. He developed an interest in filmmaking while there, and in 1979 began work as a summer intern for Columbia Pictures. Later that year he moved on to study at New York University's Institute of Film and Television, Tisch School of the Arts. He met the cinematographer Ernest Dickerson (1952–), with whom he collaborated on later films. Even early on in his career Lee focused on controversial issues: The 10-minute film *The Answer*, shot for his first-year project, was a response to D. W. Griffith's 1915 movie *The Birth of a Nation,* and received a mixed response.

▲ *Spike Lee has also directed music videos for Miles Davis, Public Enemy, Prince, and Stevie Wonder.*

Graduating from NYU with a masters in filmmaking in 1982, Lee wrote, produced, and directed his thesis film, *Joe's Bed-Stuy Barbershop: We Cut Heads*. Dickerson shot the movie and Lee's father composed the jazz score, the first of several collaborations between father and son. The film won the 1983 Student Academy Award for best director and it was selected by the Lincoln Center's New Directors and New Films series as their first student production. With his friend Monty Ross, Lee set up a production company called Forty Acres and a Mule Filmworks, named after the reparations promised by the government in 1865 to freed slaves.

Making movies

After unsuccessfully trying to find financing for a film called *The Messenger,* Lee decided to work on a script that could be produced on a low budget. *She's Gotta Have It* (1986), the first Forty Acres and a Mule production, was shot on a budget of $175,000 in a 12-day, one-location shoot, and was edited in Lee's apartment. An exploration of race, gender, and sexual issues, the movie focused on the romantic encounters of a beautiful black New York woman; Lee played the role of a bike messenger, Mars Blackmon. The film was critically acclaimed and won the Prix de Jeunesse for best film

KEY DATES	
1957	Born in Atlanta, Georgia, on March 20.
1982	Graduates from NYU Tisch School of Arts with an MFA.
1986	Makes *She's Gotta Have It.*
1990	*Do the Right Thing* wins an Oscar for best screenplay.
1992	Directs the controversial *Malcolm X.*
2002	Directs the critically acclaimed *25th Hour.*

INFLUENCES AND INSPIRATION

In an interview in 2002 Spike Lee said that it was important for African Americans to recognize and challenge stereotypes in films and to be able to follow their dreams. Lee was himself influenced by his jazz musician father, Bill Lee, and the filmmaker Martin Scorsese.

Lee has opened the gates for other African American filmmakers to pursue careers in Hollywood. His challenging movies, which present the lives of ordinary black people and celebrate the lives of heroes like Malcolm X, have challenged racial and other stereotypes and have helped give many young black people a pride in their race. *Malcolm X*, for example, generated interest in the activist. Lee said, "I think Malcolm's impact is still being felt today and it will be felt far into the future. He's influenced a lot of people.... I don't think there's anything more concrete than to change the way people feel about themselves. And Malcolm X made black folks feel good about themselves, not to be ashamed of being black, proud of their heritage, their culture, and you can't get more concrete than that."

by a newcomer at the Cannes Film Festival. It grossed more than $7 million in the United States alone. Lee later directed a series of commercials for Nike featuring the Blackmon character.

Lee's next films drew on his own experiences while commenting on serious issues. The conflict between light and dark-skinned blacks was highlighted in the box-office success *School Daze* (1988). Similarly, the racism that some black Americans felt toward other minority groups featured in the acclaimed but controversial movie *Do the Right Thing* (1989). Featuring actors Ossie Davis, Ruby Dee, and John Turturro, the film focuses on Brooklyn's Bedford-Stuyvesant area, which explodes when a white police officer kills a black man. Although Lee won an Oscar for the screenplay and the film received several Golden Globe nominations, it was criticized by some commentators for being overly violent and providing racist stereotypes of other minority groups. Lee argued that the film had been misunderstood. It grossed more than $28 million.

The 1990 *Mo' Better Blues*, about a jazz trumpeter, began Lee's long relationship with actor Denzel Washington. The 1991 *Jungle Fever* explored an interracial relationship between a black married architect (Wesley Snipes) and an Italian American secretary (Annabel Sciorra). It also featured memorable performances from Samuel L. Jackson and Halle Berry as crack addicts.

The making of Malcolm X

Although Norman Jewison was scheduled to direct *Malcolm X*, he withdrew from the project following Lee's criticism of the appointment of a white director to a biographical movie of such an important African American. Lee had problems with financing from the start, however. He wanted Warner Brothers to double the budget to $40

million, but they refused. Much to the company's embarrassment, Lee made the film by selling the foreign rights for about $8.5 million, taking a cut in his salary and getting donations from prominent black Americans including the talk-show host Oprah Winfrey and comedian Bill Cosby. Released in 1992, the film grossed $48 million. Denzel Washington, who played Malcolm X, received an Oscar nomination, but the film was largely overlooked by the movie community.

Later work

Lee's films produced after the mid 1990s include *Clockers* (1995), based on Richard Price's novel about the drug trade, and *Girl 6* (1996), which focused on a struggling actress who takes a job for a phone-sex line. The film met with mixed reviews. In 1997 Lee released *4 Little Girls*, about the 1963 16th-Street Church bombing in Birmingham, Alabama, which resulted in the deaths of four black girls: It won an Oscar for best documentary. The 2000 film *Bamboozled* focused on the blackface minstrel shows as entertainment, but again received mixed reviews. Lee also released the critically acclaimed movie *25th Hour*, although he was criticized for using a predominantly white cast, including Ed Norton. The author of several books on filmmaking, Lee established a scholarship to help ethnic minorities at his alma mater, the Tisch School of Arts.

See also: Berry, Halle; Cosby, Bill; Davis, Ossie; Dee, Ruby; Jackson, Samuel L.; Malcolm X; Snipes, Wesley; Washington, Denzel; Winfrey, Oprah

Further reading: Lee, Spike. *Five for Five: The Films of Spike Lee.* New York, NY: Stewart, Tabori, and Chang, 1991. http://www.imdb.com/name/nm0000490/ (IMDB entry).

LEIDESDORFF, William
Businessman

William Leidesdorff is believed to have been the first black millionaire in the United States. He was also the first African American citizen of San Francisco, California—he has a street named after him in the city.

Early life

William Alexander Leidesdorff was born on the island of St. Croix in the West Indies on March 26, 1810. He was the son of Alexander Leidesdorff, a Danish sugar planter, and Anna Maria Spark, an African woman. The couple never married but had six children: William, Frederik, Laurentius, Elisa, Adrianne, and Maria Christiane. William is believed to have been brought up by an English landowner who later sent him to live with his brother and his family in New Orleans.

Leidesdorff became involved in maritime trade, becoming a master of ships sailing between New York and New Orleans. He bought the 106-ton schooner *Julia Ann* with the purpose of trading sugar for animal hides with the Yerba Buena Mission (now part of San Francisco). Leidesdorff landed at Yerba Buena in 1841, and soon realized that the site had great potential as a trading port.

Mexico and California

In 1821 Mexico had declared its independence from Spain and the following year it took control of California. Seeing new opportunities American traders, trappers, and whalers soon began to arrive in California. In 1844 Leidesdorff befriended Emanuel Victoria, the black governor of Alta California, who granted him Mexican citizenship so that he would be able to operate his businesses in Spanish-dominated California. Leidesdorff became vice consul of

Mexico in 1845 and began to build up his fortune: The Mexican government granted him thousands of acres of land, located in what is now the city of Folsom, California, which he named the Rancho Rio de Americanos. In addition, Leidesdorff bought 41 lots in Yerba Buena and built the largest house in the city on a site that is now the Bank of America tower.

The new American settlers began to exert pressure on the U.S. government to annex California. In June 1846, unaware that the United States had gone to war with Mexico over Texas in May a group of settlers captured the Mexican presidio in Sonoma and declared California an independent republic. On February 2, 1848, the Treaty of Guadalupe Hidalgo formally concluded the Mexican–American War and California was ceded to the United States along with much of the present Southwest.

Californian prosperity

Leidesdorff became one of the most prominent citizens of California. He was also among the state's wealthiest people and was known as a shrewd and savvy entrepreneur. He established San Francisco's first hotel, the City Hotel. He also set up the first commercial steamship company in San Francisco Bay, and had the distinction of launching the first steamboat to sail on the bay. Leidesdorff enjoyed sports and organized the first professional horse races in California's history in 1847.

Early death

Leidesdorff died, at age 38, on May 18, 1848, probably from typhoid. He had never married, and after his death Joseph Libby Folsom, a captain in the Army, located Leidesdorff's mother and siblings in the Virgin Islands. In 1849, for the sum of $75,000, he purchased from them the absolute right and title to Leidesdorff's estate. The purchase made Folsom the wealthiest man in California, but also entangled him in legal disputes with Anna Spark that were not resolved until after his death.

KEY DATES	
1810	Born in St. Croix on March 26.
1841	Purchases the *Julia Ann*; sails to California.
1844	Granted Mexican citizenship.
1845	Appointed vice consul of Mexico.
1847	Organizes first horse race in San Francisco.
1848	Dies in San Francisco, California, on May 18.
1849	Captain Folsom buys the right to his estate.

Further reading: Palgon, Gary. *William Alexander Leidesdorff - First Black Millionaire, American Consul and California Pioneer.* Napa, CA: Lulu Press, 2005.
http://www.sfcvb.org/travel_media/press.asp?rid=175&cid=10 (Biography).

LEONARD, Buck
Baseball Player

A popular star of the National Negro League and one of the first African American players to be elected to the Baseball Hall of Fame, Buck Leonard is celebrated as an exceptional first baseman and all-round team player. Eastern booking agent Eddie Gottlieb said "The first baseman on a team in the Negro Leagues often played the clown.... Leonard was strictly baseball: a great glove, a hell of a hitter, and drove in runs."

Early life
Born in Rocky Mount, North Carolina, on September 8, 1907, Walter Fenner Leonard was the son of John, a railroad fireman, and Emma Leonard. Following his father's death in the influenza epidemic of 1919, Leonard was forced to leave school in order to help support his family. While Leonard shined shoes and worked in factories, in his spare time he played for his local semi-professional team, the Rocky Mount Black Swans.

Making the most of a brilliant talent
During the Great Depression of the 1930s Leonard lost his job, but he took the opportunity to pursue a professional baseball career instead. Playing for the Portsmouth Firefighters, the Baltimore Stars, and the Brooklyn Royal Giants in his first season, Leonard was spotted by Smokey Joe Williams (1886–1951), who recommended him to the Homestead Grays. Joining the team in the 1934 season and soon appointed captain, Leonard remained with the Grays until 1950, the longest tenure of any player in the history of the Negro leagues.

Respected and admired by fans and players alike, Leonard was nicknamed the black Lou Gehrig. The

▲ *The bronze plaque for Buck Leonard in the Baseball Hall of Fame.*

comparison was apt because both batters' hitting numbers were similar, although some people considered Leonard to be a superior fielder. Between 1937 and 1945 Leonard helped lead the Grays to nine consecutive victories in the Negro National League Championships. Generally batting in the high 300s, Leonard led the Negro League with an average of .391 in 1948. Selected for 11 East-West All-Star games and with a .317 batting average, by 1948 Leonard was reputedly the third highest-paid player in Negro League history.

Leonard left the Grays at the end of the 1950 season and played in the Mexican leagues until 1955. After retiring, he taught sports and was vice president of his hometown team. In 1972 Leonard was inducted into the Baseball Hall of Fame. He died in 1997.

Further reading: Leonard, Buck, and James A. Riley. *Buck Leonard, The Black Lou Gehrig.* New York, NY: Carroll & Graf Publishers, 1995.
http://www.aaregistry.com/african_american_history/1136/In_either_league_Buck_Leonard_was_great (Biography).

KEY DATES

1907 Born in Rocky Mount, North Carolina, on September 8.

1933 Begins career as professional baseball player.

1937 Helps Homestead Greys to win the first of nine consecutive Negro National League Championships.

1972 Inducted into the Baseball Hall of Fame

1997 Dies in Rocky Mount, North Carolina, on November 27.

LEONARD, Sugar Ray

Boxer, Entrepreneur

Nicknamed for Sugar Ray Robinson, "Sugar Ray" Leonard was one of the greatest middleweight boxers in sports history. A natural showman, Leonard won the media's hearts with his agility, skill, good looks, and charm. Stepping into the gap left by his hero Muhammad Ali, Leonard won 36 professional matches and many national titles. Once retired from the ring he became a successful businessman and producer and star of the popular boxing reality TV series *The Contender.*

Early life

Born in Wilmington, North Carolina, in 1956, Leonard was named Ray Charles after the famous singer by his mother, who wanted him to be a musician. Leonard was one of seven children born into a lower-middle class family. He began boxing when he was 14, intent on taking care of his large family through his favorite sport. As an amateur he won 145 of 150 bouts and was awarded Golden Glove championships in 1973 and 1974, Amateur Athletic Union championships in 1974 and 1975, a gold medal in the 1975 Pan-American Games, and the Olympic gold medal in 1976.

Turning professional

Leonard turned professional on February 5, 1977. His first fight was against Luis Vegas, whom he beat in a sixth-round decision in Las Vegas, Nevada.

Leonard's victory over Vegas led him to fight and beat Pete Ranzany in the North American Boxing Federation Welterweight Championship in Las Vegas on August 12, 1979. On November 30 of that same year, Leonard won the World Boxing Council (WBC) world welterweight title when he knocked out Hall of Famer Wilfred Benitez in the 15th round, again in Las Vegas. By this time, Leonard had become the most known and admired boxer in his weight and division in the world.

On June 20, 1980, however, Leonard suffered his first defeat and lost his championship title to Roberto Duran in a 15th-round decision in Montreal, Canada, only to regain it on November 25, 1980, in an exciting rematch that took

▼ *Sugar Ray Leonard defeated Marvin Hagler in a World Middleweight title fight held in Las Vegas, Nevada, on April 6, 1987.*

INFLUENCES AND INSPIRATION

Like many sports figures in the United States, Sugar Ray Leonard has been a role model for deprived inner-city black youth. Known to millions of viewers through the reality-TV boxing series *The Contender,* Ray, along with cohost actor Sylvester Stallone, gave young boxers the chance to achieve their dreams.

Leonard himself was inspired by boxing legend Muhammad Ali, and followed his style so closely that ABC journalist Howard Cosell called him the newer, lighter Ali.

Leonard experienced the problems of drug addiction in the mid–1980s but managed to kick the habit in 1989. He is now among the most outspoken

voices in sports against youth drug abuse and violence. In 1997 Leonard set up a youth foundation to educate children about the danger of drug abuse. He also campaigns for D.A.R.E. America whose antidrug and antiviolence campaign is estimated to reach 36 million children around the world.

place in New Orleans, Louisiana. During the course of the fight Duran turned around, walked to his corner, and gave up the fight with 17 seconds to go in the eighth-round, uttering the now famous Spanish words "No más" (no more). When puzzled referee Octavio Meyran asked Duran whether he meant what he had just said, Duran repeated "No más, no más."

Leonard's streak of victories continued: On June 25, 1981, he knocked Ayub Kalule out in the ninth-round in Houston, Texas. The victory earned him the world junior middleweight title. He went on to beat Thomas Hearns in the 14th round in late 1981, earning the unified world Welterweight Championship

Retirement announcements

The retina of Leonard's left eye had been injured during the fight, however, which forced him to announce in a press conference that he would retire in 1982. But after undergoing an eye operation at Johns Hopkins Hospital in July of that year, Leonard announced that he would resume fighting in 1984.

On April 7, 1987, Leonard became the WBC's middleweight champion, after beating Marvin Hagler in Las Vegas on a split decision; the fight earned him $11 million. Suffering again from a detached retina, Leonard again announced his retirement, even though most observers did not believe him.

In November 1988 Leonard returned to the ring and won the WBC Light Heavyweight and Super Middleweight titles after knocking out Canadian-born Don Lalonde, the then WBC light heavyweight champion, in the ninth round.

Leonard was eventually defeated in 1991 by WBC super welterweight champion Terry Norris at Madison Square Garden in New York City, which prompted him to once again announce his retirement. He attempted to return to the limelight but Hector Camacho, too fast and

too powerful for him, forced Ray to retire permanently after a fifth-round knockout in Atlantic City, New Jersey, on March 1, 1997. By the end of his professional career Leonard had won 36 fights—25 by knockout—lost 3 and drawn 1. In 1997 he was inducted to the International Boxing Hall of Fame.

Following his retirement, Leonard worked as a sports broadcaster for NBC, ABC, HBO, and ESPN, and appeared in several commercials for companies such as Ford and Nabisco. He founded the Sugar Ray Leonard Youth Foundation, which educates children about the danger of drug abuse, gangs, and violence, and is a spokesperson for D.A.R.E. America (*see box*).

KEY DATES

1956   Born in Rocky Mount, North Carolina, on May 17.

1976   Wins welterweight boxing gold medal in Olympic Games; fights first professional match a year later, beating Luis Vegas.

1979   Beats Wilfred Benitez and wins WBC world welterweight title.

1982   Retires owing to injury to the retina.

1984   Resumes fighting.

1988   Wins WBC Light Heavyweight and Super Middleweight titles; retires again.

1997   Comes back; but is beaten by Hector Camacho; retires from the ring; founds a youth foundation.

See also: Ali, Muhammad; Hagler, Marvin

Further reading: Haskin, Jim. *Sugar Ray Leonard.* London, England: Robson Books, 1998.
http://www.ibhof.com/srleon.htm (Article on Leonard's career).

LEWIS, Bill
Football Player, Lawyer

A star football player in his college days and the first African American to be selected to an All-American team, Bill Lewis went on to become a successful lawyer and the first black assistant attorney general.

Early life
Born in Berkley, Norfolk County, Virginia, in 1868, William "Bill" Henry Lewis was the son of former slaves. Lewis worked to raise his own college fund, first studying at the Virginia Normal Institute and then continuing his education at Amherst College, Massachusetts. Lewis consistently excelled both academically and in sports.

Football prowess
At Amherst Lewis was a starting center on the football team, which he captained in 1890 and 1891. Lewis met his future wife, Elizabeth Baker, at his graduation.

After his graduation from Amherst, Lewis enrolled at Harvard Law School. There he played football so successfully that in 1892 he became the first African American player to be selected to Walter Camp's All-American team. Camp (1859–1925) was a famous football coach who is known as the "Father of Football." He elected the first All-American team in 1889.

Lewis achieved another record in November 1893, when he became Harvard's first African American captain and led his team to victory in his first game. He was again chosen as an All-American for the 1893 season. In 1903 he wrote an essay on defense for Camp's football manual *How to Play Football*.

Law and politics
While Lewis was at Harvard a white barber in Cambridge refused to cut his hair. As a result he and fellow African American Butler R. Wilson (1860–1939), who graduated from Boston University School of Law in 1893, persuaded the Massachusetts legislature to broaden the state's antidiscrimination statute to include barbershops and other places of public accommodation.

Butler went on to have a successful legal career, starting out as an apprentice to a judge and ending as Master in Chancery. He was a cofounder of the Boston branch of the National Association for the Advancement of Colored People (NAACP) in 1912 and one of the first African Americans admitted to the American Bar Association.

On graduating from Harvard in 1895, Lewis practiced law for a Boston firm and also became involved in local politics. He was elected to the Cambridge Common Council, serving three years. In 1903 President Theodore Roosevelt (1858–1919) appointed Lewis assistant district attorney of Boston. Lewis soon became recognized for his commitment to the judicial system. In 1911 he became the first African American to be appointed to a sub-cabinet position when President William Howard Taft (1857–1930) made him assistant attorney general.

In 1912 Lewis was admitted to the American Bar Association. He remained committed to fighting racial discrimination and was respected for his work defending difficult corruption and bootlegging cases. Although Taft recommended him for an appointment to the Massachusetts Superior Court in 1913, Democratic Governor Eugene N. Foss did not appoint him.

A delegate to the Republican National Convention in 1920, Lewis was involved in Republican politics throughout the 1920s. He died of heart failure in Boston, Massachusetts, in 1949, six years after his wife.

KEY DATES

1868 Born in Berkley, Norfolk County, Virginia, on November 28.

1892 Becomes first African American All-American football player.

1893 Becomes first African American captain of Harvard football team.

1895 Graduates from Harvard Law School.

1903 Appointed as assistant district attorney of Boston.

1911 Appointed assistant attorney general.

1949 Dies in Boston, Massachusetts, on January 1.

Further reading: Low, W. Augustus, and Virgil A. Clift. *Encyclopedia of Black America.* New York, NY: Da Capo Press, 1984.
http://www.aaregistry.com/african_american_history/606/William_Lewis_displayed_physical_and_mental_gifts (Biography).
http://www.hickoksports.com/biograph/lewisbill.shtml (Short sports biography).

LEWIS, Carl
Athlete

In 1984 Carl Lewis became the first athlete since Jesse Owens in 1936 to win four gold medals at a single Olympics. In a career that spanned four Olympics, Lewis won nine gold medals in four different events. Away from the track he became an outspoken critic of drug abuse in athletics (*see box on p.118*)

Early life
Frederick Carlton "Carl" Lewis was born on July 1, 1961. Raised in Willingboro, New Jersey, he attended public schools. He was a relatively late developer as an athlete, and few people spotted him as a potential star of the future until he reached the 10th grade, when he clocked a time of 10.6 seconds in the 100 meters and made a leap of 23 feet 9 inches (7.23m) in the long jump.

Making a mark in sports
After graduating from high school in 1979, Lewis went to the University of Houston. Although he was selected for the Olympic team in 1980, the United States boycotted the games in Moscow and Lewis's Olympic debut was delayed by four years. Lewis went on to win the National Collegiate Athletic Association's (NCAA) long jump championship in 1980 and the NCAA and national outdoor 100-meter and long-jump titles in 1981.

After graduating Lewis moved to California, where he joined the Santa Monica Track Club. A year later he won the national 100-meter and long-jump championships. In 1983, after winning the 100- and 200-meter dashes and the long jump at the U.S. nationals—the first time since 1886 that a single athlete had won all three—Lewis triumphed in the 110-meter hurdles, the long jump, and the relay at the inaugural IAAF World Championships.

These achievements, great as they were, were eclipsed by Lewis's performance at the 1984 Olympics in Los Angeles, California, where he won gold medals in the same four events as the legendary Jesse Owens in the 1930s: the

▼ *At the 1984 Olympic Games, held in Los Angeles, Lewis (nearest camera) won the 100 meters.*

INFLUENCES AND INSPIRATION

The greatest formative influence on Carl Lewis was undoubtedly Bob Beamon, whose world record-breaking long jump at the 1968 Olympics in Mexico City the seven-year-old Lewis watched on television. Throughout Lewis's career, Beamon's was the achievement that he most wanted to surpass—but it was not to be.

Despite his unparalleled success, Lewis never really won the hearts of the American public, and as a result he failed to secure the massive endorsement and sponsorship deals that enriched most contemporary stars of similar stature in other sports.

Lewis did little to court affection, and when he first began to complain about drug abuse in field sports there was little or no evidence to support his claims. His accusations seemed like sour grapes to many sports fans. When Canadian Ben Johnson was stripped of his 1988 Olympic gold medal after he tested positive for drugs, Lewis was proved right; he was, however, perceived by some people as sanctimonious. Lewis nevertheless remained a shining—if not always entirely likeable—example of what could be achieved in sports without cheating.

100 meters, the 200 meters, the long jump, and the 4 x 100-meter relay. In the final of the first of his races, Lewis reached a top speed of 28 mph (45 km/h) and at the finish was 8 feet (2.43m) ahead of the runner-up, the largest winning margin in the history of the Olympic event. In just three years Lewis, who was now 6 feet 2 inches (1.88m) tall and weighed 175 pounds (79.3kg), had risen from obscurity to become the world's premier athlete. He missed most of the 1985 season owing to injury, but announced his return to fitness with another triple triumph at the national championships in 1986.

Lewis retained his long-jump title at the 1987 World Championships. In the 100 meters, however, despite equaling the existing world record, he was beaten into second place by Ben Johnson of Canada, who broke the tape in 9.83, a full second ahead of Lewis (*see box*). Both men were clocked at the same top speed—26.32 mph (42.35 km/h)—but the gap had been opened up over the first 10 meters: At the time most commentators put that down to Lewis's notoriously poor starting and Johnson's speed off the blocks, but the real explanation turned out to be far different.

At the 1988 Olympics in Seoul, South Korea, Johnson finished first in the 100 meters, finishing in 9.79 seconds, a meter ahead of Lewis. Shortly afterward, however, the Canadian was disqualified when he tested positive for steroids. Lewis was awarded the gold medal, and his time of 9.93 seconds set a new legitimate world record.

In the wake of the Johnson scandal, Lewis withdrew from the 1989 national championships to protest what he regarded as the failure of the Athletics Congress to combat drug abuse. Aged 28 and realizing that his sprinting days were numbered, Lewis decided to concentrate on the long jump and try to crown his amazing career by beating his hero Bob Beamon's world record of 29 feet 2½ inches (8.90m), which had stood since 1968. The achievement eluded him: The most famous leap in history was finally surpassed by the previously unknown Mike Powell at the World Championships in Tokyo, Japan, in August 1991.

At the 1992 Olympics in Barcelona Lewis failed to qualify for the 100 meters but won gold in the long jump. Although not scheduled for the 4 x 100-meter relay, he was called in as a late replacement for injured anchorman Mark Witherspoon: The team victory brought Lewis his eighth Olympic gold medal. He won his final gold in the long jump at the 1996 Olympics in Atlanta, Georgia, his fourth consecutive win in the event.

KEY DATES

1961	Born in Birmingham, Alabama, on July 1.
1979	Enrolls at the University of Houston, Texas.
1981	Joins Santa Monica Track Club.
1983	Wins three titles at World Championships.
1984	Wins four gold medals at Los Angeles Olympics.
1988	Wins two gold medals at Seoul Olympics.
1992	Wins two gold medals at Barcelona Olympics.
1996	Wins ninth Olympic gold at Atlanta.

See also: Beamon, Bob; Owens, Jesse

Further reading: Aaseng, Nathan. *Carl Lewis: Legend Chaser.* Minneapolis, MN: Lerner Publications Co., 1985.
www.carllewis.com (Site focused on Lewis).

LEWIS, David Levering
Historian

One of the United States's leading historians, David Levering Lewis is best known for his biography of the early civil rights campaigner and educator William Edward Burghardt (W. E. B.) DuBois. For each of the two volumes of this work, published in 1993 and 2000, Lewis was awarded the Pulitzer Prize for biography. He was the first and only African American to receive the award twice.

In his wide-ranging historical work, Lewis has often used biography as a way of exploring and understanding significant historical moments. Another of his most famous works was a biography of Martin Luther King, Jr. Lewis is currently Julius Silver University Professor and professor of history at New York University.

A wide-ranging education

Lewis was born in Little Rock, Arkansas, in 1936. His father was a college president and his mother a teacher. During his childhood the family moved around a lot, and Lewis graduated from high school in Atlanta, Georgia. Under an early-entrance program, he began to study history at the historically black college Fisk University in Tennessee. He graduated Phi Beta Kappa at age 19 in 1956.

After a brief period of study at law school Lewis chose to change direction and gained an MA in history at Columbia University, New York City, in 1959. He continued his studies in the United Kingdom at the London School of Economics and Political Science, where he was awarded his PhD in 1962.

Lewis began a career as a university teacher at the University of Ghana, West Africa, before taking up successive positions at Howard University, Washington, D.C.; Cornell University, New York; Notre Dame, Indiana; Harvard, Massachusetts; the University of California, San Diego; and Rutgers, New Jersey.

Understanding the past

Initially Lewis's research and teaching focus was on modern France, but he increasingly turned his attention to the history of African Americans. In 1970 he published an acclaimed biography of Martin Luther King, Jr. (revised in 1978). It was published only two years after the assassination of the civil rights leader and it represented the first time that King's legacy and achievements had been fully analyzed. Lewis later published a study of the racial politics of the 1920s and 1930s in *When*

KEY DATES	
1936	Born in Little Rock, Arkansas, on May 25.
1955	Graduates from Fisk University.
1962	Gains a PhD at the London School of Economics and Political Science.
1970	Publishes biography of Martin Luther King, Jr.
1993	Publishes *W.E.B. DuBois: Biography of a Race, 1868–1919.*
2000	Publishes *W.E.B. DuBois: The Fight for Equality and the American Century, 1919–1963.*
2001	Wins second Pulitzer Prize.

Harlem Was in Vogue (published in 1980 and revised in 1994). The period covered by the book is called the Harlem Renaissance, the New York-based rebirth of African American art and culture that occurred around that time.

Prize-winning work

Lewis won national fame, however, with his Pulitzer Prize-winning two-volume biography of DuBois. DuBois was an African American social reformer who helped set up the National Association for the Advancement of Colored People (NAACP). DuBois was an inspiration for many of the 20th century's civil rights activists, and Lewis was praised for his meticulous research and the complex, in-depth picture he provided of the early struggle for civil rights.

Lewis's work has won him many awards. In addition to his two Pulitzers, he is holder of the Frances Parkman Prize in History and the Bancroft Prize in American History and Diplomacy. In 1999 he received a five-year MacArthur Foundation Fellowship and in 2004 a John Hope Franklin Distinguished Contributor to Higher Education award.

See also: DuBois, W. E. B.; King, Martin Luther, Jr.

Further reading: Lewis, David Levering. *W. E. B. DuBois*: New York, NY: Henry Holt and Co, 1993 and 2000.
http://www.pbs.org/newshour/conversation/jan-june01/lewis_01-24.html (PBS interview).
http://www.thehistorymakers.com/biography/biography.asp?bioindex=1020&category=educationMakers (Biography).

LEWIS, Edmonia
Sculptor

Edmonia Lewis was the first African American artist to receive national and international recognition. Her marble sculptures, made in the neoclassical style, brought her success in Europe and the United States. She spent her working life in Rome, Italy, a city with a rich artistic heritage and a vibrant community of expatriate American artists. Although Lewis produced more than 60 sculptures during her life, fewer than half of them have been located.

Early life

Little precise biographical information survives about the early or late years of Lewis's life. Believed to have been born near Albany, New York, in 1844 or 1845, Lewis was the daughter of an African American father and a mother of mixed African American and Ojibwa (Chippewa) descent.

Orphaned at an early age, Lewis and her brother Samuel, also known as "Sunrise," lived with her mother's Ojibwa relatives: Lewis adopted the name "Wildfire." When she was about 12 she was sent by her brother to study at New York Central School in McGrawville, New York. In 1859 she entered Oberlin College, Ohio, one of the first colleges to admit women and African Americans, changing her name to Mary Edmonia.

An extraordinary life

In 1862 Lewis was accused of attempting to poison two of her white classmates. The accusation brought to a head the antiblack feeling prevalent in Ohio at the time, and a mob of vigilantes beat Lewis almost to death. The African American lawyer John Mercer Langston defended Lewis and she was subsequently acquitted of the crime. She moved to Boston, Massachusetts. Through the abolitionist William Lloyd Garrison (1805–1879), Lewis met and studied under portrait sculptor Edmund Brackett (1818–1908).

In 1864 Lewis opened her own sculpture studio in the city; she made a series of clay and plaster medallions of famous abolitionists such as Garrison and John Brown (1800–1859). She also created a bust of Colonel Robert Gould Shaw (1837–1863), a white officer from a wealthy Boston family who led the all-black 54th Massachusetts Regiment in the assault on Fort Wagner, South Carolina, during the Civil War (1861–1865). Lewis was able to move to Italy with the proceeds from the sale of the bust in 1865.

Critical acclaim

Two years later Lewis settled in Rome, Italy, becoming part of an American expatriate circle of artists and writers, including Henry James (1843–1916), and Harriet Beecher Stowe (1811–1896). She became part of a group of women sculptors led by the neoclassical artist Harriet Hosmer (1830–1908). Lewis studied ancient and Renaissance sculpture and also learned marble carving. She sculpted African American heroes and produced works inspired by the Emancipation Proclamation, including *Forever Free* (1867). Lewis also sculpted Native American subjects, such as *The Marriage of Hiawatha* (about 1868) and *The Old Arrow Maker and His Daughter* (1872), as well as religious subjects and more playful pieces such as cupids.

One of Lewis's most acclaimed pieces, the *Death of Cleopatra* (1876), was exhibited at the Philadelphia Centennial Exposition. Described by some critics as the most remarkable piece of sculpture in the American section of the exhibition, it showed Cleopatra dying or dead. The sculpture drew huge crowds and helped established Lewis's reputation as an artist in the United States. Although lost for many years, it was restored by the Smithsonian's National Museum of American Art (NMAA) in the mid-1990s. Little is known about Lewis after the mid-1880s: The last reference to her is in 1909, when she was still living in Rome.

Further reading: Patton, Sharon F. *African American Art.* New York, NY: Oxford University Press, 1998.
http://www.pbs.org/newshour/bb/entertainment/edmonia_8-5.html (PBS feature on Lewis).

KEY DATES

1844   Born near Albany, New York, at about this time.

1864   Opens her own sculpture studio in Boston, Massachusetts.

1866   Settles in Rome, Italy.

1876   Exhibits sculpture *Death of Cleopatra* to critical acclaim at the Philadelphia Centennial Exposition.

1909   Last recorded mention of Lewis is in Rome; she is believed to have died in the next few years.

LEWIS, Reginald F.
Entrepreneur

One of the most successful U.S. entrepreneurs of the 20th century, Reginald F. Lewis became chairman of TLC Beatrice International—the only black-owned company to have ever broken the billion-dollar mark in annual revenues. Lewis gave much of his wealth to social projects throughout his career. After his death the Reginald F. Lewis Foundation continued to support numerous organizations and charities, many of them active in the African American community.

KEY DATES	
1942	Born in East Baltimore, Maryland, on December 7.
1983	Buys McCall Pattern Company for $22.5 million.
1987	Sells McCall Pattern Company for $90 million; then buys Beatrice International for $985 million.
1992	TLC Beatrice International makes sales of $1.6 billion; Lewis gives $3 million to Harvard Law School.
1993	Dies in New York on January 19.

Born businessman

Lewis was born in 1942 in East Baltimore, Maryland. He began his career at age 10, when he started delivering an African American newspaper around the neighborhood. He kept his earnings in a tin can and later sold the business at a profit.

Lewis went to high school in Dunbar, West Virginia, where he did well both in the classroom and on the sports field. He was quarterback on the football team, a shortstop on the baseball team, and a forward on the basketball team. He was captain of all three teams.

Lewis's excellence as a football player won him a scholarship to Virginia State University near Richmond in 1961. However, he was soon injured, lost his scholarship, and had to work his way through college. Nevertheless Lewis graduated on the dean's list with a major in economics in 1965.

Lewis went on to study at Harvard Law School. In his third year at Harvard, Lewis found his calling after taking a course in securities law. He wrote his third-year paper on takeovers; it would be his takeovers in the 1980s that would make his name and fortune.

City lawyer

After finishing law school in 1968, Lewis found work as a corporate lawyer in New York City. Just two years later he set up his own law firm. As a lawyer Lewis was involved in many high-profile corporate takeover bids, and he came to enjoy the high-stress and high-reward lifestyle of Wall Street.

In 1983 Lewis founded TLC Group L.P., a venture-capital company (a company that buys and sells other companies). In the same year he bought the struggling McCall Pattern Company, nursed it back to health, and sold it four years later, making a $42.5-million profit.

In 1987 Lewis bought the global giant Beatrice International Foods for $985 million—a remarkable buyout even by the standards of the 1980s, a decade renowned for its flamboyant deals. Renamed TLC Beatrice International, the company flourished. In 1992 its sales topped $1.6 billion and the company reached No. 512 on *Fortune* magazine's list of the world's 1,000 largest companies. Lewis himself was regularly listed as one of the United States's wealthiest individuals.

The generous philanthropist

Lewis gave his money away generously. In 1988 he gave $1 million to the historically black Howard University, Washington, D.C. In 1992 he gave $3 million to Harvard Law School, the largest single donation the school had ever received. In January 1993 Lewis died suddenly of a brain tumor. His half-brother, former Dallas Cowboys and Washington Redskins football player Jean Fugett (1951–), took over the chairmanship of TLC Beatrice.

After Lewis's death, the Reginald F. Lewis Foundation continued to make lavish endowments. In 1999 the NAACP founded the Reginald F. Lewis Youth Entrepreneurial Institute to help young black people set up their own businesses, and in 2005 the Reginald F. Lewis Museum of Maryland African American History and Culture opened its doors in Baltimore.

Further reading: Lewis, Reginald F., and Blair S. Walker. *Why Should White Guys Have All the Fun?: How Reginald Lewis Created a Billion-Dollar Business Empire.* Hoboken, NJ: John Wiley & Sons Inc., 1994.
http://www.africanamericanculture.org/museum_reglewis.html (Biography and links to Reginald F. Museum, Maryland).

LIL Jon
Singer, Rapper, Producer

Rap performer and record producer Lil Jon is best known for his band Lil Jon and the East Side Boyz, formed with fellow Georgians Lil Bo and Big Sam. They proclaimed themselves the kings of "crunk," a form of hip-hop that arose in the southern states, notably Atlanta, Georgia. Crunk featured repetitive loud chants and drum-machine rhythms. The early 2000s in particular saw Lil Jon rise from regional success to hit collaborations with such artists as Ludacris, Ice Cube, and Usher.

Rising star
Born Jonathan Smith in Atlanta, Georgia, in 1970 Lil Jon attended Atlanta's Frederick Douglass High School, from which he graduated in 1988. As a teen Jon was an enthusiastic skateboarder and listened mainly to punk bands such as the Ramones, the Dead Kennedys, and the Sex Pistols.

On leaving school Lil Jon began work as a DJ in clubs around the South and eventually met with Jermaine Dupri of So So Def Records. Dupri was so impressed by the young DJ that he invited him to come and work for the record label. Eventually named executive vice president of A&R (Artists and Repertoire) at So So Def, Lil Jon also hosted a radio show at Atlanta's V103 during this period, and began producing records for Atlanta artists Usher, Too Short, and Xscape.

King of Crunk
In 1996 Lil Jon teamed up with Big Sam and Lil Bo to become the East Side Boyz, and introduced the nation to the southern term "crunk," derived from "crazy" plus "drunk," with the debut album *Get Crunk, Who You Wit: Da Album* (1997). Despite scoring a hit with the club anthem "Who You Wit?," the next five years saw Lil Jon and his group confined to mainly regional success. The East Side

▲ *Lil Jon's album* **Crunk Juice** *features contributions from Usher, Ice Cube, and comedian Chris Rock.*

Boyz's big break came when "Bia', Bia'" from the album *Put Yo Hood Up* (2001) became a huge national hit. The following year the group released the breakthrough album *Kings of Crunk* (2002), which remained on the charts for two years. The second single, "Get Low" (2004), featuring the Ying Yang Twins, became an international hit.

At last in demand as both an artist and producer, Lil Jon had huge success in 2004: He featured on Usher's international hit "Yeah," won a Source Award for Producer of the Year, and released a double album, *Crunk Juice.*

See also: Ice Cube; Rock, Chris; Usher

Further reading: http://www.liljononline.com/ (Official site).

KEY DATES	
1970	Born in Atlanta, Georgia.
1993	Works for So So Def Records until 2000.
1996	Links up with Big Sam and Lil Bo to form the East Side Boyz.
2002	Releases breakthrough album, *Kings of Crunk.*

LILES, Kevin
Musician, Record Company Executive

Musician and record-company executive Kevin Liles is one of the most powerful men in the entertainment industry. As vice president of the Def Jam Island Group, Liles has helped forge the careers of such stars as Jay-Z and Ja Rule.

Achieving a dream

Born in Baltimore, Maryland, on January 14, 1968, Liles was the son of a railroad conductor and an accountant for an insurance company; his upbringing was quite comfortable. Liles attended Woodlawn High, from which he graduated in 1986. He later said that the school "helped provide me with a good education and great memories."

Liles showed an early interest in music. Rap and hip-hop were becoming more popular in Baltimore, and as a teen Liles joined a 10-turntable mixing crew, performing at local clubs. Although he went on to college to study engineering, his interest in music never left him and he

▼ *Despite his support of Def Jam's gangsta image Liles insisted that the company and staff should be as professional as any other type of business.*

KEY DATES

1968 Born in Baltimore, Maryland, on January 14.

2002 Appointed vice president of the Island Def Jam Music Group.

2004 Becomes executive vice president of the Warner Music Group.

dropped out of college just before graduation. He formed Numarx, a rap group, with some friends, writing and recording such songs as "Girl You Know It's True." Chrysalis later rerecorded the song with the manufactured band Milli Vanilli to great success.

An influential man

In 1991 Liles set up MBR (Marx Brothers Records), primarily so that he could have more control over his music and business dealings. In 1992 he began work as an intern at Russell Simmons's hugely successful record company Def Jam. He impressed the management with his hard work and dedication to both the music and artists and rose quickly to become Mid-Atlantic manager, and promotions general manager for the West Coast in 1994, general manager and vice president of promotions in 1996, and finally president in 1998.

Liles's business acumen and reputation helped Def Jam to grow: Through careful branding deals and expansion into new areas such as games and clothing, the company revenues increased from $200 to $400 million during Liles's presidency. In 2002 Liles was appointed executive vice president of the Def Jam Music Group. Two years later, Liles decided to move on to become executive vice president of the Warner Music Group.

A generous supporter of charities, in 2002 Liles donated $150,000 to help complete the stadium of Woodlawn High School. The school's principal, Anthony Thompson, said that Liles was an inspiration to every student. Liles was also central to the Rock the Vote campaign to promote voting among young Americans.

See also: Jay-Z; Simmons, Russell

Further reading: http://music.ign.com/articles/517/517050p1.html (Biography).

LISTON, Sonny
Boxer

Charles "Sonny" Liston was one of the most feared heavyweights of his era. He is best remembered for his two world heavyweight title fights against Muhammad Ali, both of which ended in controversy.

Early life
Much of Liston's early life is shrouded in mystery. The date most often given for his birth is May 8, 1932, although many boxing historians believe that he was born considerably earlier, possibly in 1917. Liston grew up in Arkansas with his father, a tenant farmer, but ran away as a teenager to St. Louis, Missouri. In St. Louis the teenage Liston fell into a life of crime, and in 1950 he was jailed for robbery. While in prison he learned to box. On his release in October 1952 Liston embarked on an amateur career.

An immediate success
Liston did not wait long to turn professional. His first professional fight was a knockout win over Don Smith on September 2, 1953. Through the 1950s Liston put together a string of victories, many by knockout. He was eventually rewarded with an attempt at the world heavyweight title against Floyd Patterson on September 25, 1962. The fight was short and brutal: Liston knocked out the champion in just two minutes and five seconds in the first round. A rematch held the following year lasted just four seconds longer, with Liston again the victor.

Liston's next defense was against a young boxer named Cassius Clay. At the time Liston was regarded as unstoppable, and few observers gave Clay a chance of beating him. However, when the pair fought on February 25, 1964, Liston showed none of his usual ferocity and quit on his stool at the end of the sixth round, apparently because of a dislocated shoulder. By the time of the rematch the following year, Clay had changed his name

▲ *Sonny Liston before his 1964 match with Cassius Clay (later Muhammad Ali).*

to Muhammad Ali. Liston lost once again, this time to a first-round knockout. However, television cameras could not detect the knockout blow, which became known as the "phantom punch."

Because of Liston's ties to the mafia—he was effectively managed by a known gangster called Blinky Palermo—rumors spread that he had thrown either one or both fights. Nothing was ever proved, but Liston never fought for a world title again, although he continued to box for another six years. From 1953 to 1970 Liston had 54 fights, winning 39 by knockouts and losing only 4.

On January 5, 1971, Liston's body was discovered in his Las Vegas home. The police declared that the cause of death was a drug overdose, but many people believe that Liston was murdered by the mob.

See also: Ali, Muhammad; Patterson, Floyd

Further reading: Tosches, Nick. *The Devil and Sonny Liston.* Boston, MA: Little, Brown, and Company, 2000. http://www.aussiebox.com.au/ace/sonny.html (Article on Liston with links).

KEY DATES

1932	Born in St. Francis County, Arkansas, on May 8.
1962	Beats Floyd Patterson on September 25 to become world heavyweight champion.
1964	Loses heavyweight title to Cassius Clay on February 25.
1970	Dies in Las Vegas, Nevada, on about December 30.

LITTLE RICHARD
Musician

One of the most successful and flamboyant artists of the rock-'n'-roll era, Little Richard merged gospel with rhythm and blues (R&B) to create a unique sound that had a major influence on other rock-'n'-roll musicians.

Richard Wayne Penniman was born into a family of 12 children in Macon, Georgia, in 1932. He was brought up in a strongly religious environment—both his father and his grandfather were preachers. As a child Penniman sang with the family gospel group the Penniman Singers, and the music he performed heavily influenced his later vocal style.

Penniman ran away from home when he was still in his early teens, after his admission that he was gay led to conflicts with his parents. He went on to perform in traveling shows, where he adopted the stage name Little Richard. In 1951 Little Richard won a talent contest in Atlanta that led to a recording contract with RCA Victor; but the singles he produced were disappointing and met with little commercial success.

By 1955 Little Richard had returned to Macon and worked as a dishwasher in a local restaurant. He saved enough money to record a demo tape and sent it to Specialty Records. While Specialty owner Art Rupe was not overly impressed with the songs, he brought Little Richard in for a recording session. The initial results were not promising. However, during a break Little Richard and producer "Bumps" Blackwell went to a local bar, where Little Richard started playing a wild song on the piano. Blackwell recognized its potential and the pair returned to the studio to record "Tutti Frutti."

A string of hits

"Tutti Frutti" was released in February 1956 and reached No. 17 on the charts, selling over three million copies. It was just the first of a string of hits for Little Richard that year, including "Long Tall Sally," "Slippin' and Slidin' (Peepin' and Hidin')," and "Rip it Up."

Little Richard had became a national star. A key part of his appeal was his extraordinary voice, which peppered his songs with falsetto shrieks and wild hollers. An equally

▼ *Little Richard performs at a nostalgia rock-'n'-roll concert in 1995.*

Arguably the biggest influence on Little Richard's career was the R&B singer Billy Wright (1932–1991), also born in Georgia. In 1949 Wright released his first single, "Blues for My Baby," for the Savoy label. A number of other R&B hits followed in the late 1940s and early 1950s, including "Back Biting Woman," "Stacked Deck," and "Hey Little Girl." By this time Wright had befriended Little Richard, who was impressed by the wild vocal style and appearance of the "Prince of the Blues." Wright wore flamboyant clothes, his hair was slicked back in a giant pompadour, and he used makeup on stage. Little Richard borrowed all these attributes, which would become indelibly associated with his act. But while Little Richard became an international superstar, Wright never achieved mainstream success; his musical career petered out in the mid-1950s, although he continued to work as a master of ceremonies in Atlanta nightclubs for a number of years.

important part of his success was his outrageous appearance. A flamboyant dresser, he wore mascara on stage and sported an exaggerated pompadour hairstyle; his effeminate look hinted at his homosexuality.

Little Richard's chart successes continued in 1957 with singles such as "Jenny, Jenny" and "Keep a Knockin" making the Top 10. His profile was increased by his appearances in a number of rock-'n'-roll movies, including *Don't Knock the Rock* (1956), *The Girl Can't Help It* (1957), and *Mr. Rock 'n' Roll* (1957).

A change of direction

When Little Richard was at the height of his fame his career came to an abrupt, self-imposed halt. In October 1957 he began a tour of Australia with fellow rock-'n'-roll stars Gene Vincent and Eddie Cochran. While on board an airplane, Little Richard had a sudden vision of an impending apocalypse. He immediately pledged to give up rock 'n' roll and devote himself to God. He quit the tour and returned to the United States, planning to become a preacher.

Little Richard's contract with Specialty meant that he had to record one more session for the label before turning his back on rock 'n' roll. Once the session was over he enrolled at Oakwood College in Huntsville, Alabama, where he studied to become a Seventh Day Adventist minister. While Little Richard was attending bible college, Specialty released a succession of singles, including "Good Golly, Miss Molly," which reached the Top 10 in 1958.

For the next five years Little Richard dedicated himself to the church but combined preaching with the performance and recording of gospel music.

Eventually, however, Little Richard returned to his rock-'n'-roll roots. In 1962 he crossed the Atlantic to tour the United Kingdom. A second UK tour the following year saw him appearing on the same bill as the Beatles. The British

KEY DATES

1932	Born in Macon, Georgia, on December 5.
1956	"Tutti Frutti" becomes Richard's first hit record; it goes on to sell three million copies.
1957	Abandons rock-'n'-roll career in the middle of an Australian tour.
1962	Begins performing rock 'n' roll again.
1986	Inducted into the Rock and Roll Hall of Fame.

group were big fans of Little Richard and many other British early 1960s groups recorded covers of Little Richard's songs. The exposure reinvigorated his career and in 1964 he had a minor hit with "Bama Lama Bama Loo."

Fading career

After the mid-1960s Little Richard's career began to wane. He continued to release new material, such as the 1970s albums *The Rill Thing* and *King of Rock 'n' Roll*, but met with little commercial and critical success. However, the strength of his output in the mid-1950s ensured that he was always able to pull crowds at nostalgia shows.

In 1986 Little Richard appeared in *Down and Out in Beverly Hills* and a single from the movie, "Great Gosh a Mighty," reached No. 42 on the charts. He was inducted into the Rock and Roll Hall of Fame the same year. Little Richard continued to make occasional cameo appearances on television and in movies into the 21st century.

Further reading: White, Charles. *The Life and Times of Little Richard: The Quasar of Rock.* New York, NY: Da Capo, 1994. http://www.allmusic.com/cg/amg.dll?p=amg&sql=11: l2jm7i5jg71r (Biography). http://www.kolumbus.fi/timrei/lre.htm (Fan site).

LLEWELLYN, J. Bruce
Lawyer, Businessman

Businessman J. Bruce Llewellyn is among the wealthiest and most successful African Americans in the nation. In 2005 his Coca-Cola bottling plant in Philadelphia, Pennsylvania, was the fifth-most profitable in the United States and the fourth-largest black-owned U.S. business; He also owned a cable and broadcasting corporation, Queen City Broadcasting, Inc., and *Essence* magazine.

Early life

The son of Jamaican parents, Llewellyn was born in Harlem, New York, in 1927. His father was a newspaper printer and pushed the young Llewellyn hard. After graduating from high school, Llewellyn attended City College of New York, from which he received a BA. He went on to study law at New York Law School, graduating in 1960. He also received an MBA from Columbia University and a Masters of Public Administration from New York University.

While attending law school and business school, Llewellyn managed to save $30,000 as a down payment on a liquor store in Harlem. He later said that, "It taught me to watch the books, pay everybody on time and not to think of yourself as a black businessman. I'm a businessman, that's all."

Making something out of nothing

From 1960 to 1962 Llewellyn worked as a prosecutor in the office of the Manhattan district attorney. He also became increasingly involved in politics and the civil rights movement. By 1965 Llewellyn had been appointed as New York's regional director of the U.S. Small Business

▲ *J. Bruce Llewellyn believes in education and has established several scholarships for minority students.*

Administration. He said the position helped him learn "about the realities of what works and what doesn't." In 1969, realizing that there were business opportunities around for black Americans, he took a great risk, mortgaging his house and borrowing money to buy the Fedco Food Stores, a chain of 10 food stores situated in the economically deprived South Bronx. No one else wanted to buy the stores at the time and many people thought Llewellyn was crazy. The move proved to be a lucrative one, however: By 1983 Fedco was the largest minority-owned retail business. Two years later Llewellyn borrowed large sums of money to buy the Philadelphia Coca-Cola plant, becoming the only African American among Coca-Cola's more than 100 U.S. bottlers.

In 1986 Llewellyn became the principal stockholder and chair of the ABC television network affiliate in Buffalo, New York. From 1989 through 1994 he served as chair of Garden State Cablevision, Inc. He has received several honorary degrees.

Further reading: http://www1.hbs.edu/leadership/database/leaders/536 (Biography).

KEY DATES

1927	Born in Harlem, New York.
1948	Attends City College, New York.
1960	Graduates from New York Law School.
1969	Buys the Fedco Food Stores, South Bronx.
1985	Becomes the first African American to own a Coca-Cola bottling plant when he buys one in Philadelphia.
1986	Becomes principal stockholder and chair of ABC television network affiliate, Buffalo, New York.

LOCKE, Alain
Intellectual, Educator

Alain LeRoy Locke was one of the most influential American intellectuals of the first half of the 20th century. A respected educator, writer, and philosopher, Locke, through his study of African culture and its influence on western civilization, helped show how much black people had contributed to the modern world; his work also helped promote pride and self-respect among African Americans themselves. He is probably best remembered as one of the leaders of the Harlem Renaissance, the black arts movement centered in Harlem, New York, that took place in the 1920s.

The road to Africa
Born in Philadelphia, Pennsylvania, on September 13, 1886, Locke was the son of Pliny Ishmael and Mary Hawkins Locke. Both Locke's parents were teachers; Pliny Locke was principal of the Institute for Colored Youth in Philadelphia. Locke's parents were engaged for almost 16 years, marrying in middle-age. When Locke was six years of age, his father died; his mother supported her son through teaching.

A clever child, Locke was also sickly; he contracted rheumatic fever when quite young, which weakened his heart and prevented him from doing many physical activities. He retreated into books and music. After studying at Central High School and the Philadelphia School of Pedagogy, Locke enrolled at Harvard University, a great achievement for a black American at that time; this enabled him to study under some of the leading philosophers of the time, including Josiah Royce (1855–1916).

After graduating magna cum laude in 1907, Locke had the distinction of becoming the first African American scholar to study at Oxford University in the United Kingdom from 1907 to 1910, after which he decided to do advanced research in philosophy at the University of Berlin in Germany. He stayed there for a year and met and mixed with people from different cultures, including Pa Ka Isaka Seme, a young South African law student and future founder of the African National Congress, and Har Dayal, a student who was involved in India's nationalist movement. Locke was also exposed to new developments in literature and the arts, some of which drew their inspiration from African culture (*see box*). All these elements helped Locke develop his theories about the "New Negro" in the 1920s.

▲ *Locke visited Egypt in the 1920s and was present at the opening of Tutankhamen's tomb in 1924.*

On his return to the United States Locke quickly realized that his race and superior intellectual capabilities set him apart from most of his peers. As a black man, the jobs available to him were limited to posts at African American educational institutions, but he was much better educated than many other black academics at the time. In 1912 Locke joined Howard University, Washington, D.C., as assistant professor of English. Although he tried hard to make Howard an eminent black teaching facility, he ran into problems with the board of directors, which insisted that Howard should be a nonracial university.

In 1915 Locke took part in a series of lectures sponsored by the NAACP called "Race Contacts and Interracial Relations." Locke argued that race was a socially formed concept. A year later he went to study for a doctorate in philosophy at Harvard, returning to Howard in 1918 as a full professor of philosophy.

Although Locke became an influential member of the faculty and was much respected by his students, he and other African American scholars were fired from their positions in 1925; the move was said to have been necessitated by the need to cut costs. The 1920s had,

INFLUENCES AND INSPIRATION

Even before Locke wrote his groundbreaking book *The New Negro* (1925), there had been much discussion about the need to transform the often negative stereotypical images of black people as mentally deficient, inferior beings into that of a race of people that had influenced the development of western civilization.

Several prominent white and black people supported this idea. In the 1880s, for example, the Czech composer Antonin Dvorak (1841–1904) claimed that spirituals were the United States's first real contribution to world culture. Similarly at the turn of the 20th century the Spanish artist Pablo Picasso (1881–1973), one of the leaders of the cubist movement, drew on African art and culture, in particular the African masks, in his work, as seen in his seminal painting *Les Demoiselles d'Avignon* (1907). Such artists helped transform the way in which African culture was viewed, changing it from something primitive and dark to something brave, proud, and even regal.

In 1920 filmmaker Oscar Micheaux produced *Within Our Gates*, which highlighted racism in U.S. society and challenged representations of black people as seen in such films as D. W. Griffith's controversial *The Birth of a Nation*. Micheaux's work influenced Locke's thinking.

however, seen a rise in black consciousness among the student body. This was at odds with the direction that the white president and the board of directors wanted Howard to take: They still believed that Howard should be a nonracial institution. In September 1925 Locke published "Negro Education Bids for Par" in the *Survey Graphic* magazine. Locke argued that black American education ought to be able to to develop its own aims and interests without interference. Locke was subsequently reinstated at Howard, although he only returned to teach there in 1928, after Mordecai W. Johnson became the university's first black American president in 1926.

Harlem and beyond

The years between leaving and returning to teach at Howard were productive ones for Locke. He published articles in the leading black journals of the time, including *Opportunity* and the *Survey Graphic*, for which he edited a special issue devoted completely to the Harlem Renaissance. He expanded that work into a volume called *The New Negro: An Interpretation.*

Featuring Locke's own work, *The New Negro* also showcased other black Americans' work, including that of Countee Cullen, Arna Bontemps, and Langston Hughes. It illustrated how perspectives of race were changing. The book was critically acclaimed for contributing not only to how black Americans saw themselves but also to the way in which white people viewed African Americans. A cohesive arts movement based on black American culture began to emerge and critics finally started to take contemporary African American culture seriously. Locke became the leading expert on the subject, and he used his

KEY DATES	
1886	Born in Philadelphia, Pennsylvania, on September 13.
1904	Studies at Harvard University.
1907	Goes to Oxford University as a Rhodes Scholar.
1912	Teaches at Howard University; remains there for almost 40 years.
1925	Publishes *The New Negro: An Interpretation.*
1954	Dies in New York on June 9, 1954.

status position to help promote the careers of several young artists and writers, Richard Wright and Zora Neale Hurston among them. Locke arranged exhibitions and wrote about art so that other black Americans might take pride in their heritage and culture. In 1927 Locke returned to teaching, spending a year at Fisk University, Tennessee. He returned to Howard in 1928, but his efforts to establish a separate African studies program did not reach fruition until 1954. Locke wrote several influential books on black art, philosophy, and history. He was visiting professor at several prestigious universities before his death in 1954.

See also: Bontemps, Arna; Cullen, Countee; Harlem Renaissance; Hughes, Langston; Hurston, Zora Neale; Micheaux, Oscar; Wright, Richard

Further reading: Steward, J. C. (ed.). *Alain Locke: Race, Contacts, and Interracial Relations.* Washington, D.C.: Howard University Press, 1992.
http://www.dclibrary.org/blkren/bios/lockea.html (Biography).

LOGUEN, Jermain
Abolitionist

Jermain Wesley Loguen escaped from slavery in Tennessee in 1834 and fled north, later settling in Syracuse, New York, where he became an important figure in the Underground Railroad, a secret network that helped escaped slaves reach freedom in Canada.

Loguen was born in 1813 to an African American slave named Cherry and her owner, David Loguen. At first he led a relatively privileged life, but when financial problems induced David Loguen to sell Jermain and his family, the young man experienced the full horrors of a slave's existence.

Escape to freedom

In 1834, at age 21, Loguen escaped from his owners and their Tennessee plantation. He made his way through Kentucky and Indiana to Detroit and then to the safety of Canada. With the help of local citizens, Loguen settled in Hamilton, Ontario, where he worked as a farm laborer and gained a basic education at Sunday school.

Loguen spent three years in Canada before traveling to Rochester, New York, where he worked as a hotel porter. Two years later he went to study at the Oneida Institute

▼ *Jermain Loguen estimated that by 1859 he had helped about 1,500 fugitive slaves reach freedom.*

near Whitesboro, New York. Oneida was an integrated college run by Beriah Green (1795–1874), a leading abolitionist and reformer. After a couple of years at Oneida, where he met his future wife, Caroline Storum, Loguen set up a school for colored children in Utica, New York, and became increasingly involved with the African Methodist Episcopal Church (AME).

In 1841 Loguen moved to Syracuse, but he spent three of the next few years in Bath, Steuben County, and two in Ithaca, Tomkins County, as an AME Zion minister. In 1848 he bought some land in Syracuse, built a house, and started a school for colored children. He also became involved in the antislavery movement, making public speeches about his own experiences.

Loguen turned his home into a principal "station," or place of refuge, for fugitive slaves making their way to freedom on the Underground Railroad. He also became a leading figure in the Fugitive Aid Society through his public speaking, lobbying in newspapers, and efforts to find escaped slaves jobs, shelter, and a passage to safety.

In 1851 Loguen was forced to flee to Canada when he was indicted for his role in the "Jerry Rescue." He and other Syracuse residents had rescued an escaped slave named Jerry, whom the police had arrested under the Fugitive Slave Act (1850), and helped him escape to Canada. Loguen returned to Syracuse the following year and continued his abolitionist work. In 1859 he published his biography, *The Rev. J. W. Loguen As a Slave and As a Freeman*. Loguen died in Syracuse in 1872.

KEY DATES	
1813	Born in Tennessee.
1834	Escapes from slavery and flees north to Canada.
1851	Indicted for his role in the Jerry Rescue.
1872	Dies in Syracuse, New York.

See also: Slavery

Further reading: Sernett, Milton C. *North Star Country*. Syracuse, NY: Syracuse University Press, 2002. http://docsouth.unc.edu/neh/loguen/menu.html (Electronic version of Loguen's biography on University of North Carolina's site).

LONG, Nia
Actor

Award-winning actor Nia Long was listed as one of the 50 Most Beautiful People in the World by *People* magazine in 2000.

Nitara Carlynn Long was born in Brooklyn, New York, in 1970 to Doc and Talita Long. Her parents divorced when she was two years old, and Long and her mother moved to Iowa City, Iowa. When she was seven they moved to a South Central Los Angeles neighborhood.

Long showed an interest in acting at an early age and began taking acting lessons from Betty Bridges, mother of Todd Bridges, child star of *Different Strokes*.

As a teenager Long appeared in several stage productions. In 1996 she landed a role in *The B.R.A.T. Patrol*, a "Disney Sunday Movie," and made appearances in music videos. She graduated from Westchester High School in Los Angeles in 1989, and after attending Santa Monica City College for two years, quit her studies to focus on acting full time.

Acting career

In 1990 Long made her movie debut in *Buried Alive*. In 1991 she was cast in a three-year role on the television soap opera *Guiding Light*. That same year she was cast as Brandi in John Singleton's powerful drama *Boyz N the Hood*. Although the film received critical acclaim, it was her two-year role as Will Smith's girlfriend on *The Fresh Prince of Bel-Air* that brought Long national recognition.

Long began to establish herself as a strong presence in romantic dramas and comedies. In 1993 she worked with Will Smith again in *Made in America*. In 1995 she appeared in *Friday*, alongside the rapper Ice Cube. She also made guest appearances in television series such as *Living Single*, *ER*, and *Moesha*.

Long's first leading role was in *Love Jones* (1997), in which she also performed two songs. That same year Long formed her own film production company and played a role in *Soul Food*, costarring Vivica A. Fox. In 1999 Long won an NAACP Image Award for Outstanding Actress in a Motion Picture for *The Best Man*. She also had supporting roles in *Stigmata*, *In Too Deep* (1999), and *Boiler Room* (2000). In 2000 Long's role in the comedy-thriller *Big Momma's House*, which costarred Martin Lawrence, earned her even wider recognition.

In 2002, after a two-year break, Long returned to television in a made-for-TV movie *Sightings: Heartland*

▲ *Nia Long attends the premiere of* **Alfie** *in 2004. She played Lonette, one of Alfie's "conquests."*

Ghost and began a regular role in the show *Judging Amy*. In 2003 Long began starring in the NBC drama *Third Watch*. In 2004 she starred in *Alfie* with Jude Law, and *Are We There Yet?* In 2005 Long won an NAACP Image Award for Outstanding Actress in a Drama Series for her performance in *Third Watch*.

KEY DATES	
1970	Born in Brooklyn, New York, on October 30.
1990	Makes her movie debut in *Buried Alive*.
1991	Begins acting in the TV soap opera *Guiding Light*.
1997	Gains her first leading role in *Love Jones*.
2005	Wins an NAACP Image Award for Outstanding Actress in a Drama Series for her performance in *Third Watch*.

See also: Ice Cube; Lawrence, Martin; Singleton, John; Smith, Will

Further reading: http://www.celebopedia.com/nia-long/ (Nia Long tribute page).

LORDE, Audre
Poet

Audre Lorde defined herself as a "black, lesbian, mother, warrior, poet," and devoted herself to dealing with the injustices caused by racism, sexism, and homophobia (prejudice against gay people). She published many books of poetry and, after being diagnosed with breast cancer, wrote frankly about her battle with disease.

Audrey Geraldine Lorde was born in Harlem, New York, on February 18, 1934. The youngest of three, Lorde was the daughter of Frederic Byron Lorde, who came from Barbados, and Linda Bellmar, from Grenada. Lorde's parents were saddened by the fact that they could not afford to return to the West Indies to start up a business as they had originally planned; they were forced to live in America in exile from friends and family. This influenced how Lorde perceived herself in terms of her racial and cultural identity, themes that occur repeatedly in her writing. Lorde also had extremely poor eyesight, was slow to read and write, and did not speak until she was four years old, after which she was still very quiet. At school Lorde was at first teased for being slow.

A love of literature

Lorde loved poetry, however. She wrote her first poem in the eighth grade and had a piece published in *Seventeen* magazine while still at school. In 1951 she went to Hunter College, New York, graduating in 1959 with a BA. In 1954 she spent a year as a student at the National University of Mexico. Five years later she studied for an MA in library science at Columbia University, from which she graduated in 1961. Lorde began working as a librarian at Mount Vernon Public Library and then became the head librarian

▲ *In 1991 Audre Lorde was appointed New York State's Poet Laureate.*

of Town School Library, New York, between 1966 and 1968. After publishing the poetry collection *The First Cities* she quit her job. With a grant from the National Endowment for the Arts Lorde became poet-in-residence at Tougaloo College, Mississippi. Her second volume of poetry, *Cables to Rage* (1970), contained "Martha," Lorde's first poetic expression of her homosexuality.

In 1978 Lorde was diagnosed with breast cancer; she poured her feelings into prose writing. *The Cancer Journals* (1980) reached a wide audience and was acclaimed for its honesty. The book won the American Library Association Gay Caucus Book of the Year Award (1981). In 1980 Lorde and writer and activist Barbara Smith created a new publishing house, Kitchen Table: Women of Color Press. In 1989 *A Burst of Light* (1988) won a National Book Award. Lorde died in 1992, in St. Croix, U.S. Virgin Islands. Her last volume of poetry was published in 1993.

Further reading: Lorde, Audre. *The Cancer Diaries.* San Francisco, CA: Aunt Lute Books, 1992.
http://www.albany.edu/writers-inst/lorde.html (New York State Writers page on Lorde).

KEY DATES	
1934	Born in Harlem, New York, on February 18.
1959	Receives a BA from Hunter College, New York.
1968	Publishes first book of poetry, *The First Cities*.
1978	Becomes a professor of English at John Jay College of Criminal Justice; is diagnosed with cancer.
1981	Becomes professor at Hunter College, New York.
1992	Dies at St. Croix, in the U.S. Virgin Islands, on November 17.

LOUIS, Joe
Boxer

Joe Louis was heavyweight boxing champion of the world from 1937 to 1949 and became the first title holder to retire undefeated, having defended his title 25 times, more than any other champion in any division. His nickname was "the Brown Bomber."

Early life
Born Joseph Louis Barrow in 1914, he dropped his last name in 1933 on the instructions of his manager, who thought plain "Joe Louis" was snappier. Louis was the son of an Alabama sharecropper, or tenant farmer, who died when Louis was about four. Three years later his mother remarried and the family moved to Detroit. When he was 16 Louis used the money his mother had given him for violin lessons to pay for a locker at the Brewster Recreation Center, where amateur boxers trained.

In 1934 Louis won the Amateur Athletic Union 175-pound championship and turned professional. In 54 amateur fights Louis had lost only four, all by decision. From then on his rise to the top was almost inexorable, although he suffered a setback in 1936 when he was knocked out in 12 rounds by the German Max Schmeling.

World title
Although Louis won the world title in 1937 by knocking out James J. Braddock in the eighth round, he said, "I don't want nobody to call me champ until I beat Schmeling." On June 27, 1938, he knocked out the German after only two minutes and four seconds of the first round. In the context of the rising international tension that was to lead to World War II (1939–1945) Louis became a national hero for his victory over the white boxer backed by the Nazi government.

▲ *Joe Louis (left) prepares for a training match. He was renowned for his accurate knockout punches.*

Over the next 13 years Louis conducted a series of memorable defenses of his title, most notably those against Billy Conn, whom he knocked out in 13 rounds in 1941 and again in eight rounds in 1946, and Jersey Joe Walcott, whom he outpointed in 15 rounds and later stopped in 11. In 1942 Louis enlisted in the Army and gave 96 exhibition matches to U.S. troops around the world. He retired undefeated in 1949. Although Louis had earned a lot of money during his career, he gave most of it away and was then was forced back into the ring to pay back taxes. His comeback was disappointing: His 1950 bid to regain the crown from Ezzard Charles ended in a 15-round defeat, and his last-ever fight, against Rocky Marciano in 1951, was stopped when he was knocked out in round eight.

Louis continued to have money problems after his second retirement and served as a greeter at Caesar's Palace in Las Vegas. He died of a heart attack in 1981.

See also: Color Bar and Professional Sports; Walcott, Jersey Joe

Further reading: Bak, Richard. *Joe Louis: The Great Black Hope.* New York, NY: Da Capo Press, 1998.
http://www.cmgww.com/sports/louis/louis.html (Official site).

KEY DATES	
1914	Born in Lafayette, Alabama, on May 13.
1934	Turns professional.
1937	Wins world heavyweight boxing championship.
1949	Retires undefeated.
1981	Dies in Las Vegas, Nevada, on April 12.
1990	Inducted to International Boxing Hall of Fame.

LOURY, Glenn C.
Economist, Social Commentator

Glenn Loury is one of the United States's leading academics and intellectuals. During the 1980s and early 1990s his outspoken opposition to affirmative action, the program of active intervention by government to improve minorities' employment and educational opportunities, made him a deeply controversial and even unpopular figure in the African American community.

The conservative thinker

Glenn Cartman Loury was born on the South Side of Chicago, Illinois, in 1948. In 1972 he graduated from Northwestern University with a degree in mathematics. In 1976 he gained a PhD in economics from Massachusetts Institute of Technology (MIT). He taught at Northwestern University (1976–1979), the University of Michigan (1979–1980), and Harvard University (1982–1991), where he was the first tenured black professor of economics.

▲ *Glenn C. Loury relaxes at his home in Brookline, Massachusetts, in 2002.*

KEY DATES

1948   Born in Chicago, Illinois, on September 3.

1982   Becomes professor of economics and of Afro-American studies at Harvard University.

1991   Becomes professor of economics at Boston University.

During the 1970s Loury had become disillusioned with the politics of the civil rights movement. He believed liberal black thinkers and leaders had failed African Americans because, in analyzing the causes of black poverty, they focused only on white racism rather than looking at failings within the black community itself. He argued that African Americans should help themselves rather than depend on intervention by the government to achieve better lives. He argued that policies such as affirmative action were detrimental to the dignity of black people, who did not need "special favors."

During the 1980s Loury became closely associated with Republican thinkers and politicians, including President Ronald Reagan (1911–2004). For many African Americans, however, his conservative views amounted to a betrayal of the civil rights generation. Loury's estrangement from the mainstream black community may have contributed to his personal problems, which included a much publicized cocaine addiction.

Changing views

In 1991 Loury became a professor of economics at Boston University. In 1996 his book *One by One, From the Inside Out: Essays and Reviews on Race and Responsibility in America* won the American Book Award. In 1997 he became the founding director of the university's Institute on Race and Social Division. By now Loury had begun to rethink many of his opinions. In *The Anatomy of Racial Inequality* (2002) he argued that African Americans are still suffering from the consequences of their nation's historical racism and that "racial stigma" persists.

See also: Affirmative Action; Civil Rights

Further reading: www.bu.edu/irsd/loury/lourybio.htm (Short biography).

SET INDEX

Set Index

Set Index

Picture Credits

Front Cover: Library of Congress: Van Vechten, Carl (top); **Steven Dunwell:** Lordly and Dame, Inc (top center); **Robert Hunt Library:** (center); **NASA:** (bottom center); **Library of Congress:** Battey, Cornelius M. (bottom)
Air Force Link: 005; **Baseball Hall of Fame:** 027; **Corbis:** 098; Bettmann 007, 025, 040, 094, 099, 113; D'Angelo, Rebecca/Sygma 035; Downing, Larry/Sygma 073; Freidman, Rick 134; Kaszerman, Nancy/Zuma 041; Leynse, James 074; Muhammed, Jeffrey 101; Reuters 081, 090; **Empics:** Cavaretta, Joe/AP 054; Marshall, Tony 064; **Getty:** Allocco, Dave/DMI 047; Hulton 089; Mcgough, David/Stringer 108; MPI/Stringer 039; Schumacher, Karl 042; Silk, George/Stringer 030; Thai, Ted 127; Yamasaki, Taro 078; **History Makers:** 070; **Jill Posener:** 059; **Lebrecht:** NYPL Performing Arts 022, 066, 128, 130; **Library of Congress:** 024, 065, 132; Bachrach, Fabian 062; Metropolitan Printing Co. 055; Parks, Gordan 017; Van Vechten, Carl 106; **Mary Randlett:** 016; **Minnesota Historical Society:** 045; **NASA:** 011; **Queens Borough Public Library:** 103; **Redferns:** 031, 101; **Rex:** Barklie, Nigel R. 008; BL/Keystone USA 018; Brooker, Peter 122; DWM 014; Nukari, Jussi 006; Rocha, Alfredo 100; Rothenberg, D L. 009; Sipa Press 004, 029; THH 060; Von Holden/DMI; **Robert Hunt Library:** 023, 058, 068, 080, 084, 088, 124,133; **Robin Kelly:** 071; **Photographs and Prints Division, Schomburg Center for Research in Black Culture, The New York Public Library, Astor, Lenox and Tilden Foundation:** 044, 048; **Topham:** 114; Arena PAL Picture Library 079, 095; CC 056; ESC 125; Fastfoto Picture Library 110; Hindley, Tommy 117; IMW 033, 076; Lipnitzki/Roger-Voilet 052; National Pictures 077; PAL 046; Steele, Michael 049; Universal Pictures 109; UPPA 082, 131; **United Methodist Communications:** 072.